WOMEN, INFANTICIDE AND THE PRESS, 1822–1922

T0304150

This book is dedicated to my mother – my inspiration
Maureen Jean Miller (née Gayton)

Women, Infanticide and the Press, 1822–1922

News Narratives in England and Australia

NICOLA GOC

University of Tasmania, Australia

Routledge
Taylor & Francis Group

LONDON AND NEW YORK

First published 2013 by Ashgate Publishing

Published 2016 by Routledge
2 Park Square, Milton Park, Abingdon, Oxfordshire OX14 4RN
711 Third Avenue, New York, NY 10017, USA

First issued in paperback 2016

Routledge is an imprint of the Taylor & Francis Group, an informa business

British Library Cataloguing in Publication Data
Goc, Nicola.
   Women, infanticide and the press, 1822-1922 : news narratives in England and Australia.
   1. Infanticide--Press coverage--England--History--19th century. 2. Infanticide--Press coverage--Australia--History--19th century. 3. Women murderers--Press coverage--England--History--19th century. 4. Women murderers--Press coverage--Australia--History--19th century.
   5. English newspapers--Language. 6. Australian newspapers--Language. 7. Journalism--Political aspects--England--History--19th century. 8. Journalism--Political aspects--Australia--History--19th century. 9. Journalism--Social aspects--England--History--19th century. 10. Journalism--Social aspects--Australia--History--19th century.
   I. Title
   070.4'493641523'0852-dc23

Library of Congress Cataloging-in-Publication Data
Goc, Nicola.
   Women, infanticide and the press, 1822-1922 : news narratives in England and Australia / by Nicola Goc.
      p. cm.
   Includes bibliographical references and index.
   ISBN 978-1-4094-0604-4 (hardcover)
   1. Infanticide--Press coverage--England--History. 2. Infanticide--Press coverage--Australia--History. 3. Unmarried mothers--Press coverage--England--History. 4. Unmarried mothers--Press coverage--Australia--History. I. Title.
   PN5124.I554G63 2013
   074--dc23
                                                                            2012026156

ISBN 13: 978-1-138-25155-7 (pbk)
ISBN 13: 978-1-4094-0604-4 (hbk)

Contents

Contents

Acknowledgements

This book could not have been written without the support of Professor Lucy Frost whose passion for bringing the lives of nineteenth-century women to readers today has been a continuing inspiration to me. To Ann Donahue at Ashgate who has been the personification of patience and to Elaine Couper and the Ashgate editorial team – thank you for your support. A special acknowledgement to the readers for their thoughtful suggestions – you made this a better book. Finally where would any writer be without the support of those who, through no fault of their own, are taken on the journey of discovery? Thank you to my sons Tristan and Xavier for their love; to Tamlyn for a summer Sunday, a Greek festival and Foucault, and thank you especially to Romak for tolerating my obsession(s) and for creating this beautiful space in which I write.

Introduction

It is hard to imagine a woman, recently delivered, taking her newborn child's life, and yet mothers have been killing their babies for millennia. In nomadic tribes infanticide was a routine practice, a form of contraception for hunters and gatherers constantly on the move. Today sensational news stories alert us to mothers who have killed their newborn babies and we are still confounded and uncertain about how to 'deal' with the infanticidal woman. She is either demonized or pathologized, but rarely understood, because how do you make sense of such a brutal act?

This book examines how societies in England and Australia, at different moments in time from 1822 to 1922, made sense through news discourse of the act of infanticide and of the woman who killed her newborn baby. News texts are an important resource in historical studies as they are often the only surviving texts, or the only comprehensive texts to survive, on an issue such as infanticide. News texts are regularly used in historical studies as uncomplicated reflections of a historical reality, while what they offer is one reporter's view of a newsworthy event. However, as this study will show, through a close reading of news it becomes clear that news texts are the nexus of multiple discourses, they are far more complex texts than they may at first appear and offer fertile ground for researchers. By applying Critical Discourse Analysis to this study of infanticide news the ways in which knowledge and power were acquired, maintained and understood discursively at given moments in time is better understood. All discourses interact with other discourses in the social moment in which they are produced and consumed, and news texts are an important record of the formation of influential infanticide discourses in the period 1822–1922. Infanticide news, as this study shows, was woven into interconnected discourses about the regulation of women through the family, through law and justice, and through welfare and medicine, reinforcing the central role of discourse in the creation and maintenance of power relations. News texts are, as Kieran McEvoy argues, 'active participants and vital contributors in an ongoing dialectic with their readers' (1996, p. 179). It is through an analysis of this dialectic between newspapers and their readers that insight is gained into how infanticide was understood in the nineteenth and early twentieth centuries and how power was influenced over the infanticidal woman and how the infanticidal woman herself held power through news discourse.

This study takes Foucault's perspective that the production of knowledge, of 'facts' and truth claims, and the exercise of power, are inextricably connected to discourse. Newspaper discourses provide a way to investigate the discursive practices that brought the nineteenth-century infanticidal woman – known as 'the Infanticide' – into being. Infanticide news also created oppositional ways of viewing the 'players' in infanticide courtroom dramas and by discursively placing the young transgressive female up against a body of male authoritarian figures male authority over all women was reinforced.

Press discourse did not, however, entirely suppress and constrain the infanticidal woman and in this book I will argue that the prominent reporting of a woman's infanticidal actions also provided her with a public presence that (unintentionally) politicized her actions and transformed her from a docile subject into a political being. Central to my argument is the premise that at various moments in history particular news discourses in specific newspapers (the London *Times*, the *Colonial Times*, the *Hobart Town Courier*, the *Tasmanian Austral Asiatic Review*, the Hobart *Mercury* and the *Leicester Mercury*) were formative in the creation of public opinion on the act of infanticide and on the infanticidal woman. Infanticide was used explicitly and persuasively by the London *Times* to argue the inequities of the 1834 New Poor Law (see Part I) in England and this coverage saw parliamentarians, local politicians, magistrates, medical and legal coroners, ministers of religion and all manner of public speakers across the nation draw upon leading articles and news reports from *The Times* to form opinions on various aspects of infanticide, the infanticidal woman and the law. In Part II the analysis of individual case studies exposes the formative role the press played in the creation of public opinion on individual infanticidal women – Mary McLauchlan, Sarah Masters, Harriet Lovell and Lilian Wakefield in Australia and Edith Roberts in regional England.

The years from 1822 to 1922 were a time in which infanticide news resonated so particularly because the actions of young mothers threatened the domestic ideal of womanhood, and were seen as a direct threat to the family, and therefore the very foundations of a 'society of blood' (Foucault 1991a, p. 269) where power was rooted in 'blood relation'. While it was an age when women were eulogized in literature and put on a pedestal as Madonnas of immaculate purity, it was also a time when lurid newspaper reports on infanticide, laden with pathos, inscribed with illicit sex, with love turned sour, with sexual assault and seduction, with betrayal and with murder, were highly marketable news products. In line with Foucault's thesis on power as omnipresent (Foucault 2008a, p. 93) rather than hierarchical, an analysis of infanticide news reports shows how sensationalized infanticide discourses not only entertained the masses but also educated society on the deviancy of young unmarried women, compounding anxieties about the 'women question' and the changing role of women in an increasingly industrialized and urbanized society.

Infanticide – A Historical Overview

Around four hundred years ago Western societies came to understand the act of infanticide through a legal framework and in England infanticide was brought under tighter control through the enactment of the 1624 Infanticide Act. This act, which was brought in 'to prevent the destroying and murthering of bastard children', determined that any woman who concealed the death of her bastard child was presumed to have murdered the child and was condemned to death even in the absence of a body (Oberman 2003, p. 4). It was automatically presumed that the mother of a bastard was guilty of murder if she tried to conceal the birth by secreting the corpse, with the onus put on the mother to prove that her child died from natural causes. In 1690 the first Scottish law specifically related to infanticide was passed making it a capital offence for a woman to conceal her pregnancy should the baby subsequently be found dead or missing. This law was the theme of Sir Walter Scott's *The Heart of Midlothian* (1818) set in 1736, in which Effie Deans was capitally convicted for concealment of pregnancy (the baby disappeared, but it was not dead), but she was subsequently pardoned. Scott's literary work reflected community feeling that the law was too harsh. In 1803 Lord Ellenborough's Act (43 Geo III c 58) decreed that infanticide was to be proceeded with like any other form of murder; the mother was innocent until proven guilty, therefore reversing the 1624 Act. Up until 1803 women suspected of killing their newborn children were tried according to common-law rules of evidence, requiring the prosecution to provide proof that the child had been born alive. Where a murder charge failed the jury had the option of returning a verdict of 'concealment of birth' with a penalty of up to two years' imprisonment (Rose 1986, p. 118).

The late eighteenth and early nineteenth centuries in Britain was a time marked by an unprecedented population explosion. Between 1801 and 1851 the population of England and Wales doubled from nine to 18 million (Rose 1986, p. 5), due mainly to a decline in the infant death rate. This increase also saw the number of illegitimate children surviving infanthood rise dramatically, creating a burden on parish relief. By the 1830s there were calls to introduce legislative reform to reduce the numbers of bastard children being paid for by the parishes. This increasing burden on the wealthy to provide for what was seen as the 'licentious profligacy' of the poor, allowed for the theories on population control of economist and social reformer, Reverend Thomas Malthus, to become widely accepted. Malthus's solution to the high rate of illegitimacy was to shift the responsibility onto the mother, denying her the support of the Poor Law (Malthus 1798, p. 183). He argued that the human population was increasing much faster than agricultural production, and that unless policies were introduced to control the increasing population there would be inevitable social unrest. He warned that the current laws were a 'pernicious stimulus to unnecessary births' (p. 183) and his theory allowed society to place the blame for the rising rate of illegitimate births directly upon unmarried working-class mothers.

In 1834 the popularity of Malthusian policies saw the New Poor Law with its pernicious Bastardy Clause introduced as a way of controlling the sharp rise in illegitimate births. Under the new law all illegitimate children were the sole responsibility of their mothers until they were 16 years old, and it was this act that had the most significant impact on the increase in infanticide in nineteenth-century England. Under the new law there was no reduction in the rate of illegitimate births and unmarried mothers (more often than not unemployed and unemployable servants), denied parish relief, were now in a desperate situation. Their options were few: the dreaded workhouse, prostitution or infanticide. Workhouses were overcrowded and unsanitary places where disease was rife and death a daily reality. As we will see in Chapter 2 in the Sevenoaks workhouse inquiry, exposed in nine leading articles in *The Times*, women gave birth in appalling conditions. The dread of the workhouse offered a very real motive for desperate unmarried women to kill their newborn babies. Prostitution was a dangerous and uncertain occupation, women were forced to work long hours in appalling conditions, and prostitution led to further unwanted pregnancies. Malthus's belief that by denying mothers of illegitimate children charity unmarried working-class women would be persuaded against profligate behaviour, and that no woman would harm her child for economic considerations, proved to be a fallacy. Within months of the introduction of the New Poor Law in August 1834 the rate of infanticide had increased across the country and Chapter 2 analyses the response in the London *Times* newspaper, with its editor Thomas Barnes's campaign to repeal the law. By the 1860s the rate of infanticide in England was said to have reached epidemic proportions with the medical coroner for central Middlesex, Dr Edwin Lankester, the focus of Chapter 3, claiming that at least 16,000 London mothers had the blood of their infants on their hands.

The medical profession, looking to colonize the birthing room, found medical answers to the problem of infanticide. In 1820 William Hutchinson wrote his influential *A Dissertation on Infanticide in its Relations to Physiology and Jurisprudence*, which summarized the laws on infanticide and was highly influential in informing both the legal and medical professions on infanticide. Forty years later another tract by Dr William Burke Ryan influenced another generation of lawmakers and medical men: *Infanticide – Its Law, Prevalence, Prevention and History* (Ryan 1862a). These texts, along with the presence in the courtroom of the medical expert witness to provide evidence of live birth in cases of infanticide, saw medical discourse privileged in infanticide legal and news discourse.

The medicalization of infanticide also influenced social and religious discourses on infanticide and the role of women within the family. The infanticidal woman, emblematic of woman's unregulated sexual activity, was seen as a sinister threat to that bulwark of Victorian paternal authoritarianism, the Family. In public discourse the ideal woman was a chaste and obedient wife, mother, or daughter within the family home. The ideal Victorian woman inhabited the private, domestic sphere, nurturing her family's – and the nation's – values. She was the 'angel in the house', a term coined after one of the most popular poems of the age by Coventry Patmore (1854–56), which placed the ideal woman firmly within the home where she must obey her husband and raise his children:

> Man must be pleased; but him to please
> Is woman's pleasure; down the gulf
> Of his condoled necessities
> She casts her best, she flings herself. (Patmore 1863)

Women were framed in discourse as 'innocents', untouched by public life and in need of male protection; they were also expected, because of their virtue, to be the moral guardians of family life, of 'that domestic temple which it is women's natural duty to guard' (Nochlin 1982, p. 226). The infanticidal mother subverted the domestic ideal in the most confronting manner, by destroying a man's lineage. Even when the child was illegitimate, and rejected by the father, the mother's actions were seen as a fundamental threat to the Family.

The nineteenth-century infanticidal woman speaks most powerfully to Michel Foucault's notion of blood and the 'society of blood' (Foucault 1991a, p. 269) and the power of 'blood relation' (ibid., p. 268). The woman who kills her newborn child subverts the age-old privilege of the sovereign power, and through the sovereign power, all male power. Foucault tells us that 'for a long time, one of the characteristic privileges of sovereign power was the right to decide life and death' (Foucault 1991a, p. 258). He traces this power back to ancient Rome 'in a formal sense, it derived no doubt from the ancient *patria potestas* that granted the father of the Roman family the right to "dispose" of the life of his children and his slaves; just as he had given them life, so he could take it away' (ibid., p. 269). Foucault talks about 'a society of blood' where 'power spoke *through* blood' (ibid.). 'Clearly, nothing was more on the side of the law, death, transgression, the symbolic and sovereignty than blood' (ibid.). My reading of Foucault situates the primary site of blood relation, and therefore blood power, with the female. All of us are rendered human through our mother's bodies and when a woman kills her newborn child she destroys a man's lineage and therefore his place in a society of blood. The blood relation in nineteenth-century monarchical England, as it was in France before the Revolution, was an important element in 'the mechanisms of power, its manifestations, and its rituals' (ibid., p. 268). Lineage determined who sat on the throne of England, but also who sat in the House of Lords, who inherited vast wealth and property, both industrial and domestic, and who ruled in an elitist class-based society. The blood relation remained a powerful force in class-based nineteenth-century England. Infanticide news texts, with their vivid imagery of puerperal blood converging with the blood of the slain newborn, provided a potent and shocking symbol of maternal power and of a mother's ability to subvert blood relation. Women, predominantly from the underclass – illiterate servants girls and prostitutes – were the main perpetrators of infanticide, and it was these disenfranchised young women whose all-powerful actions, documented in news texts, deeply shocked and threatened patriarchal society. The unmarried pregnant woman was at one and the same time disenfranchised and powerless, and an all-powerful political being. A woman's 'disorderliness' was perceived as power (Wiltenberg 1992, p. 7) and when nineteenth century news stories told of the secret, desperate actions of parturient women killing their babies in the back lanes and alleyways, attics and garrets of England, it was deeply unsettling because these stories demonstrated to a patriarchal society that parturient women had the ultimate power over life.

The infanticidal woman also represented unregulated – and therefore deviant – sexual activity and sex, Foucault argues, was 'put forward as the index of society's strength, revealing of both its political energy and its biological vigour' (Foucault 2008a, p. 146). While Foucault is silent on the maternal figure, his work can be usefully employed in analysing the politics of sex and the infanticidal woman and provides the theoretical framework for this study. The politics of sex was tied up with female regulation and the control of women. Chastity – that is male sexual control over female sexuality – was the pre-eminent virtue of a respectable woman, linked as it was to the economics of a patriarchal society that required a man to ensure the succession of his legitimate heirs. The infanticidal woman, rejecting her role as a procreator, refusing to be controlled, and forsaking order, represented sexual disorganization and abandonment. The woman who killed a man's child at birth, regardless of whether the father acknowledged the child or wanted it to survive, spoke to a fundamental loss of the power of the male sex act and a loss of male power over the birthright to control lineage, and also to society's loss of a future labour force. In reading infanticide from this perspective it becomes clear that the infanticidal woman in nineteenth and early twentieth century England and Australia was profoundly involved in the political field. Foucault posits that 'political investment of the body is bound up, in accordance with complex reciprocal relations, with its economic use; it is largely as a force of production that the body is invested with relations of power domination' (Foucault 1991a, p. 173). Furthermore sex is 'at the pivot of the two axes along which developed the entire political technology of life' (Foucault 1991a, p. 267–8). Sex is the 'theme of political operations, economic interventions (through incitements to or curbs on procreation), and ideological campaigns for raising the standards of morality and responsibility' (Foucault 2008a, p. 146). Viewed from this perspective the infanticidal woman is a powerful and threatening political figure indeed.

Infanticide during the nineteenth century also comes within Foucault's axis of modern power, the bio-politics of the population, known simply as 'bio-power' (Foucault 2008a p. 140). In the nineteenth century infanticide shifted from primarily being understood through a juridical discourse to be part of a broader state discourse on population control and management that was influenced by the dogma of Malthus and reflected through the burgeoning science of statistics, with its focus on birth and death rates, on health, discipline and education. By shifting the focus from a purely legal framework infanticide and illegitimacy became inextricably enmeshed in the new politics of population control and management. The rise of the medical expert witness in infanticide trials, the role of medicine in social welfare and in the care of the parturient woman, the creation of the Social Science Association in 1857, the rise of the medical coroner and the advancement of scientific statistics all fed into what Foucault called 'bio-power'. 'Bio-power' is the transformation in the nature of the sovereign's power over its subjects from one of prohibition and legal authority to what Foucault called a 'normalizing society' where the focus was on the birth rate of a population and on a society's health, its discipline, the longevity of its citizens and the education of its children.

Foucault's bio-power and what he calls the 'socialization of procreation' offers a useful framework for an analysis of infanticide.

Why Foucault? It may seem more than a little strange that this study looks to Foucault for an understanding of infanticide and infanticide press discourse when in Foucault's work on power, language and knowledge he not only largely ignores the female subject, but is also silent on news journalism and the power of press discourse (apart from a brief mention of sensational eighteenth-century broadsides). Foucault has rightfully been charged with 'gender blindness and androcentrism' (Simons 1996, p. 179) in his great canon and it is no surprise that feminist scholars have been known to reject Foucault's work. Sandra Bartky argues that Foucault treats 'the body throughout as if it were one, as if the bodily experiences of men and women did not differ and as if men and women bore the same relationship to the characteristic institutions of modern life' (Bartky 1988, p. 132). Foucault's 'failure to acknowledge the gendered character of many disciplinary techniques' (McNay 1992, p. 11) and the gendered nature of power does not sit well with me, nor with most feminist scholars. I nevertheless argue that Foucault's work on power/knowledge and discourse, when applied to a study of infanticide and the press, provides for a far more nuanced understanding of how press discourse made meaning of the infanticidal actions of desperate young women.

This study analyses infanticide intertextually, that is it examines the multiple discourses – legal, medical, judicial, political, religious, economic and social – that are embedded within news texts. It looks at the connections between these discourses, and at how these interconnections created a particular way of knowing the act of infanticide and the infanticidal woman and saw infanticide become one of the significant social issues in the period 1822–1922. In Foucault's work discourse is a social force (Foucault 1994), it has a central role in what is constructed as 'real' and therefore what is possible. This study draws on Foucault's work on how language embodies systems of thought which structure what can be understood, and how language works to not only produce meaning, but also to produce 'particular kinds of objects and subjects upon whom and through which particular relations of power are realized' (Luke 1999, cited Graham 2005, p. 4). Newspaper discourse in the pre-electronic age had a central role in determining what society understood as 'real'. For many it determined how the world was seen, and therefore what was possible, and what was known about that world and what was done in it. Nineteenth-century newspaper discourses offer insight into how the social subject was positioned and limited in society.

The ideological role of the press in communicating beliefs, values and opinions that shape the way individuals and groups think, act and understand the world, speaks directly to Foucault's concerns with the relationship of language to other social processes, and how language works within power relations. In 1803 in England when journalists were allowed for the first time into the halls of Parliament to directly observe and report parliamentary proceedings, 'Parliament no longer stood alone as the exponent of opinion, and was obliged to share its privilege with a number of gifted men whose names it could hardly ever find out'

(*Leisure Hour* 1863, p. 542). What had been 'an intellectual exercise, practiced in a random way by thousands' in the coffee houses was now 'turned into a branch of industry and pursued with great skill by a few' (Ibid., pp. 541–2). The journalistic framing of political, religious and social debates, including issues of crime and criminality, and the reporting of court proceedings, make journalism texts particularly suited to Foucault's work on the relationships between regimes of power. The journalistic framing of infanticide through political, legal, medical, religious and social debates, and the reporting of coronial and judicial proceedings and other news events speaks directly to Foucault's work on discourse and power.

In *Archaeology of Knowledge* (2002a) Foucault studies common documents to listen to the submerged voices and in this analysis of the discursive practice of news I look for the submerged voices, particularly for the submerged voices of the desperate young women who stood accused of killing their newborn children. The 'Infanticide' who is rarely given voice through direct quotes in press discourse, who rarely spoke in the judicial proceedings beyond a pathetic 'not guilty', can nevertheless still be heard in courtroom discourse through the mediated voices of witnesses and journalists, and importantly through her own actions, brought into the courtroom discursively by expert witnesses, by lawyers and by judges and coroners and reconstituted into news discourse by journalists. In other press discourses, in leading articles and news features, in letters to the editor, and in the reports of coroners and members of the Social Science Association, the submerged voices of the 'Infanticide' can also be found.

Throughout his work in analysing discourse, Foucault claims that 'one sees the loosening of the embrace, apparently so tight, of words and things, and the emergence of a group of rules proper to discursive practice' (Foucault 2002a, p. 54). In all of Foucault's analyses he attempts to understand the rules that were used when various objects of knowledge were born and adopted (2002a). These rules define, within each discursive formulation, 'the ordering of objects' (Foucault 2002a, p. 54). 'Discursive practices' Foucault claims, 'systematically form the objects of which they speak' (Foucault 2002a, p. 54). Analysing press discourse provides one way of understanding how the rules that governed unmarried women were formed discursively and how through these rules women were categorized as 'good' or 'bad', as 'angels of the house' or as 'fallen women'.

At a time when discussion on sex in polite society was taboo, prurient infanticide news brought sex and scandal into the drawing rooms of the middle class through news stories in the London *Times*. Victorians, unlike their grandparents (who were familiar with lurid literature through the gothic novel which had evolved in the mid-eighteenth century), were, outwardly at least, a chaste lot. However, the conservative *Times*, along with other 'serious' newspapers, reflected the practice of the popular presses by showing little restraint (although these news texts were censored as I will discuss later) in reporting the salacious details of infanticide inquests and trials, providing readers with compelling narratives detailing illicit sexual liaisons, childbirth, bloody murder and the inference of intimate medical examinations carried out on sexually active women.

While young women may have been forbidden from reading newspapers because of their lurid content, such was the dramatic quality of infanticide news stories published in the press that several well-known novelists appropriated these lurid narratives – without the gore – as the basis of the plots for sensational novels. And despite warnings that novels were unsuitable for the moral development of young women, several of these novels were best sellers and are considered classics today. Victorian infanticide novels sanitized infanticide and relocated it from its traditional working-class environment into the world of 'respectable' classes through novels such as Frances Trollope's *Jessie Phillips* (serialized 1842–43), George Eliot's *Adam Bede* (1859), Elizabeth Gaskell's *Ruth* (1853), Mary Elizabeth Braddon's *Lady Audley's Secret* (1862) and Wilkie Collins' *The Woman in White* (1860). Trollope's novel eloquently illustrates the cause and effect of the Bastardy Clause of the 1834 New Poor Law, the focus of Part I of this study.

Infanticide and Medicine

Medicine became a dominant voice in infanticide with the entry of the medical expert witness into courts of law in England in the seventeenth century when doctors's testimony provided crucial evidence on live birth in infanticide trials. Medical voices framed as scientific, and therefore as the voices of quantifiable 'truths', were privileged in the witness box, with the medical voice alone holding the power to determine the outcome of infanticide trials and inquests. By the eighteenth century medical men had become a powerful influence over family life and the family was the 'target for a great enterprise of medical acculturation' (Foucault 1991a, p. 280). Medical politics in eighteenth-century Europe, according to Foucault, not only formed the framework for medicine's influence over the 'organization of the family, or rather the family children complex', but also established 'the first and most important instance for the medicalization of individuals' (Foucault 1991a, p. 281). A 'medico-administrative knowledge' began to develop 'concerning society, its health and sickness, its conditions of life, housing, and habits', which served as the 'basic core for the social economy and sociology of the nineteenth century' (Foucault 1991a, p. 283). Doctors had a politico-medical hold on populations 'hedged by a whole series of prescriptions relating not only to disease but to general forms of existence and behaviour (food and drink, sexuality and fecundity, clothing and the layout of living space)' (Foucault 1991a, p. 283). Because sex was seen as a 'means of access both to the life of the body and the life of the species' (Foucault 2008a, p. 146) what was regarded as 'deviant' sexual relations (sex outside marriage, sex with prostitutes, homosexual acts) was discursively problematized to a point where society decided the sexually deviant woman needed to be brought under legal and medical control and by pathologizing female sexuality medicine was able to take control of the infanticidal woman. Foucault in *Archaeology of Knowledge* (2002a, p. 205) maintains that to 'tackle the ideological function of a science in order to reveal and modify it' (2002a, p. 205) one should question it as a 'discursive formation' which involves mapping the system by which particular objects are formed and the types of enunciations implicated.

Foucault's analysis of the ideological function of medical science provides a useful frame for reading the role of medicine in the 'treatment' and control of infanticidal women and the role of reporters in privileging medical voices in the creation of news texts. The powerful rhetoric of the man of science in the witness box persuaded magistrates, lawyers and jurors of the rigor and truth of his evidence, and also allowed the court reporter to further privilege the position of the medical man in the eyes of his readers through news discourse. Court reports influenced the public's understanding of the powerful role of the medical man and the veracity of the 'truth' of medical science – an example of Foucault's idea of shifting the source of power to language itself.

In the overwhelming majority of discourses on infanticide studied in this book the evidence of the medical expert witness was critical to a woman's conviction or dismissal. The universal acceptance of the statements of medical men allowed the voice of the eminent medical coroner and medical health officer for central Middlesex, Dr Edwin Lankester (see Chapter 3) to dominate the infanticide debate in England in the 1860s. In locating Lankester's highly influential statement, that there were 16,000 women living in London alone who had committed infanticide, and identifying its function in a particular power/knowledge nexus, this study exposes how a potent but false statement, broadcast through news discourse, led to the formation of a maternal panic.

This study also exposes ruptures in the dominant legal-medical position. At particular moments medical men struggled in the public spotlight to maintain their authority over the infanticidal woman as disputes erupted between the legal and medical professions over the infant's corpse and the issue of 'live birth'. The evidence of the medical expert witness on the question of live birth often created a dilemma for juries. After the introduction of the 1834 New Poor Law with its Bastardy Clause, which denied mothers of illegitimate children parish relief, the numbers of young women brought to trial on charges of infanticide increased and juries were often reluctant to send a young infanticidal women to the gallows. By the middle of the century juries were routinely ignoring the evidence of the expert medical witness who attested to a live birth having taken place, and either found a woman not guilty, not guilty because she was of unsound mind, or guilty of the lesser crime of concealment of birth, a process Mary Beth Emmerichs describes as 'pious perjuries' (1993, p. 105). One magistrate in Kent, Justice Bramwell, said juries in infanticide trials were 'always told there is a possibility of the child not having been born alive despite the medical evidence, therefore you must acquit her. Such direction is not reasonable but it is always given and the jury is always glad to acquit' (cited Conley 1991, p. 110).

Medicine looked to madness to control the infanticidal woman. The rationale behind the madness defence was that the act of giving birth, or the act of breastfeeding, could so affect a woman's mental state as to reduce her culpability if she killed her infant. This defence allowed infanticidal women to be spared from the death penalty, while at the same time removing them from society and placing them under medical control in asylums. The 'hysterization of women, which involved a thorough medicalization of their bodies and their sex, was carried out in the name of the responsibility they owed to the health of their children, the solidity of the family institution, and the safe-guarding of society' (Foucault 1991a, p. 268). Where marriage constituted for woman 'a kind of preservation against the two sorts of insanity which are most inveterate and most often curable' (Foucault 1991a, p. 149), that is, 'debauchery, misconduct' and 'vicious habits such as drunkenness, limitless promiscuity' (Foucault 1991a, p. 149), unmarriageable women (such as women recently convicted of infanticide) were confined to the proxy matrimonial home, the asylum, by their fathers, and occasionally by their husbands, although infanticide within marriage was rare. And in this asylum doctors, 'wearing the mask of Father and of Judge' (Foucault 1991a, p. 161) had the ultimate power to control and to 'treat' these women:

> Family Child relations, centered on the theme of paternal authority; Transgression-Punishment relations, centered on the theme of immediate justice; Madness-Disorder relations, centered on the theme of social and moral order. It is from these that the physician derives his power to cure … . (Foucault 1991a, p. 162)

Infanticidal madness and the notion that medicine provided the way to control infanticide was wholly embraced by nineteenth-century society, and remains with us today as the preferred reading of a woman's infanticidal actions.

The Press

The advent of the press as a powerful institution in the late eighteenth century for the first time allowed a widely dispersed mass audience to be informed on issues of national interest and therefore gave citizens a sense of nationhood and of being able to participate in democratic debate through public discourse. The press, as an influential communicator of news, information and knowledge, speaks to Foucault's notion of power operating through knowledge. Press discourses, both in popular and serious newspapers, educate the citizenry on matters of health, law and order, politics, the economy, transport, welfare, religion and all manner of topics, including sport and recreation, providing citizens through enculturation with models for how to behave and how not to behave in a society, creating what Foucault termed in *Discipline and Punish* (1991b) 'docile bodies', that is a population of subjects who conform to the ruling hegemony through socialization. In the nineteenth-century court reports published in newspapers were perfect ideological morality tales, particularly those where the outcome was capital punishment, warning people of the consequences of behaving badly.

However, the ideological control of newspapers was hidden behind the public service notion of the press as the 'Fourth Estate', a term coined by the Anglo-Irish statesman Edmund Burke who said: 'there are three Estates in Parliament, but in the Reporter's Gallery yonder, there sat a Fourth Estate more important than they all (cited Carlyle 1907, p. 147). The other three estates in nineteenth-century England were Parliament, the Judiciary and the Church. Jeremy Bentham saw the formation of public opinion through news texts as a safeguard against the abuse of power by the legislator, as a tribunal that unites 'all the wisdom and all the justice of the nation' (Boyce 1978, p. 24). In 1866, at the height of the panic about an alleged infanticide epidemic in London, Thomas Carlyle claimed that the press was 'superseding the Pulpit, the Senate, the *Senate Academicus* and much else' (1907, p. 148). Carlyle argued that printing was equivalent to democracy. Invent writing, he said, and democracy is inevitable: 'Whoever can speak, speaking now to the whole nation, becomes a power, a branch of government with inalienable weight in law-making, in all acts of authority' (Carlyle 1907, p. 147). Carlyle also believed that the nascent press allowed men of all ranks to have a tongue 'which others will listen to' (ibid.). Carlyle's belief, however, did not extend to women and there is little evidence to show that working-class women, in particular the domestic servants who became newsworthy through their infanticidal actions, were given a direct and unmediated voice in the press outside brief utterances from the dock in court reports.

In the 1850s the press – with its span from serious broadsheets such as *The Times* and the *Morning Chronicle* to scurrilous scandal sheets such as the *News of the World* – was established as an instrument of social control, with lasting consequences for the development of modern British society (Curran 1978, pp. 79–103). At the same time as England's population doubled the number of literate citizens quintupled from about one-and-a-half million to between seven and eight million. By 1830 R. K. Webb estimates working-class literacy was running at between 65 per cent and 75 per cent (Chibnall 1980, pp. 10–36).

Foucault argued that in the highly regulated printing industry crime texts (he was speaking here of salacious broadsheets) were allowed to be printed and distributed 'because they were expected to have the effect of an ideological control' (2008b, p. 90). Newspaper proprietors saw it as their public duty to report on police and legal matters, in particular court proceedings, talking back to their readers and reinforcing society's expectations in terms of law and order. In Victorian England, 'respectable society increasingly depended on printed texts to educate and inform it about good behaviour in various situations, and newspapers provided regular and detailed commentary on what constituted this' (Stevenson 2005, pp. 242–3), reflecting Foucault's notion of 'docile bodies' and disciplining and controlling lives through the influence of cultural discourse.

The fact that crime and legal reports attracted widespread interest and bolstered circulation and advertising revenue, which saw this genre become a core component of the newspaper business model in both popular and serious newspapers, reinforced the relationships between knowledge, power and capitalism. In the first half of the nineteenth century mainstream newspapers increasingly turned to crime reporting, with its ability to engage the reader through a sense of dramatic immediacy, to boost their circulation. One 'running patterer' (a writer of gallows literature that was sold in single sheets at the gallows) told Henry Mayhew in 1862 that he was not impressed when newspapers began to encroach on his territory: 'we once had a great pull that way over the newspapers. But Lord love you, there's plenty of 'em gets more and more into our line. They treads in our footsteps sir, they follows our bright example' (Mayhew 1862, p. 225).

Crime narratives increased newspaper revenue to such an extent that newspapers were established on the crime and scandal genre alone. *Lloyd's Weekly* exploited the crime formula so successfully in the 1850s it became the first newspaper in the world to reach a sale of a million. In the 1840s the entry of several popular newspapers into the market (*Lloyd's Weekly Newspaper*, the *Illustrated London News*, *News of the World*, the *Daily Express* and the *Daily News*) pushed the established newspapers such as *The Times*, the *Observer*, the *Advertiser* and the *Standard* to publish more crime news (Gregory 2003, p. 36). Richard Altick even suggests the advent of crime news motivated the masses to learn to read (1970, p. 288). From its beginning the down-market *News of the World* exploited crime news and scandals and was rewarded with a large circulation, which it continued to enjoy until 2011. 'Extraordinary Charge of Drugging and Violation' was the sensational lead headline in its first edition in 1834, establishing an editorial line of reporting scandal and crime which immediately found a substantial audience and saw *News of the World* achieve the largest circulation of any newspaper before the final repeal of the Stamp Duty in 1855 (Chibnall 1980, p. 205). Communicated to a mass audience through press reports, crime news allows the public to participate in a shared voyeuristic experience, and at the same time, as Judith Knelman argues, 'as we watch and read about trials and weigh the stories told, we are adjusting the shared beliefs that constitute society's value system' (Knelman 1998, p. 38). She says it is not surprising that, once newspapers began publicizing the arguments and issues in murder trials, their readers responded with 'rapt and constant attention' (Knelman 1998, p. 39), again reflecting Foucault's idea of an omnipresent power (2008a, p. 93) which in terms of news discourse socialized readers, teaching them the 'rules' of society while it entertained and informed.

Crime news, 'true stories of everyday history' (Foucault 1991b, p. 68) were received avidly by the lower classes 'because these people found in them not only memories, but also precedents; the interest of "curiosity" is also a political interest' (Foucault 1991b, p. 68). Foucault regarded the division from salacious broadsheets to the 'grey, unheroic details of everyday crime and punishment' reported in newspapers as a point of departure in the publishing of crime. 'The great murders', he wrote, 'had become the quiet game of the well behaved' (Foucault 1991b, p. 69). While it is true that reports of trials published in the 'respectable' newspapers were often turgid reports with the appearance of verbatim texts, and defendants were rarely represented as heroic characters, nevertheless infanticide newspaper reports were far from grey. Infanticide news, like all judicial reports, was constrained by judicial and journalistic practice, and was shrouded in judicial language, however these news texts were lifted out of the mundane, the 'grey', by their very subject matter. Graphic reports of the testimony of medical practitioners examining the bodies of fecund young women, and lurid accounts of autopsies on dead babies, combined with the salacious evidence of witnesses, brought scandalous sex regularly to the public arena, even in the most respectable of newspapers, the London *Times*, through the bold headline: 'SHOCKING INFANTICIDE!' These scandalous reports, despite censorship erasing the most graphic details, were part of the reason why even *The Times*, the newspaper of record for the middle and upper classes, was regarded as unsuitable reading matter for wives and daughters. The husbands and fathers, however, sat back in comfortable lounges at their elite clubs, publicly titillated, shocked and entertained by reports of illicit sex, secret childbirth and murder. There is a good chance that educated, resourceful wives and daughters sought out copies and were not as ill-informed as their husbands and fathers imagined.

The publication of trials and police reports was used as a way of performing surveillance on and controlling the penal population of Van Diemen's Land in the first half of the nineteenth century (see Chapter 4). The island was a giant jail known as the 'Botany Bay of Botany Bay', it was a place where convicts and former convicts overwhelmingly outnumbered free settlers. During the half century of transportation between 1803 and 1853 the island housed more than 74,000 convicts and while Bentham's panopticon worked at enforcing self-surveillance amongst the prisoners in the Silent Prison, at Port Arthur, the press in the colony also operated to effect self-control and self-surveillance amongst the colonies free, emancipated and convict population. There was an urgent imperative to keep the convict class under strict control and importantly to inform the growing free settler class that the authorities had control of the convict masses and this was done through newspapers reporting, at great length, the trials of convict men and women convicted of both petty and serious criminal offences.

Infanticide was understood in both England and colonial Australia in terms of class, the infanticidal woman was overwhelmingly working class – more specifically servant class – and news stories about infanticide fed into bourgeois concerns and interests, particularly the 'servant problem', which was of particular concern to the growing middle classes. At a time when the London *Times* ran to just four double-sided pages (in the 1820s growing to 12 by the 1870s) infanticide was systematically given priority over other crimes. While after 1834 this had much to do with the newspaper's persistent campaign to bring about reform of the 1834 New Poor Law, it was also due to the widespread interest in the topic. Infanticide reports in *The Times* embedded class into the discourse, speaking to a middle-class audience of the dangers of the sexual impropriety of the working class, particularly servants. Mistresses were lectured about their responsibility to control their female servants and when infanticide occurred under their roofs the news reports often named the mistress of the house who had failed in her duty to provide adequate surveillance of her female servants. (Rarely mentioning the master who was at times the cause of the unwelcome pregnancy.)

Through the creation of intertextual infanticide news narratives from one particular trial, through political, religious and welfare news stories, and through letters to the editor and the highly influential leading articles, readers were alerted to the importance of law and order issues, assuring infanticide a privileged place on the public agenda.

Critical Discourse Analysis

Critical Discourse Analysis follows on from Michel Foucault's groundbreaking discourse analysis work that uncovered how knowledge and power are articulated in discourse. In this analysis of infanticide news from 1822 to 1922 Foucault's approach to discourse analysis provides a way to elucidate how news discourse explained, positioned and limited and politicized, and therefore empowered, the young woman charged with infanticide, and the ways in which society controlled and disciplined her. Drawing upon Foucault's theorization of the 'constitutive and disciplinary properties of discursive practices within socio-political relations of power' (Luke 1999, cited Graham 2005, p. 4) also exposes the means by which particular legal, medical, political, religious and social perspectives on the act of infanticide were legitimized and achieved dominance through news discourse. Foucault, in shifting the source of power to language itself, and his concerns with the relation between regimes of power and discursive formations, provides a particularly relevant theoretical framework for a study of news discourse. To date there has been a reticence among journalism scholars to draw upon Foucault's work when analysing news discourse. Foucault often becomes all too difficult, as Graham argues (2005, p. 4) for those researchers working in more 'practice-oriented fields'. However, Andrejevic (2008, p. 605) is more hopeful, arguing that it is 'somewhat surprising that Foucault's work has not enjoyed a more thorough or enthusiastic reception in journalism studies' and points to the reason for this 'missed encounter' as perhaps the legacy of the 'subterranean antipathy between French theory and more applied forms of practice'. A key question Foucault highlights is: 'how are we constituted as subjects who exercise or submit to power relations?' (Foucault 1991a, p. 49). The ideological role of the press in communicating beliefs, values, and opinions, which shape the way individuals and groups think, act and understand the world, speaks directly to Foucault's concerns with the relationship of language to other social processes, and how language works within power relations.

In this study I have looked to John E. Richardson's application of Critical Discourse Analysis to elicit meaning from historical news texts. Importantly Richardson's methodology 'allows for an interpretation of the meanings of text rather than just quantifying textual features and deriving meaning from this' (Richardson 2007, p. 15). Richardson argues that the analyst of news texts needs to 'situate what is written or said in the context in which it occurs rather than just summarizing patterns or regularities in texts' (Richardson 2007, p. 15) and it is from this perspective that I have approached this study of how infanticide news discourse made meaning of the crime of infanticide and the infanticidal woman in the period 1822–1922. While Richardson's focus is on contemporary newspaper texts, his methodology is also relevant and useful to apply to a study of historical news texts. Richardson argues that textual meaning is constructed through interaction between producer, text and consumer rather than simply being 'read off' the page by all readers in exactly the same way (Richardson 2007). Scholars focusing on contemporary news discourse have access to cross-media texts and significantly they have access to audiences and therefore through Critical Discourse Analysis they can make a more comprehensive analysis than can those of us using historical texts where the archive imposes (frustratingly) particular limits. Nevertheless, the application of Richardson's intertextual and close textual analytical methods, along with his interpretative, contextual and constructivist approach, allow those of us analysing historical texts to make far more nuanced judgements about the meanings behind those texts.

Journalists, Richardson (2007, p. 54) reminds us, make choices in the way they create texts and that 'every text which has been produced could have been produced differently'. I have been interested for some time in the way journalists create meaning from events of the day, how they create news stories narratively, and how journalists at particular moments in time have created news texts that have had a significant negative impact on those they are writing about, particularly mothers whose children die or go missing while in their care (see Goc 2004, 2007, 2009a, 2009b, 2012). Journalists tell stories, they communicate new information and events to the public through stories; they are the professional storytellers of their age, yet journalists reject the notion that they are storytellers, they argue they are merely reporting the events, the 'facts' of the day. The journalist's practice of creating news texts is concealed from both the audience and the journalist alike through the process of 'naturalisation' (Hall 1978). As a young female news journalist in the late twentieth century I was trained to create news texts, to create 'copy', to reflect society back to itself. In the early years I was unconscious of just how much the process of socialization within a male-dominated newsroom, and a patriarchal editorial policy, framed the way I represented the world to readers and viewers. That does not mean to say that I created false or inaccurate texts, but rather that I created texts with a particular ideological (patriarchal) stance and it is from this viewpoint that this book analyses news texts. However, it is important to acknowledge that respected journalists do not deliberately falsify information; to do so would be to destroy their professional credibility and that of their news organization and to undermine the role of the Fourth Estate within democracies. Scholars analysing news texts as historical documents can be reasonably confident that the events published in credible newspapers did actually happen, and for this reason alone news stories are a valuable historical resource because they provide a snapshot of a society at a given moment in time, they tell us what happened, when it happened and whom it happened to. News texts are in the overwhelming majority of cases the only surviving documentation on the lives of the women in this study. Without news texts many of these women would cease to exist beyond being names on a birth, death or marriage certificate uncovered by a family historian or genealogist, reinforcing the power of discourse. Historic news stories provide a, albeit limited, view into the lived experiences of past generations, and as this study hopes to demonstrate, a critical analysis of historical news texts also provides valuable insight into past journalism practices and into the creation of public discourse at particular moments in time.

This book provides two approaches to the analysis of infanticide news. Part I studies infanticide news discourse in the London *Times* over four decades from the 1820s to the 1860s. The routine practice by the national English newspaper of providing regular reports on infanticide inquests and trials provided a corpus of infanticide texts for analysis, allowing for a comprehensive analysis on how the crime of infanticide and the infanticidal woman were represented in England's most influential nineteenth-century newspaper. The practice of *The Times* from 1834 of appropriating infanticide reports from the assizes columns and embedding these reports into the influential leading articles as part of a press campaign to reform the New Poor Law provided me with an insight into the ways in which multiple discourses: parliamentary, legal, religious, medical, welfare and press discourses, influenced public policy on unmarried mothers and also how press discourses informed public opinion on infanticide and the infanticidal woman.

While the national English newspaper rarely provided prolonged or extensive coverage of individual infanticide cases, regional newspapers in England and Australia, with their focus on local news events, did provide comprehensive coverage of individual cases of infanticide. This point of difference provides the focus of Part Two which takes a case study approach in examining five infanticide cases and their press coverage in small, but influential, regional newspapers in Australia and England at various moments between 1830 and 1922.

In colonial Australia I did not find the same consistency and regularity of infanticide news in court and coronial reports that I found in *The Times*. It was not that infanticide did not occur in colonial Australia, the annual returns for births, deaths and marriages tell us that it did, but the relatively small number of cases that came before the public through the court reports in newspapers meant that the crime of infanticide remained off political and social agendas. The focus of court reports in the nascent penal colony of Van Diemen's Land was escaped convicts, bushrangers, stock thefts and violent crimes, but when infanticide was occasionally the subject of brief reports in the court columns, not unsurprisingly, the style and format mirrored the English press, providing no new insight into the representation of infanticide and the infanticidal woman in colonial press discourse. However, the individual cases of at least two young women in Van Diemen's Land – Mary McLauchlan and Sarah Masters – did become the focus of political news discourse and these two women and the press coverage of their infanticide trials are the focus of the first chapter (Chapter 4) in Part II of this study. The second chapter (Chapter 5) examines two very different cases of infanticide, the cases of Harriet Lovell who killed her nine-year-old daughter and was suspected of killing her four infant children in the previous decade, and Lilian Wakefield who allegedly killed her three infant children before killing herself. These two young mothers from the same rural district were the focus of prominent, by disparate, press coverage in the Hobart *Mercury* in 1912. My analysis of these two cases provides an insight into how the grand narrative of nationhood in Australia influenced the way infanticide was reported in the Australian press in the first decade after Federation.

The final case study in Part II, and in this book, is the significant case of 21-year-old factory hand, Edith Roberts, who killed her newborn baby in the attic bedroom of her home in rural Hinkley, near Leicester, in the spring of 1921. It was the desperate act of this quiet, respectable young woman, and the press campaign by the *Leicester Mercury*, that was the catalyst for change to the 300-year-old infanticide act. In England in 1921–22 this case became the cause célèbre for infanticide law reform and Edith Roberts became the first 'celebrity Infanticide'. This case study provides insight into how a regional newspaper, at a moment of great change for women and the press, established a national infanticide discourse through its coverage of Edith Roberts's infanticide.

The marked differences in the coverage of infanticide news between the large circulation national newspaper, *The Times*, and small print run regional newspapers the *Colonial Times*, the *Tasmanian Austral Asiatic Review*, the *Hobart Town Courier* and the *Leicester Mercury* provided the opportunity for an in-depth and comprehensive analysis of infanticide news in England and Australia from 1822 to 1922. The start date for this study, 1822, was chosen to enable an analysis of infanticide news coverage in the decade before the introduction of the 1834 New Poor Law, to understand how political and social discourses articulated into the draconian legislative reform of 1834 that denied unmarried mothers and their offspring parish relief. This decision saw a sharp increase in the number of infanticide cases after August 1834 and until 1872 when reforms to the New Poor Law made the father equally liable for the support of the illegitimate child until the age of 16. The study ends in 1922 when infanticide was on the national political agenda in England for the first time since the 1860s with the case of Edith Roberts. The 100-year timeframe of this study should not be seen as a linear study of progress in the way the press reported infanticide or the infanticidal woman, but rather this study provides examples at different moments across a 100-year timeframe of the diverse ways in which the press represented young women accused of killing their babies.

PART I
Infanticide News in the London *Times*: 1822–1871

Part I of this study provides a comprehensive overview of the representation of infanticide and the infanticidal woman, and the complex ways in which The *Times* played a formative role in the creation of public opinion on unmarried mothers, illegitimacy and infanticide, at various moments between 1822 and 1871. Through access to *The Times Digital Archive 1785–1985* infanticide reports 1822–71 are quantified and then analysed using Critical Discourse Analysis and close textual analysis and contextualized through historiography. Chapter 1 provides the context for understanding how English society understood illegitimacy and the 'fallen woman' and infanticide in the decade before the introduction of the 1834 New Poor Law. This chapter shows how various strategic discourses aligned to create the political climate that allowed the New Poor Law with its harsh Bastardy Clause to be passed in 1834 by both Houses of Parliament. Chapter 2, again drawing upon multiple infanticide court and coronial reports, as well as leading articles and other infanticide discourses, analyses *The Times*'s campaign to amend the New Poor Law and to remove the Bastardy Clause. The final chapter in this section examines the way *The Times* privileged the voice of medical men, and in particular how the privileging of one medical coroner, Dr Edwin Lankester, allowed for the creation of a maternal panic in the 1860s.

Chapter 1

Personal Tragedies, Public Narratives: 1822–1833

In nineteenth-century England the feminine ideal of chastity was considered the pre-eminent virtue of a respectable woman, linked as it was to the economics of a patriarchal society that required a man ensured the succession of his legitimate heirs. An illegitimate child tainted a man's lineage and threatened his position in a 'society of blood' (Foucault 1991a, p. 269). The illegitimate child was in law *filius nullius* (a son of nobody). Illegitimacy was named and defined by a set of rules and conditions that were established between institutions, economic and social practices and patterns of behaviour. Illegitimacy was framed as a great social evil. A report to the House of Lords in 1844 pronounced 'illegitimacy is in itself an evil to a man' for 'without any crime whatever of his own, the illegitimate child is often exposed to dangers, hardships, and ignominy from his infancy'.

A woman who gave birth to an illegitimate child was framed as a 'fallen' woman, an allusion to the original 'Fall' of Eve from God's grace. (On the other hand a 'fallen' man was a heroic figure, a soldier who had literally fallen dead on the battlefield.) The 'good woman' in the nineteenth century was 'constructed as a model for women to aspire to; but their natural propensities, as daughters of Eve, were believed to run counter to it' (Ajroud 2001, p. 23). From early times woman's normal inclination was believed to be unruly, her obedience and virtue was only sustained by 'vigilant suppression of her unruly drives' (Wiltenberg 1992, p. 98). Susan Clark (2001) argues that the preoccupation with a woman's chastity in the nineteenth century was also a 'reflection of the view that a woman's being was centered in her sexuality' and that 'her representative vice was adultery', therefore 'if a woman lost her reputation for chastity, then nothing else mattered' (Clark 2001, p. 14).

Accepting Foucault's argument that both the discursive and the non-discursive are inextricably intertwined, the first chapter in this study of women, infanticide and the press looks at the 'fallen women' and infanticide in *The Times* newspaper in the period from 1822 to 1833. Through an analysis of press discourse in the decade leading up to the legislative changes of 1834 this chapter provides the political and social context for the introduction of the New Poor Law and its Bastardy Clause which had such a disastrous impact on the lives of unmarried mothers and their illegitimate children. Through a combination of historiography and discourse analysis, drawing from John E. Richardson's Critical Discourse Analysis methodology, this chapter will analyse court reports, coronial inquiries, law and police reports, editorials, political reports and letters published in the correspondence pages of the London *Times* to understand how in this period English society came to understand the 'fallen woman', illegitimacy and infanticide.

Gail Reekie argues (1998, p. 7) that the 'illegitimate child' and the 'unmarried mother' are 'particular social identities or subjectivities extruded as part of the cultural process of making and maintaining the illegitimate birth category'. In nineteenth-century England the illegitimate child and the unmarried mother were discursively framed as a problem in society and when the new science of statistics tabulated the numbers of illegitimate children and quantified the economic burden unmarried mothers and their bastard children imposed on society through the distribution of parish relief they became the subject of vociferous political, religious and social debate. Newspapers reflected these concerns through moral discourses about the dangers of dissolute women, often articulated through reports of mothers killing their illegitimate babies. When newspapers published the annual returns for districts and included data on illegitimate births the public awareness of the 'issue' of illegitimacy led to demands for legislative control.

The problem of illegitimacy was not new to nineteenth-century English society. England had been legislating to control illegitimacy and the economic burden it posed on society for centuries. The first legislation to manage the cost of upkeep of illegitimate children was in the Elizabethan era when a statute governing 'chargeable bastards' was passed ('Poor Act' 1575). This initial act compelled the mother and the 'putative' (reputed) father of a bastard child to maintain the child by weekly payments. Subsequent Acts ('An Act for the Due Execution of Divers Laws and Statutes' 1610; 'An Act to Prevent the Destroying and Murthering of Bastard Children' 1624) allowed overseers of parish relief and churchwardens to recover the costs through parental rents. In 1810 a new law to control the problem of illegitimacy was passed ('Bastards Act' 1810), which explicitly placed the burden of upkeep onto the father. The 1810 law allowed a single woman to declare herself pregnant to any justice and to charge a man with being the father. Upon a woman's word an overseer, or a 'substantial householder', could issue a warrant for the putative father's arrest and his committal to jail unless he could provide surety to indemnify the parish. If unable to provide surety he remained in jail until the child was a month old, at which time paternity was determined on family likeness. It was not long before there was a male outcry over the 'injustices' of this new law. This female power over men was reported in the press as a gross inversion of the natural powers of humanity and led to Poor Law Commissioners gathering a corpus of anecdotal evidence on mothers making 'a kind of enterprise' out of bearing illegitimate children (this is discussed in Chapter 2). When this discursive 'evidence' was published in *The Times*, there was public outrage at the duplicity of unmarried women and increasing pressure to change this 'abhorrent' law.

Infanticide News

Infanticide news reports worked as ideological texts on several levels. Through the choice of content, language, rhetorical style, tone and layout these texts reinforced the patriarchal hegemonic position of the female in society. Infanticide news reports reinforced the mental and physical inferiority of women and the dangers unmarried mothers and their illegitimate offspring posed to society. Infanticide news reminded men of the need for eternal vigilance over their wives and daughters and female servants. Foucault talks about how 'the literature of crime transposes to another social class the spectacle that has surrounded the criminal' (Foucault 1991b, p. 69) and by publishing infanticide stories about poor working class women in the pages of *The Times* under such attention-grabbing headlines as 'Extraordinary Case of Infanticide' (*Times* 18 November 1823, p. 3); 'Shocking Infanticide!' (*Times* 30 June 1830, p. 3); 'Shocking Case of Infanticide' (*Times* 19 December 1831, p. 4), upper and middle-class readers gained an insight into the lives of desperate, poor unmarried women. The publication of coronial inquiries and trials exposed the stereotypical 'infanticide' as a young unmarried female domestic servant, alerting society to the close proximity of this moral danger and reinforcing the duty of mistresses to constantly keep their female domestic servants under surveillance.

Foucault describes the 'literature of crime' as a 'locus in which two investments of penal practice meet – a sort of battleground around the crime, its punishment and its memory' (2008b, p. 90). He argues that in the highly regulated printing industry crime texts were allowed to be printed and distributed 'because they were expected to have the effect of an ideological control' (2008b, p. 90). While Foucault was referring primarily to the publication of crime reports in broadsheets, the publishing of less hyperbolic accounts of crime in *The Times* had the same ideological effect. In 1799 Justice Lawrence, presiding in a libel case (*Rex* v. *Wright*, 8 T.R. 293 [K.B.1799]) explicitly acknowledged the ideological effects of newspapers publishing court reports:

> it is of vast advantage to the public that the proceedings of courts of justice should be universally known; and the general advantage to the country in having these proceedings made public more than counterbalances the inconvenience to private persons whose conduct may be the subject of such proceedings. ('Privileged Parliamentary Reports and Comments' 1 December 1868, Andrews 1869, p. 6)

When looking at the ideological function of news it is important to understand who created the texts and in the nineteenth-century press reports of criminal trials and coronial inquests and police reports were, in the main, not produced by journalists but by lawyers and law clerks. The following account from 1863 provides insight into just who was providing courtroom copy for the newspapers:

> In our Law and Police Courts may be seen, sitting in a privileged compartment,
> a busy penman taking down notes of the proceedings. This person is likewise
> preparing copy for the press. He is generally a barrister not overburthened with
> briefs, who is glad to eke out an uncertain income 'by just doing a little reporting'.
> As a rule, he receives a weekly stipend, and, with one or two exceptions, is in
> the service of three or four journals, receiving a limited salary from each. (King
> 1863, p. 372)

Most nineteenth-century citizens had no personal experience of courtrooms, and
most were informed of the goings on inside the courts through news stories. The
fact that lawyers and law clerks, with a vested interest in law, were predominantly
creating court reports for newspapers had a significant influence on their lexical
structure and ideological effect. The privileging of legal language and the framing
of courtroom participants within a legal framework created a sense of authority
and a perception of 'truth' that allowed court reports to be privileged by readers
and interpreted as the reality of law and justice, providing clear evidence of the
consequences for those breaching society's rules.

The format for reporting trials developed from the eighteenth century and
provided a fairly uniform style for court and coronial reports across all newspapers
from the popular presses to the serious newspapers. While the development of
this style was hegemonic, and reflected particular ideological perspectives, the
practicalities of just how law clerks reported on court proceedings also impacted
on the content, style and format, and had ideological implications. King's 1863
description of the court reporter illustrates these effects: 'He writes upon very
thin prepared paper with a pencil also specially adapted to the paper, and is thus
enabled to produce six or seven copies of his reports at once. This saves, time,
labour, and expense' (King 1863, p. 372). The ability to duplicate a report for
publication in multiple newspapers across the country, and the Empire, reinforced
the ideological power of these texts to inform and influence mass audiences.

With the popularity of Pitman's shorthand, devised by Sir Isaac Pitman (1813–
1897) in 1837, journalists were able to create lengthy news reports that had the
appearance of being full verbatim transcripts. The fact that these court transcripts
were rarely verbatim, or full transcripts, and were in fact highly mediated texts
was a moot point. The perception was that reports of court proceedings, with
their perceived neutrality through the use of legal language, were read as 'true'
accounts. Court reporters, educated men with stenographic skills and legal
knowledge, created reports that allowed readers to feel a part of the judicial
process. Nineteenth-century newspaper readers, according to Judith Knelman:

> were quite prepared to plod through masses of peripheral detail on the way to
> the verdict and sentence. 'The theory of *The Times*,' said one chronicler of the
> period, was 'that every reader knew by experience that every word in the paper
> was indispensable, he worked his way through the entire solid and black print,
> from the first page to the last.' (Knelman 1998, p. 39)

While shorthand promised the '*ipsissima verba* of a speech' (A. Smith 1978, p. 154) in reality it rarely delivered that promise. Before the advent of the inverted pyramid reporters with shorthand ability to capture the words of sources verbatim rarely created news narratives with direct quotes. Rather they used 'constructed dialogue' (Richardson 2007), creating discourses from indirect reported speech, paraphrasing and summarizing what the speaker actually said, overtly mediating the courtroom discourse. The words uttered in the courtroom, and appropriated by the reporter, ceased to be those of the speaker, reminding readers of the reporter's central role in the delivery of news. When direct speech was used in infanticide court reports it was always the exception rather than the rule. These brief utterances were used in the news discourse for dramatic effect to add weight and solemnity to the spoken words.

In *The Times* report of the coronial inquiry into the death of Mary Lazenby's newborn baby in 1823 ('Infanticide', *Times* December 15, 1823, p. 3), for example, direct speech is used just once and attributed to the medical expert witness, reinforcing the importance of the medical voice in infanticide court discourse. Nineteenth-century readers were told that when the physician examined the girl he said to her, 'You must at least have had a miscarriage'. Mary's response is not reported. In the very next sentence the reader is told: 'every part of the house was searched, but nothing was found'. When Mary finally confessed the court reporter mediated her crucial testimony: 'She confessed that she had been delivered of something, but said it was very small. She would not say that it was alive she had never heard it cry'. Beyond a pithy response such as 'may God forgive me', or a simple 'sorry', the voice of the female in the dock was rarely unmediated. Was the infanticidal woman silenced because to allow her to speak of her infanticidal actions was to allow her to broadcast her agency to the world?

The law had legal authority over court news discourse and this authority impacted on the verbatim style of court reports. The laws of libel required that reporters provide 'full and fair' accounts of court proceedings or run the risk of a libel action. In actions of libel 'a jury must be satisfied that the article was an honest and fair comment on the facts; in other words, that in the first place they must be satisfied that the comments had been made with an honest belief in their justice' (see *Rex* v. *Wright*, 8 T.R. 293 [K.B.1799]; and *Davison* v. *Duncan* 7 E and B 229, 1857; Andrews 1869, p. 6). Court reporters were required to provide a full (with one exception which will be discussed later in this chapter) and fair account of court proceedings. 'A garbled or partial report, or detached parts of proceedings, published with intent to injure individuals, will equally be disentitled to protection' [from libel] (Andrews 1869, p. 8). This imperative resulted in the long-winded, verbose format of nineteenth-century court reports, which reinforced the authority of legal proceedings and the influence of judicial discourse.

Despite the requirement for reports to be 'full and fair', there was a clear class division in the reporting of trials in the nineteenth-century press. The trials of the poor published in *The Times* were regularly truncated, while the trials of prominent citizens, or those who had the resources to take out a libel action against a newspaper, were meticulously comprehensive. A cursory examination of press reports in nineteenth-century London newspapers, and a comparison with the lists for the Old Bailey, also shows that there was a selection process for publishing trials based on news values and that not all trials were reported. Capital offences and the more salacious violent crimes such as infanticide received more coverage than other offences.

Court news was also constrained by an overt censorship that reflected the patriarchal hegemony of the time. Blackstone reminded court reporters in 1832 that it was a requirement of law 'that certain offensive material not be published' and that newspapers were exempt from libel suits for withholding particular news, namely 'the publication of trials, where indecent evidence must from necessity be introduced; for it would be in vain to turn women and children out of court, if they are afterwards permitted to read what has passed in their absence' (Blackstone 1832 p. 111–12). This exception reflects the ideological control legal and news discourses (and other discourses) had over women, reinforcing the nineteenth-century view that women had to be 'protected' from certain aspects of society, particularly sexual knowledge. This restriction, Blackstone (1832, p. 38) argued, 'in no way' infringed or violated the '*liberty of the press*'. As women had no privileged right to knowledge or information, this form of censorship was seen as a way to protect society from the corruption of female morals.

The Times

The London *Times*, known in the nineteenth century as the 'newspaper of record', was chosen as the newspaper for analysis in Part I of this study because it was the most influential nineteenth-century English newspaper. As early as 1823 the highly respected *Edinburgh Review* somewhat begrudgingly acknowledged the powerful position of *The Times* as the pre-eminent newspaper in England: 'The Times newspaper is, we suppose, entitled to the character it gives itself, of being the "Leading Journal of Europe", and is perhaps the greatest engine of temporary opinion in the world' (S. Smith 1823, p. 363). Acknowledging that *The Times* was not to the *Review*'s taste, Sydney Smith claimed it was 'stuffed up with official documents, with matter-of-fact details' and that it was 'pompous, dogmatical, and full of pretensions, but neither light, various, nor agreeable. It sells more, and contains more, than any other paper, and when you have said this you have said all.' *The Times* saw its primary audience as businessmen from the rising middle class, something Smith, as a journalist on a literary magazine, found disagreeable:

> It is a commercial paper, a paper of business, and it is conducted on principles
> of trade and business. It floats with the tide: it sails with the stream. It has no
> other principle, as we take it. It is not ministerial; it is not patriotic; but it is not
> civic. It is the lungs of the British metropolis; the mouthpiece, oracle, and echo
> of the Stock Exchange; the representative of the mercantile interest. One would

think so much gravity of style might be accompanied with more steadiness and weight of opinion. But *The Times* conforms to the changes of the time ... It is valiant, swaggering, insolent, with a hundred thousand readers as its helm; but the instant the rascal rout turns round with the 'whiff and wind' of some fell circumstances, *The Times*, the renegade, inconsistent *Times*, turns with them! (S. Smith 1823, p. 363)

When Thomas Barnes became editor of *The Times* in 1815 he prided himself on his ability to move with public opinion and he was never apologetic for changing the newspaper's editorial policy. (One of the newspaper's most dramatic changes of opinion after the introduction of the Bastardy Clause in the 1834 New Poor Law is the focus of Chapter 2.) In 1855 the industrialist and reviewer, W. R. Greg, warned of the potential 'despotism' of the London *Times*, arguing that *The Times*, was 'a journal read every morning by hundreds of thousands who read nothing else, who imbibe its doctrines, who accept its statements, and who repeat both to every one they meet', and that the newspaper alone formed 'the public opinion of the country' (Greg 1855 pp. 492–3). In 1871 Grant wrote that the 'prestige' of *The Times* was 'remarkable', claiming: 'The same articles, if they were to appear in other papers, would not produce the same effect as if they had appeared in the "Times"' (Grant 1871, p. 36). This, he argued, was because 'a prestige has, for nearly half a century, attached to the "Times" which has not been attached to any other paper ever published in this country' (p. 37).

Infanticide in 'The Times' 1822–33

Between 1 January 1822 and 1 August 1834 *The Times* published four leading articles which included discussions of infanticide, two relating to infanticide in India, one which made mention of infanticide in North America, and one which made cursory mention of infanticide in a debate on the death penalty. In the same period there were eight letters to the editor on the topic of infanticide, seven of these were on infanticide in India and the eighth was a letter from 'A Member of the Royal College of Surgeons' on the medical efficacy of the hydrostacy test. Infanticide in England was yet to spill out from the court reports and into leading articles and correspondence pages as a focus of political discourse – that was to come after the introduction of the New Poor Law in August 1834. In the period January 1822 – August 1834 there were 24 headlined infanticide reports on trials and coronial inquiries and in news articles in *The Times*; however, there were 74 reports on infanticide embedded in court and assizes reports, foreign news and parliamentary reports. Infanticide was also a preoccupation of the Indian news discourse between 1822 and 1833 and fed into a larger debate on the expansion of the British Empire and the colonization and civilization of India and concerns with the maintenance of law and order and the promotion of British laws. Three *Times* reports on colonization in India in this period focused on infanticide. The House of Commons report on 'The Papers upon Hindoo Infanticide' was published in full over three editions of *The Times* (25 October 1824; 30, December 1824; 6 January 1825). This report positioned India as a country where 'infanticide continued for centuries, through good fortune and through bad, to be the bloody characteristics of the tame, and quiet, and submissive natives of India', but that 'it is pleasing' to reflect that, 'within the short period that English power has been established in India, more has been done to eradicate the abominable superstition of its inhabitants than all the long series of years which have proceeded it' ('The Papers upon Hindoo Infanticide', *Times* 25 October 1824 p. 3). This colonial framing of Indian society as uncivilized and barbaric in contrast to the civilized English colonial power saw cases of infanticide in England (before the 1834 New Poor Law) framed within news discourse as aberrations of individual deviant females and not a reflection on society.

The close textual analysis of infanticide court reports in this chapter is restricted to 14 prominent reports where the word 'infanticide', or the phrases 'child murder', 'unnatural act' or 'inhuman atrocity', (coded language for infanticide) were contained in the headlines. News headlines are ideological – they embody a particular point of view and provide readers with a preferred reading of the text that follows. Headlines provide a macro-reduction of content and background and in terms of this study they reduced the actions of desperate young women who murdered their newborn babies to inflamed headlines such as 'Shocking Infanticide'. Van Dijk argues (1991 pp. 34–5) headlines act as a major control on the way readers interpret the text that follows. In the nineteenth century the word 'infanticide' in a news headline primarily signified the shameful act of an immoral and shameful unmarried woman, although it could also connote a 'heathen' act if the text that followed was a report on infanticide in India, China or Australia.

'Inhuman Atrocity'
The only headlined infanticide report published in *The Times* in 1822 was a police report in October republished from the *Stirling Journal* under the capitalized headline 'INHUMAN ATROCITY' (*Times* 29 October 1822, p. 3). The headlines were designed to attract a reader's attention with the connotation of a shockingly violent or cruel act; readers also understood it was 'inhuman' for a mother to kill her own infant. The violent act was an alleged infanticide and the report that followed this lurid headline reinforced the dominant view of domestic infanticide at the time, that young unmarried women murdered their babies motivated by shame. The woman's identity is framed through the descriptor: 'a young woman residing at Sunny-brae', her identity not considered necessary as she is representative of a particular deviant female, the 'infanticide'. Conflating her state of mind and her actions into 'the wretched infanticide' she becomes the personification of female disgrace through a referential strategy (Reisigl and Wodak 2001; Richardson 2007) which ascribes her deviant characteristics. The descriptive text reinforces this perspective as readers are told that she had 'an illegitimate child, and in order to avoid the shame which an exposure of her

situation might have drawn upon her, barbarously murdered the innocent infant in a manner at which human nature shudders'.

The indexical meaning of the term 'illegitimate' was widely understood in a society where the sense of shame and fear of abandonment from having to face the birth of an illegitimate child was held by all sexually active unmarried women in a society governed by the rule of blood. Finally the coupling of 'illegitimate child' and 'shame' emphasizes her exclusion from society. An illegitimate child was a burden to society; it had no social value, and was thus always represented in press discourse in a negative light. Both the unwed mother and her bastard child were placed outside the 'ideological square' (Teun van Dijk 1988, 1991, 1997) in *The Times* news discourse. Van Dijk's 'ideological square' predicts that 'outsiders' of various types will always be represented in a negative way in news discourse, while insiders will always be represented in a positive way, and while illegitimacy was primarily seen as a problem of the poor, particularly the rural poor, illegitimacy was a potential threat to all members of society, therefore all women who broke society's moral rules were shamed and excluded.

Collocation, that is the coupling of words that tend to occur next to or close to each other in phrases, is a rhetorical strategy used in infanticide reports. Collocations such as 'barbarously murdered' when placed close to other collocations such as 'innocent infant' and 'unspeakable horror' with 'hapless victim' and 'unnatural parent' produce an ideological effect through the connotations and the assumptions which they embody (Stubbs 1996, p. 172) reinforcing society's abhorrence at the young woman's actions. In *The Times* report republished from the *Stirling Journal* readers were told that an 'old woman was surprised to find a very disagreeable smell issuing from the fire and after repeatedly interrogating the sick female, without obtaining a satisfactory answer, turned up the coals, and to her unspeakable horror, found in the midst of them, the half-consumed remains of the hapless victim of the unnatural parent's inhumanity' ('Inhuman Atrocity', *Times* 29 October 1822, p. 3). In this report the collocations 'old woman'; 'sick female', 'unspeakable horror', and 'unnatural parent' provide a specific reading of the news text. The young woman from Sunny-brae is a shameful, 'unnatural parent', the code for a mother who kills her child. The 'old woman' descriptor connotes perceived wisdom, while 'sick female' was a nineteenth-century code for a parturient woman and 'unspeakable horror' was a common collocation used by the press to describe infanticide. The report is finally transformed from a morality tale into a warning discourse informing readers that 'every exertion' to find her had met 'without success', alerting society to the dangers of an 'infanticide' making her 'escape'.

'Child Murder'

Infanticide reports also acted as ideological texts by speaking directly to household mistresses whose role it was to manage and control the morality of female servants as well as their domestic labour. At times news discourse explicitly placed the blame for infanticide on the mistress of the house for failing in her duty to society. According to Milner 57 per cent of the illegitimate births in London in 1857 were from mothers who worked as domestic servants (Milner 2000, p. 298) and it was the servant women in the wealthiest sections of London who killed their newborn infants in the greatest numbers.

In a 1823 news report headlined 'Child Murder' (*Times* 4 February 1823, p. 3) on the inquest of a newborn infant conducted at the Skinners' Arms in London the focus was not the 17-year-old servant girl, but the mistress of the house who on 'considering the girl in labour, sent for her aunt; but before she arrived the child was born, no person being with the girl in the room at the time'. The mistress not only failed in her duty to properly manage her servant's morality, but also failed in her duty to provide surveillance of the unmarried birthing woman whose infant was at risk of infanticide. In reporting the jury's verdict of 'Wilful Murder' against the girl, *The Times* concluded with a blaming discourse that told readers the jury 'were unanimously of opinion there was a great neglect on the part of the mistress in suffering so young a girl to be left alone'.

'Extraordinary Case of Infanticide'

The third headlined infanticide report in 1823 was framed as an 'Extraordinary Case of Infanticide' (*Times* 18 November 1823, p. 3). It was the unusual case of a married woman killing her three children. Such was the rarity of infanticide cases involving married women that this case warranted the headline descriptor of 'extraordinary' connoting something bizarre, unusual and strange. The report represents the mother, Ann Tildesley, the wife of Thomas Tildesley, a joiner, as the antithesis of the ideal mother – she is a suicidal alcoholic living in an unhappy relationship. Ann Tildesley 'administered' poison to her children due to 'domestic unhappiness'. She is a deviant maternal figure who had 'given way to liquor' and who 'wished her own demise'.

'Surrey Winter Assizes: Charge of Infanticide'

In 1824 there were five headlined reports, the first was the case of Sarah Read ('Surrey Winter Assizes: Charge of Infanticide', *Times* 3 January 1824, p. 3) a servant from Newington charged with having thrown her 'newborn female bastard child' into a ditch at Wandsworth. Sarah's ignominy was laid out at unusual length across two columns of *The Times*. Her sorry tale, mediated through constructed dialogue, tells readers that she arrived at her aunt's home in Surrey where she secretly gave birth during the night. Using an evaluative linguistic strategy the reporter informs readers that Sarah was already the mother of another young child, ascribing to her the pejorative 'fallen woman' frame. The aunt's evidence, however, presents Sarah as 'a kind-hearted, good girl in all other respects'. After a long descriptive paragraph on the evidence of family and neighbours Sarah is fore-grounded briefly: 'the prisoner declared her innocence. The constable put a great many questions, to which she said 'Yes,' without knowing what they were'. With that she was silenced. The summation by the magistrate, Mr Justice Park, was presented in formal legal language, reflecting the reporter's familiarity with the syntax of the bench. This stylistic variation in language also symbolizes the authority and knowledge of the magisterial role: 'Mr

Justice Park proceeded to charge the jury – in all inquisitions for blood, the greatest particularity must be observed in the evidence'. Through the didactic, constructed dialogue of the reporter Mr Justice Park provides readers with the historical context of infanticide laws: 'The old law was jealously guarded, that the bastard being absent and not to be found, the mother would have been tried for murder. Thank God, the law was not so severe now; for at least the body must be found. To convict the prisoner, it was necessary to prove malice prepense, or, in plainer speech, malice aforethought ...'. The reporter then describes the mother's actions, as told by Mr Justice Park, which create a positive reading of Sarah Read who provided her baby with clothes and fed the infant 'with her own milk', reflecting her nurturing nature. This evidence opened up the possibility that her infanticidal actions were the result of momentary madness rather than malice aforethought. Park's summary frames the young woman sympathetically, explaining that there had been proof that 'she was of a humane and kind disposition' and finally, through the reporter, the magistrate offers madness as the explanatory framework for her actions: 'women after that particular state of suffering were subject to inflammatory affections, from the fluctuation of their milk. This woman had suffered extreme agitation, and had undergone almost incredible fatigue, considering her situation; being delivered in her aunt's house at night, in 14 hours after she left Newington on the top of a stage coach on a very rainy day, to go to Streatham'. In his summation to the jury Park reiterates the evidence of constable Levet who had earlier stated that Sarah said she was 'bewildered, that she did not know what she was doing' and then he purposely offers the jury the madness defence: 'the jury would determine whether or not the act, if proved to their satisfaction, was the effect of momentary aberration of mind'.

The trial is brought to a conclusion in the press discourse within six lines and the jury, 'consulted for a few minutes and pronounced a verdict of *Not Guilty*'. The last words are Justice Park's: 'who called back Levet, and severely rebuked his cruel impertinence in rigorously questioning the women while she was in almost a distracted state of mind'.

Magistrates and judges, faced with the unpalatable duty of handing down death sentences on young women found guilty of killing their newborn babies, while the absent and non-culpable fathers escaped sanction, were often sympathetic from the bench, and immediately after passing down the dreaded death sentence wrote to the Home Office requesting the commutation of the sentence. Justices Park and Baron were represented in *Times* reports as both condemning the 'unnatural actions' of young women who killed their babies, and also when addressing juries their words were often sympathetic towards the young woman in the dock. Juries were rarely so generous and regularly convicted women of murder, leaving it to the magistrate to don the black cap and hand down the death sentence.

'Suspected Infanticide'
In February 1824 the coronial inquest into the death of an infant child 'supposed to have been murdered under circumstances of great atrocity' was reported under the bold capitalized headline 'SUSPECTED INFANTICIDE' (*Times* 12 February

1824, p. 4). Elizabeth Alert, a servant at the Swan-with-Two-Necks was charged with having murdered her newborn bastard child. The trial received press coverage despite a verdict of 'still-born', which reflects the news values of infanticide trials, regardless of the verdict.

'Papers upon Hindoo Infanticide'

Towards the end of the year infanticide was embedded into the racist discourse of reports from the House of Commons 'Papers upon Hindoo Infanticide'. In the publication of these reports *The Times* made no attempt to mediate the texts, preferring to publish these lengthy reports verbatim in serialized form over three months (*Times* 25 October, 30 December 1824, 6 January 1825). This imperial racist discourse contrasts the binary opposition between the 'heathen' Hindoos and the 'Christian' English. In the first report published in *The Times* infanticide is utilized as an exemplar of the barbarity of Hindoos: 'the moral principles and the religious ordinances of the Hindoos have led to so many incongruities in their general conduct ... The wretch who is so absurdly parsimonious of animal life as to scruple to crush an insect, or tread upon a worm, will not hesitate to give his child to the sharks of the Ganges.' This opening sentence established the narrative's overarching frame that India was a nation of uncivilized heathens in need of the civilizing Christian influence of the colonial power.

In the years 1825 and 1826 there were no local infanticide reports in *The Times* under the headline 'Infanticide'; however, there were infanticide reports embedded in court reports and assizes reports.

'Infanticide'

In 1827 two cases of infanticide were given prominent coverage, the first was Sarah Scorey's infanticide trial ('Infanticide', *Times* 15 February 1827, p. 4) which was presented to the readers as a case of 'peculiar interest' not because it was another case of the 'too frequent crime of child-murder', but because it involved 'circumstances of peculiar interest both of the commission of the deed and its discovery'. This case was considered an exemplar of the dangers unmarried women, particularly from the servant class, posed to all men. With constructed dialogue the court reporter weaves a suspenseful infanticide story from the coronial proceedings adopting the chronological plot sequence of a fictional account, rather than the usual format of a coronial report. The reporter builds the tension by layering the multiple voices of the witnesses and his interpretation of their accounts of the events. Using transformed indirect quotation (Richardson 2007, p. 104), removing the quotation marks and attributions, the reporter presents the events not as opinion statements, as the witnesses' versions of the events, but *as the events*. Significantly the focus of the report is not the young woman charged with 'Wilful Murder' but rather:

> A young man of the adjoining village of Bishop's Stoke, by the name of Charles
> Benham [who] had paid his addresses, for about six months, to Sarah Scorey, a

servant girl, whose friends resided in Stoneham parish and nothing appeared to stand in the way of their intended union, except one suspicion, which arose from the following cause: ('Infanticide', *Times* 15 February 1827, p. 4)

The characterization of Charles Benham as a 'poor young man' and Sarah Scorey as a duplicitous maidservant creates the framework for a familiar press discourse on the evils of the 1810 law that gave women power over men. Sarah's actions, described in the dominant deviant female news frame, were read by *The Times*'s readers as further evidence of the need for changes to the old poor laws. The reporter transformed the judicial discourse into a compelling narrative that reinforced the perceived wisdom of the duplicity of unmarried servant women. His breathless prose continues, with little punctuation, to weave a tale of deception that begins when Charles Benham 'overheard a female neighbour tell his mother that Sarah was in the family way':

> Alarmed at this Benham immediately inquired what reason there could be for such a suspicion, which was confirmed by his mother, who earnestly advised him to have no more to do with Sarah, who, by-the-by, as Benham well knew, was the mother of one child, a fine boy, in Stoneham poor-house. But as that occurred some years ago, it had not been regarded as an indelible stain, and Benham was even yet willing to believe that his mother's suspicions were unjust. ('Infanticide', *Times* 15 February 1827, p. 4)

The verbal process chosen to characterize reported speech frames the reader's understandings of the reported event and, in some cases, Richardson argues (2007, p. 103) 'this may be ideological'. The specific use of the vernacular aside, 'by-the-by', draws the reader into an intimate, privileged conversation with the anonymous reporter, the authoritative 'we' of *The Times*. He gives readers crucial 'facts' about the character of the woman, which reinforces the preferred reading of Sarah Scorey as an immoral and duplicitous woman. The style of this report, which weaves witnesses accounts with the reporter's own voice, creates a powerful ideological discourse that frames the reader, the journalist and Charles Benham as inside the ideological square, the 'us', and Sarah Scorey as the 'them' outside the ideological square. Sarah is portrayed as the stereotypical immoral unmarried and therefore dangerous rural servant. The use of the metaphorical phrase 'indelible stain' to denote moral ruin, a mark against her character that cannot be effaced, was a coded message the readers of *The Times* would have been very familiar with.

The narrative next informs readers how on the night of the fair Sarah went to Charles's father asking for a bed for the night, but was denied, so she went to her uncle's and as 'there being no spare room', she slept 'on the outside of her brother's bed'. The reporter continues his narration, without attribution, creating a compelling story of desperation:

> Between 11 and 12 on the latter night the brother heard her get up and go down
> stairs. As he soon fell asleep for a short time, he could not say how long she
> was gone, but supposed she must have been absent about an hour, or more. On
> her return, he asked her what was the matter, and she merely observed that she
> was cold; upon which he desired her to cover herself with some clothes, and
> nothing further passed. About the middle of the next day (Monday), she abruptly
> left her uncle's and went to her mother's a mile distant. On Tuesday morning,
> a young man in the employ of her uncle was removing some sheaves of wheat
> from mow to the floor of a small barn near the house, he found a handkerchief,
> tied up as a bundle, in which was the body of a newborn female child. Being
> much frightened, he immediately ran to his master and told him what had
> happened; upon which the child was removed into the house and properly laid
> out. ('Infanticide', *Times* 15 February 1827, p. 5)

In this prose Sarah Scorey is only referred to using the personal pronouns 'she'
and 'her' further distancing the young woman from her community in a potent
blaming discourse.

The final paragraph transforms the narrative. The tone here is formal with the
authoritative and attributed voice of the surgeon again being privileged in the
discourse: 'he had minutely examined the body, both externally and internally,
and had no hesitation in pronouncing that the child had been born alive. He further
stated that he had examined the person of Sarah Scorey, whom he found to have
been recently delivered of a child'. The reader is assured, through the authoritative
voice of the surgeon, of the truth of the case and is in no doubt that Sarah Scorey
gave birth to and killed her infant child. However, the final layering of the 'truth' is
given over to another reliable witness, victim Charles's sister, Hannah Benham. In
a theatrical flourish the bloody handkerchief was tabled as evidence and Hannah
identified the handkerchief as Sarah's. With this damning evidence the jury, 'with
little hesitation', returned a verdict of 'Wilful Murder' and Sarah Scorey 'was
immediately committed to the County Gaol to take her trial at the next assizes'.

This not unfamiliar infanticide tale from regional England made its way into
the influential *Times* because, while Sarah's story in itself was not remarkable,
it was an exemplar of a cautionary tale of the duplicity of women, in particular
female servants, at a time when politicians, clergy and others were calling for
changes to the 1810 Bastards Act. Sarah's infanticide was emblematic of that
universal danger all men faced from women – being tricked into a marriage that
would threaten their bloodline. Infanticide news provided a potent warning to
society of the threat of sexually active single women.

This was not the end of Sarah Scorey's infanticide story in *The Times*, her trial
at the Winchester Assizes was reported ('Winchester Assizes – Infanticide', *Times*
12 March 1827, p. 4) as a legal sensation with Sarah Scorey again in the deviant
female frame, but this time as a woman who 'got off in rather a *singular* manner'.
The use of the vernacular 'got off', coupled with the phrase 'in a *singular* manner',
with the typographic inflection on '*singular*', was calculated to send a message to

the reader that this was an extraordinary example of the failure of justice and inadvertently represented Sarah Scorey as a triumphant Medea-like female. The report told readers 'A bill which was preferred against her, being thrown out by the Grand jury, it was resolved to try her upon the coroner's inquisition'. The lexical construction is calculated to infer the shrewdness of Sarah's legal counsel:

> Now, coroner's inquisitions not being in general renowned for accuracy, the counsel, who was employed to defend the prisoner, thought that it would be a short way of relieving his client, if he could pick a hole in this one, through which the prisoner might make her escape. ('Winchester Assizes – Infanticide', *Times* 12 March 1827, p. 4)

The use of colloquial language rather than formal legalese and the choice of verbs with depreciatory connotations, emphasizes the message the reporter intended to communicate to his readers – here is an example of the failure of the legal system that allowed an immoral woman who had killed her newborn child to escape justice. Stylistic variations in language relate to the social context and the social roles which people both symbolize and play in communication (Richardson 2007, p. 95) and as the court reporter was most likely a law clerk jobbing as a court journalist, it is not surprising that he took such a dim view of the failed legal proceedings and wanted to impress his point of view on *The Times*'s readers.

Mills (1995) and Richardson (2007) argue journalists make choices in the way they create texts and that 'every text which has been produced could have been produced differently' (Mills 1995 pp. 143–4; in Richardson, p. 54). Taking Mills's concept of 'transitivity', which is 'concerned with how actions are represented; what kind of actions appear in a text, who does them and to whom they are done' (Mills 1995, pp. 143–4), an analysis of this report illustrates how journalists make subjective choices in creating news discourses and it also illustrates the social construction of infanticide news and its ideological functions. Richardson (2007) argues transitivity forms the very heart of representation, describing the relationships between participants and the roles they play in the processes described in the reporting. If we look at the verbs attributed to each of the main players in this report: Sarah Scorey, the Grand Jury and Sarah's legal counsel, we can see the role transitivity, that is the relationship between the participants and the roles they played in the processes described in the reporting, played in creating a preferred reading. From the dock Sarah Scorey is portrayed as playing an active part in the legal proceedings, in actively subverting the legal process. She 'got off' and she was able to 'make her escape' from the law. To those upper- and middle-class *Times* readers with a classics training, or an interest in theatre, her actions may have brought to mind that most dangerous of all mothers, Medea, as portrayed by the ancient Greek playwright, Euripides. Versions of Euripides' play were played to packed houses in London during the nineteenth century (see Goc 2009b). Medea, after slaughtering her children, escaped being brought to justice by fleeing in a chariot pulled by fire-eating dragons.

Sarah's legal counsel is portrayed as a shrewd operator; the verbs used connoting slipperiness. He found a 'short' legal way to 'pick a hole' in the crown's case by exposing a flaw in the way the coronial report was tabled as evidence:

> After one or two objections, which were over-ruled by the learned judge (Burough), it was admitted, that, inasmuch as the inquisition appeared to be the findings of thirteen jurors, the words, 'upon their oath,' (*per coram sacramentum*) were clearly wrong, as thirteen men could not have been sworn by one oath, but by thirteen oaths. ('Winchester Assizes – Infanticide', *Times* 12 March 1827, p. 4)

The predicate 'learned' bestowed on the judge was perhaps a deliberate rhetorical strategy to soften criticism of the legal process. The lawyer reporting this trial, no doubt cognizant of the long history of legal action taken against journalists and publishers by court participants, is careful not to be seen to criticize the judge's decision. However, his report makes it clear that Sarah's counsel forced the learned judge to admit that the manner in which the coronial evidence was brought before the court was 'clearly wrong'. The addition of the Latin phrase *per coram sacramentum* in parenthesis emphasizes legal authority at the same time as it highlights the procedural failing. The report concludes:

> His Lordship immediately pronounced this objection fatal, and the inquisition was therefore quashed. This, though of course perfectly correct, was quite a novel decision, and is, therefore, worth particular notice, as a caution to coroners, and the legal profession, in future cases. ('Winchester Assizes – Infanticide', *Times* 12 March 1827, p. 4)

The 'fatal' objection from Sarah's counsel had forced Judge Burough to quash the inquisition, and while the reporter, in an obsequious tone, hastens to note that the judge's decision was 'of course perfectly correct', he provides the warning to coroners and the legal profession that this 'novel', ruling should never again allow an infanticidal woman to escape the law.

'Infanticide'

The second case reported in 1827 was that of a stereotypical infanticide committed by an unmarried servant, Eliza Young, near Bristol in November 1827 ('Infanticide', *Times* 27 November 1827, p. 3). The reporter narrates her story through constructed dialogue and begins by taking the unusual step of naming the master of the household in the opening sentence: 'A case of infanticide occurred last week at Kings-weston, near Bristol, at the house of Mr Henry Jones.' Foregrounded as the master of a disreputable family home, Mr Henry Jones is removed from the discourse and his wife, the mistress of this dishonoured home, is framed as a central player in the infanticide tale. Mrs Jones, readers are told through constructed dialogue, had 'suspected [Eliza] to be in a state of pregnancy', but to her 'repeated interrogatories [Eliza] strongly and positively denied it'. Eliza Young disappeared from the house and when she returned Mrs Jones' suspicions were 'strongly excited' and she immediately sent for a 'medical gentleman' to examine the servant girl who 'confirmed the opinion of Mrs Jones' that Eliza Young had recently given birth. Eliza continued to deny she had given birth until the following morning 'when she confessed that she had been delivered and told where the child was. On a search being made the body of the unfortunate child was found in the garden, slightly concealed by some mustard plants.' What the reader is not told, and what we can only surmise, is the interrogation Eliza was subjected to and her rationale for hiding her pregnancy, secretly giving birth and killing her newborn child. The young maidservant was, of course, all too aware that as soon as she disclosed her pregnancy she faced immediate dismissal, which left her with few options other than the streets or the workhouse. The narrative takes the reader directly from the baby found under the mustard plants to 'William Joyner Ellis Esq.' who 'held an inquest and a verdict of "Wilful murder" was returned against the unnatural mother and the coroner issued a warrant of committal to gaol' ('Infanticide', *Times* 27 November 1827, p. 3). In this report both the master and the mistress of the house are named, and shame is brought upon the household for failing to live up to the expected standards of domestic life. But it is Mrs Jones who is the focus of the infanticide discourse with the inference that what went on under her roof challenged her family's and the nation's values. In her role as mistress of the house it was her duty to see that her household was run in an orderly fashion and that she provided moral guidance for her servants. While Mrs Jones failed in her duties her failure provided *The Times* with an opportunity to create a didactic discourse that named and shamed both Eliza Young and Mrs Jones as transgressive women. This news report, and the one that follows, reiterates how the institutions of the Family and the Law came together in the nineteenth century to control domestic servants.

'Shocking Infanticide'
While mistresses were not infrequently criticized in infanticide news discourse for failing in their duties to adequately supervise maidservants, the master of the house was rarely brought into the news coverage. However, in the report of Sarah Elliot's infanticide trial, reported in *The Times* in June 1830, the master of the household was at the centre of the hyperbolic discourse:

> The commission of the most dreadful crime that ever disgraced the annals of Guernsey has lately taken place there – namely the inward laceration and murder of a newly born male infant; for the perpetration of which M. Marie Joseph Fancois Beasse and his servant, Sarah Elliot, were taken up on Monday and committed to goal. ('Shocking Infanticide', *Times* 30 June 1830, p. 6)

The report, republished from the *Hampshire Advertiser* in England's leading newspaper, elevated a regional infanticide to the national stage as a cautionary tale of the dangers of female servants, but also as a warning to the masters of households to behave within society's moral boundaries. The report, however, gives 'M. Marie Joseph Fancois Beasse' his full title in the first instance, denoting his French ancestry, and separating him from English men. Thereafter he is described as 'Mr Beasse' – the honorific a class code – while the servant Sarah is simply 'Sarah Elliot'. The style of this report reflects that used at the inquest over the body of Sarah Scorey's child, creating a compelling chronological retelling of the events through constructed dialogue. In this case the voices are almost wholly unattributed, producing a seamless narrative in which the words have ceased to be those of the speakers, but have been appropriated by the court reporter. Readers are no longer reading a report on a coronial inquiry but on the actions that brought the witnesses before the coronial enquiry. The reporter manufactures a discourse that is imbued with a sense of uncontested 'reality', taking the reader into the lives of Sarah Elliot and M. Marie Joseph Francois Beasse.

Beasse's domestic arrangements are exposed as morally unsound, readers are told that 'Mr Beasse resided at Ruettes Brayes; and Sarah Elliott and a little boy were the only persons who lived with him', the modifying clause inferring impropriety in Mr Beasse's domestic arrangements. The placement of the phrase 'a little boy' after Sarah Elliot's name connotes an unmarried mother and therefore a 'fallen woman'. An 'old woman named Waterman' enters the discourse as the all-knowing charwoman, the 'old' descriptor denoting her as outside suspicion of sexual impropriety and therefore non-threatening, but also as a person with knowledge if not wisdom. The 'old woman' is further desexualized by the absence of her first name. However, her actions in policing the morals of this household earn her a key role in the judicial proceedings and therefore in the constructed news discourse. According to the report on the Friday morning 'this old woman not seeing the servant about the home as usual, inquired what was become of her, and *was told she was gone to town* to see her brother, who was ill', the typographical emphasis alerting readers to question this statement. The reporter has overtly removed the voices of the witnesses to these events and through transformed indirect quotation and constructed dialogue he created a narrative that informs readers: 'This report having been made to the brother, who was in perfect health and had not seen his sister, he thought it his duty to wait on Mr Beasse and ascertain what had become of her.' The brother, not satisfied with the response to his queries from Mr Beasse, who is reported as saying Sarah had gone to town, 'made his case known to the constables' of the town. The narrative continues with the constable's arrival with Sarah's brother. Beasse received them but asked for time to 'consult some of his friends before he gave them any positive information respecting the girl'. The constructed dialogue continues with Beasse reported as sending a message 'shortly afterwards' to the constables that 'she might be seen at his house whenever they chose to call'. The narrative rushes to its conclusion, conflating the events into five potent sentences:

and accordingly they proceeded to his residence, accompanied by the brother, when Sarah Elliott informed them that she had been confined several days to her room with a sprained ancle [*sic*]. The constables suspecting all was not right, represented the case to the Crown office, when Mr Beasse and the girl were immediately apprehended; and the latter confessed she had been delivered of a stillborn child, which was buried in the garden. The infant was immediately exhumed; and on a *post mortem* examination, by Drs O'Brien and Hoskins, it appeared that it had been most barbarously murdered by the introduction of some instrument into its body through the mouth, which had lacerated the root of the tongue and the passage of the throat, causing an interior effusion of blood; and also by the introduction of a [unclear] instrument into the body through the anus. An inquest has been held on the body and a verdict of willful murder recorded against both the prisoners. It is expected their trial will take place before October – *Hampshire Advertiser*. ('Shocking Infanticide', *Times* 30 June 1830, p. 6)

The second last sentence of this report arrives at the confronting details which explains the coded term, used at the beginning of the report, 'inward laceration', and the rationale for the hyperbolic statement that it was 'the most dreadful crime that ever disgraced the annals of Guernsey', which saw the narrative of this infanticide brought into the national spotlight through its publication in *The Times*. However, any claims that the report's news values lay in it being a particularly shocking example of the crime of infanticide are hard to sustain as the subsequent trial was not reported by *The Times*.

'Worcester – Infanticide'
In 1832 the one headlined account of infanticide was a pithy seven-line report 'Worcester – Infanticide' (*Times* 9 March 1832, p. 3) which named and shamed 22-year-old Mary Burford, 'a good looking country girl' who had been charged with the wilful murder of a female bastard child, but was found 'not guilty' by the jury after 'a few minutes'. Mary was found guilty to concealing the birth and sentenced by Mr Justice Littledale to two years' imprisonment with hard labour.

'Infanticide and Suicide'
In 1833 four cases were published under prominent headlines in *The Times*. The first, republished from the Tory newspaper, the *Leeds Intelligencer*, under the headline 'Infanticide and Suicide' briefly recorded 'one of the most distressing occurrences' to come to the notice of the Leeds press 'for some time past', 'the murder of an infant by its unfortunate mother, who afterwards destroyed herself' ('Infanticide and Suicide', *Times* 19 January 1833, p. 4).

'Adjourned Coroner's Inquest – Infanticide'
In February 1833 the 'Adjourned Coroner's Inquest – Infanticide' (*Times* 23 February 1833, p. 2) headlined the reconvening of an inquiry into the death of

a 'fine male infant, about a week old, found barbarously murdered in Weaver's Lane'. New evidence had come to light, which now pushed this previously inconsequential inquest into the news. The news narrative focuses not on the dead baby at the centre of the inquiry, but on an anonymous letter received by the twopenny post. The reporter weaves an intriguing narrative around the malicious letter, presented as evidence at the inquest, which 'contained an insinuation that a young woman residing in the neighbourhood was the mother of the infant'. However, the reporter does not reveal the name of the young woman and readers are informed that upon inquiry the accusation 'turned out to be wholly false'. The jury 'expressed the opinion that the letter had been sent by some designing person with the view of putting them upon a wrong scent'. The reporter's constructed narrative informed readers that 'suspicions' now turned to a witness, 'Manser', a man of 'indifferent character' who 'prevaricated so grossly that it was the general belief that he knew more about the affair than he was willing to disclose'. Without further details readers are curtly informed that the court was 'again adjourned while further inquiries were made'. Frustratingly, for readers wishing to know the outcome of the letter saga, there were no further reports, reinforcing the inconsistencies in the manufacture of infanticide news discourses.

'Infanticide – The King v. Mary Smith'

In July 1833 the report of an infanticide trial at Staffordshire Crown Court was exceptional in the first instance for the fact that it placed the defendant in the capitalized headlines: 'INFANTICIDE – *THE KING* V. *MARY SMITH*' (*Times* 31 July 1833, p. 6). It was rare for a defendant to be identified in the headlines, this was the only instance between 1822 and 1833. This anomaly may have been nothing more than a particularity in the way the court reporter at Staffordshire Crown Court wrote up his records. Mary Smith was no one of note, so there seems little reason for her name to appear in the headlines. The report of Mary Smith's case is noteworthy for several reasons: it deviates from the usual constructed dialogue format, the defendant is not represented as a stereotypical infanticidal woman, and the defendant's voice comes clearly, if briefly, through the mediated discourse. The structure of this report is similar to court records, the court reporter has not taken the multiple discourses within the courtroom and created a news narrative using constructed dialogue, rather he has created a discourse on the event that was the infanticide trial and it is not the reporter who takes the reader outside the courtroom and into the world where the infanticide took place, but the individual witnesses at the trial. The layout of this report immediately informs the reader that they are reading an account of a trial. The evidence of individual witnesses is lexically and typographically separated through the use of paragraphs, and the prefacing of witness statements by their full names before the witness's truncated, and at times awkwardly mediated, evidence is presented.

This infanticide news discourse also has the feel of a court reporter unfamiliar with the practice of creating news stories from a trial as he occasionally slips himself explicitly into the narrative. He first introduces the prisoner through the formal court language of '*The King* v. *Mary Smith*' before informing readers 'the prisoner was indicted for the murder of a certain male child, to the jurors unknown, by drowning it in the canal at Bloxwich, in this county'. He then goes on to inform readers of the legal representatives in the case: 'Mr Corbett, Mr Phillips, and Mr Cooper conducted the prosecution; and Mr Gordon and Mr Lee the defence'. With a new paragraph he provides a précis of the court proceedings, in chronological order, at times providing no details but rather a singular statement: 'Mr CORBETT stated the case for the prosecution to the jury'.

Mrs Fowler is the first witness to be introduced, in a new paragraph, and a précis of her evidence is provided outside direct quotations, but in an attributed manner that convinces readers, despite its obvious conflation and the slippage in and out of direct speech, that it is an accurate representation of what she said:

> Mrs Fowler examined by Mr COOPER. – Is a midwife. Knows the prisoner. She came to witness to make an arrangement for her delivery. I delivered her on the 21st of June of a male infant. I attended her four days, till the 1st of July, when she went off. Saw her again at the inquest. The child had an opening in the upper gum. I did not believe it to be the same at first, but examined it; and finding that mark, I knew it to be the same.
>
> Cross-examined – She got up on the second day after her delivery and was then somewhat light-headed. I saw the baby four times alive. The infant when found had all its proper clothes on it. The mother said it should be called Mary Ann, and it was so called. She was as kind and tender to it as a mother could be. ('Infanticide – *The King* v. *Mary Smith*', *Times* 31 July 1833, p. 6)

The evidence, as reported in the press discourse, provides a narrative of an infanticide that sits outside the 'usual' discursive frame of an unmarried servant desperate to hide her pregnancy, secretly giving birth and killing her child. The coded language here informs readers that in seeking a midwife, and thereby disclosing her pregnancy, Mary Smith did not premeditate the killing of her child; and by providing clothes for her infant (a considerable expense for a servant) she intended to care for her child. Finally the explicit observations of the midwife, in Mary naming her child and the descriptors of 'kind and tender', speak to Mary Smith being a nurturing mother. The next witness, Maria Cockin, is the friend at whose house Mary gave birth. She is reported as telling the court that on the third of July she observed the child was 'lapped up' and Mary was dressed in a red cloak and white bonnet: 'She said she was going home to Harrison's where she lived.' Under cross-examination Maria Cockin said she heard the prisoner call the baby 'Mary'.

It is in the report of the evidence of the next witness, Sarah Cockin, that Mary's voice comes briefly through the news discourse. Sarah said she saw some baby's clothes 'were on a line before the fire' at Maria Cockin's house, a baby's 'long bed-gown with white sleeves of calico unbleached' which Sarah was going to put on the baby when Mary said, '"Oh, bless it, it will go to bed when I get home"'.

Under cross-examination Sarah said Mary 'spoke fondly to her child'. The next witness, Maria Cockin's husband is merely ' – Cocking, husband of Maria', an unusual descriptor in the patriarchal nineteenth-century English press. His evidence is presented in a disjointed manner, forcing readers to connect the dots:

> Was working from his home near Wosley and Essington canal. Harrington lives at Walsall. The direct road from my house to his is along the turnpike road. Wall's-end bridge is out of the road. I saw a woman going along the towing-path towards Walls-end-bridge in a red cloak and a white straw bonnet.
>
> Cross-examined. – The towing-path is very much frequented. ('Infanticide – *The King* v. *Mary Smith*', *Times* 31 July, 1833, p. 6)

Through the reports of the seemingly inconsequential evidence of witnesses in the courtroom readers form a picture of the events that brought Mary before the courts. The evidence of a boatman and another witness placed Mary by the canal. Hannah Cockin is the next witness on the stand and her evidence creates a fuller picture of Mary Smith's life:

> Went to James Harrison to supply prisoner's place. He came home on Wednesday, the 3rd of July, between 10 and 11 o'clock at night. She had a red cloak and a white straw bonnet. She had no child with her. I asked how the child was; she said it was very well. She went to her master's bed-room; my room is near. He asked her how the child was: she said safe; she had put it out to nurse. He said, 'There let it be; I'll pay for anything for it, or you may fetch it home.' She said, 'It is at nurse.' She fetched him some wine, and went to bed. I went away on the Saturday.
>
> Cross-examined. – I have heard Harrison say he is of the Baptist religion. ('Infanticide – *The King* v. *Mary Smith*', *Times* 31 July, 1833, p. 6)

The coded meanings embedded in this discourse, such as Harrison's religion (and the possible motive for him not marrying Mary and making an 'honest woman' of her) provided nineteenth-century readers with a rich account of an infanticide and despite its précised evidence, this prominent 1,289–word report provides researchers in the twenty-first century with insight, through *The Times*, into the lived experience of a young woman on trial for infanticide.

The roll-call of witnesses continues with a farmer, Luke Hard, finding a bundle in the water beyond Pratt's bridge, which he rescued with his pitch fork and discovered it was a dead female child; the landlord of the Spread Eagle public house, Philip Somerfield, laying the child out for examination; and the midwife's husband, Richard Fowler, going to Harrison's on 6 July to ask Mary 'how she was'. According to Fowler's evidence, Mary said she was as well as could be expected and 'no', he could not see the child as she was at nurse six miles off:

I asked her the name of the place, or of the people. She said she could find it. I said I doubted it. I told Harrison a child had been found in the canal, and brought to the Spread Eagle. He said he would rather have lost all his money than anything should have happened to it. He asked her if she had not told him it was at nurse. She said nothing. Witness went away to the Spread Eagle and on his return to Harrison's she was gone. ('Infanticide – *The King* v. *Mary Smith*', *Times* 31 July, 1833, p. 6)

This news narrative, unembellished by the reporter, simply maps out the multiple discourses of the witnesses at Mary Smith's infanticide trial. Because her 'story' was outside the usual infanticide news frame it was given prominence in *The Times* and today provides us with a fuller understanding of the motivations of one unmarried servant girl who killed her newborn infant. The report continues:

Foxall, the police-officer, had her in custody and asked her if the father had anything to do with the drowning of the child. I asked how she come to do such a horrid deed. She said the devil must have put it into her head. She loosed the child in the water and it sunk. She put her hand in for it, to get it out again, but she could not feel it or draw it out again. I took her to the station-house. ('Infanticide – *The King* v. *Mary Smith*', *Times* 31 July 1833, p. 6)

The superintendent of police at Walsall, Mr West, gave evidence that he placed Mary Smith and James Harrison in adjoining cells and overhead Harrison say to Mary:

'Good God, Mary, see what you have brought me to.' She said she was very sorry for it, as he was innocent. She could not tell what had induced her to do it – it came into her head all at once. Witness told his men not to ask her any questions, and cautioned her not to say anything to implicate herself. Afterwards he asked her if her child had a flannel petticoat on with a stone. She said no. She said she put her child under one of the bridges. I said 'Good God, what were your feelings when you saw it struggling in the water?' She said she was very wretched, and had a great mind to throw herself in. She tried to get it out, but could not. ('Infanticide – *The King* v. *Mary Smith*', *Times* 31 July 1833, p. 6)

This report also differs from the others analysed in this chapter in the way the evidence of the medical expert witness is presented. In this report it is not privileged, and the voice of the surgeon, Henry Paget, is represented in two brief sentences: 'It is a female child, and had been drowned. It has a fissure in the upper gum.' Without any secret pregnancy or birth there was no need for the surgeon to examine the defendant, but nevertheless his detailed post mortem evidence on the child, evidence that was regularly privileged in news discourse, was absent.

The news report then comes to a close with Mr Godson and Mr Lee, for the prisoner, objecting on a technicality that the 'indictment was not supported because the child was described there as being unknown, whereas it appeared on the evidence that the child was called Mary Ann, and its surname was either Harrison or Smith'. The judge said he would reserve this point for the consideration of the other judges' and then the report concludes with two short sentences:

> The prisoner said nothing in her defence, and the learned Judge having summed up the evidence,
>
> The Jury found a verdict of Guilty.
>
> The sentence was deferred until next assizes. ('Infanticide – *The King* v. *Mary Smith*', *Times* 31 July 1833, p. 6)

In this report the voice of the young woman on trial for infanticide rings clear through the mediated voices of the witnesses, as does the voice of the father of her child. The evidence, as provided in this news discourse, creates a tragic (if disjointed) narrative of illicit sex between a master and servant, the master's initial failure to stand by the pregnant servant girl and her seemingly misguided (or not) belief that she was alone without financial and moral support.

Mary Smith's refusal to speak in her defence was not unusual in infanticide trials. Her counsel would have instructed Mary not to give evidence, the hegemonic thinking being that a woman, particularly a young woman recently delivered of a child and in a highly emotional state, facing a charge of murder, was not capable of providing evidence that would be in her favour. The silencing of women in the dock, however, had other motivations rooted in a patriarchal society that worked on multiple levels to silence the infanticidal woman and to stop her from naming the father of her deceased child (see Chapter 5 for a further discussion on the silencing of the infanticidal woman).

Conclusion

This chapter provided the context for understanding how in the period 1822–33 English society understood illegitimacy, the 'fallen woman' and infanticide. Through an analysis of infanticide news discourse in *The Times* we have seen the ways in which infanticide news reports worked as ideological texts. The rhetorical style of court reports was overtly judicial, reinforcing the authority of the courts and reflecting the practice of newspapers to contract law clerks to provide courtroom copy. The courtroom discourse was framed in news reports from the prosecution's perspective, providing readers with a preferred reading that framed the pathetic young woman in the dock, whether she was found guilty or innocent of infanticide, as the personification of the 'fallen woman'. In the years 1822–33 infanticide was primarily seen as the crime of dissolute single servant women and a didactic press discourse was directed at the mistress of the home, warning her of the need for constant surveillance of her female servants.

We have seen how the pithy headline 'Infanticide' was a powerful trope for the infanticidal woman's actions and represented the young woman who killed her newborn baby as both the personification of maternal deviancy and as a woman rendered mad by parturiency. In the judicial proceedings both the defence and the prosecution often worked to silence the infanticidal woman, but even when a woman did give evidence at her trial her voice was excised from the press report, her discursive agency denied by the reporter's use of constructed dialogue. All that remains of her voice today are a few pithy utterances that frame her as submissive and pathetically contrite before the patriarchal judiciary at her moment of reckoning. However, as this chapter has shown, through a close textual reading of infanticide news texts, through a teasing out of the constructed dialogue of witnesses, these young women are lifted out of the anonymity of the descriptor 'the Infanticide' to become distinct individuals. Their stories of unwanted pregnancies, of secret childbirth, of suffering and abandonment, while common to almost all women who committed infanticide in nineteenth century England, are transformed into unique stories of the lived experiences of individual young women.

Finally this chapter provided an understanding of how a draconian law that punished mothers of illegitimate children, and aimed at controlling the sexuality of unmarried women, could come into existence. In 1832 the Government appointed a Royal Commission to investigate the application of the Poor Law and to make recommendations for improvement. The Poor Law Commissioners were given a remit to conduct a nationwide inquiry into the present state of poor laws in England and they visited more than 3,000 parishes. Their evidence, presented to Parliament in early 1834, would provide the basis for the introduction of the new 1834 New Poor Law with its Bastardy Clause, which would have such a dramatic negative impact on mothers of illegitimate children. The impact of this new law, and how *The Times* reported these changes, and how the newspaper's editors ran a campaign to amend the law, is the focus of Chapter 2.

Chapter 2

A Press Campaign and the
1834 New Poor Law

In early 1834 the Poor Law Commissioners published their 'Report into the Present State of the Poor Laws' a report which presented formidable testimony on what the Commissioners saw as the social demoralization which emanated from the abuses of the existing 1810 law. Two pages of anecdotal evidence provided examples of 'loose women' perjuring themselves and tricking 'unfortunate young men' into marriage by naming a particular man as the father when that was not the case. These women were seen as a direct threat to the institution of the Family. The report's evidence of the 'grossest inequities for men' in regards to illegitimacy flamed public outrage and led to Lord Henry Peter Brougham, the Lord Chancellor, presenting the New Poor Law Bill with its Bastardy Clause to Parliament in July 1834.

As already outlined in the previous chapter, under the 1810 Bastards Act a single woman was simply able to declare to any justice that she was pregnant and name a man as the father for a warrant to be issued for his arrest. He was then committed to jail unless he could provide surety to indemnify the parish. If unable to provide surety, and unwilling to marry the woman, the man remained in jail until the child was a month old, at which time paternity was determined on family likeness. The mother of a child having power over the putative father was perceived as a gross inversion of the natural powers of humanity. The reality was, however, that the landlord or community official who heard the woman's claims regularly rejected her assertions, which was invariably the case when a maidservant made a claim against the master or the son of a wealthy household. However, in their nationwide investigation the Commissioners claimed to have found 'case after case' of women who had tricked men into marriage. One Oxford Magistrate, Mr Simeon, claimed that 'any woman could use these laws to provide herself with what every woman looks upon as the greatest prize – a husband'; and furthermore 'a woman of dissolute character my pitch upon any unfortunate young man whom she has inveigled into her net, and swear that child to him; and the effect of the law, as it now stands, will be to oblige the man to marry her' ('Poor Law Commissioners' Report into the Present State of the Poor Laws' 1834). The metaphorical code embedded into this language of the 'dissolute' woman who *inveigled into her net* the *unfortunate young man* was immediately understood by a 'society of blood' (Foucault 1991a) where society's rules ordained that the only way to insure a legitimate lineage (bloodline) was through marriage.

In this chapter I will analyse the act of infanticide and the infanticidal woman through *The Times* campaign to amend the 1834 New Poor Law with its Bastardy

Clause which had such disastrous consequences for unmarried mothers. It will firstly demonstrate how various strategic discourses, namely parliamentary debates and the 'Poor Law Commissioners' Report into the Present State of the Poor Laws' (1834), aligned to create the political climate which allowed the 1834 New Poor Law with its Bastardy Clause to be passed by both houses of Parliament. I will then analyse the press campaign established by the editor of *The Times*, Thomas Barnes, to amend the new law and remove the Bastardy Clause. I will also analyse the part the newspaper played in the formation of public opinion that saw the Bastardy Clause become one of the most unpopular aspects of the entire Poor Law Amendment Act leading to petitions regularly being put before the House of Commons over the rest of the decade to amend the clause or remove it from the Act. The focus of this analysis will be the leading articles in *The Times* and letters in its correspondence pages, which will be analysed drawing from Richardson's (2007) work on Critical Discourse Analysis. Finally in this chapter I will examine court and coronial reports to understand how the newspaper embedded multiple infanticide discourses into its leading articles as part of its strategy to bring about changes to a '*bad* law' and expose how in so doing *The Times* politicized infanticide and the infanticidal woman.

As already outlined the introduction of the 1834 New Poor Law with its pernicious Bastardy Clause, which made all illegitimate children the sole responsibility of their mothers until they were 16 years old, had the most significant impact on the increase in infanticide in nineteenth-century England. The late eighteenth and early nineteenth centuries were marked by an unprecedented population explosion due mainly to a decline in the infant death rate. This increase also saw the number of illegitimate children surviving infanthood rise dramatically, creating a burden on parish relief. By the 1830s there were calls to introduce legislative reform to reduce the numbers of bastard children being paid for by the parishes. This increasing burden on the wealthy to provide for what was seen as the licentious profligacy of the poor, allowed for the theories on population control of economist and social reformer Reverend Thomas Malthus to become widely accepted. Malthus's solution to the high rate of illegitimacy was to shift the responsibility onto the mother, denying her the support of the Poor Law (Malthus 1798, p. 183). Drawing from Foucault's idea of the 'statement' as things said that privilege particular ways of seeing, not as a linguistic unit like the sentence but as a 'function' (Foucault 2002a, p. 97; Graham 2005, p. 7), Malthus's statement on illegitimacy and his policies for population control can be read as statements that worked to influence the construction of the 1834 New Poor Law. Malthus argued that the human population increased much faster than agricultural production, and that unless policies were introduced to control the increasing population there would be inevitable social unrest. He warned that the current laws were a 'pernicious stimulus to unnecessary births' (Malthus 1798, p. 183) and his theory allowed society to place the blame upon unmarried working-class mothers.

However, with the introduction of the 1834 New Poor Law and its Bastardy Clause, Malthus's belief that women would not harm their babies for monetary reasons proved to be a fallacy. Soon after the introduction of the New Poor Law in August 1834 *The Times* began reporting an increase in infanticide and a widespread public and judicial discomfort that women, forced by the iniquitous law to kill their babies, were sentenced to death for infanticide while their lovers escaped censure.

Leading Articles

Readers of *The Times*, without the time or inclination to read through the copious parliamentary and other news reports in the newspaper, or to attend public meetings, could form their own opinions by reading the influential *Times* editorial and could also participate in public discourse on political and social issues through the correspondent's pages. Editorials in nineteenth-century newspapers were the paper's engine room. It was in the leading articles that newspapers, particularly *The Times*, had influence over public discourse and fed into and reflected public opinion by providing the framework for people to situate themselves within society and the wider world. Leading articles offered a shortcut to taking a position on a particular issue of the day. The intertextuality of leading articles, which drew upon authoritative reports from political, legal, scientific, religious, welfare and social groups, privileged particular discourses and elevated the voices of the patriarchal elite.

The term 'editor' was in use from 1802 and was used specifically to describe the man in charge of a periodical publication (Smith 1978). Henry Crabb Robinson, who briefly held the editorship of *The Times* in 1807, (although the first man to fulfil the duties of an editor as we understand the role was Thomas Barnes), explained the nascent role of editor:

> After a time I had the name of editor and as such opened all letters. It was my office to cut out odd articles and paragraphs from other papers, decide on the admission of correspondence etc, but there was always a higher power behind. While I was in my room, Mr Walter was in his, and there the great leader, the article that was talked about, was written. (Woods and Bishop 1983, p. 34)

In the early years of the newspaper John Walter II, the first proprietor of *The Times*, wrote the leading article, but after 1817, after his appointment as the editor, Thomas Barnes was given considerable editorial control, including the writing of the leaders. As well as writing the leading article himself, Barnes brought on board a number of leading writers, including Edward Sterling whose leading article in 1830 brought the newspaper its famous moniker, 'The Thunderer'. Barnes was keenly interested in news content and in furthering the role of the press as a watchdog of government, and regularly rewrote or modified leading articles written by others to make them more in line with his point of view. He viewed *The Times* as a single, powerful voice; a voice representative of the quintessential English gentleman, and his aim was to provide contents that reflected *his* anxieties and concerns. The editorial 'we' of *The Times* newspaper spoke for the middle and upper classes, and through this 'we' *The Times* was regarded as 'the Colossus of the press, and the chief exponent of public opinion' (*Leisure Hour*, 1863, p. 541). Aled Jones argues that the 'collective presence of the editorial 'we' lends the 'rhetorical power of a collective, supposedly objective authority' (Jones 1996, p. 120 in Gregory 2003, p. 73) to news texts. An anonymous reader, writing on the influence of *The Times* in 1863, believed people:

> found out that an essay in print – an essay strong and terse, but, above all, opportune – seemed to clear their minds more effectually than the sayings which they heard in conversation, or the letters they received from their friends; and at length the principle of divided labour became so complete in its application to the forming of political opinions, that by glancing at a newspaper, and giving swift assent to its assertions and arguments, many an Englishman was saved the labour of further re-examining his political conscience, and dispensed from the necessity of having to work his own way to a conclusion'. ('*The Times* Newspaper', *Leisure Hour*, 1863, p. 541)

In 1858 John Hilson claimed that to be a writer 'in the leading journal' [*The Times*] was 'to possess a power which any potentate on earth might envy' (1858, p. 11). He said *The Times* was 'a great fact' and the financial returns to such an undertaking must be equal to those of a German Princedom' (Hilson 1858, p. 15). Furthermore he spoke directly to the power of *The Times* to influence politics: 'How few public questions which have risen from small beginnings to be consummated by legislation have been indebted in their earlier stages to the *Times* ... The *Times* is the symbol of the free-born habitudes of English thought, and all confess the potent share it exercises in gathering up the materials of our daily history, by means of which the press shapes our actions as a people' (Hilson 1858, p. 17).

Parliamentary Debate and the New Poor Law

In the House of Lords, a place of 'Christian gentlemen', the forthright Lord Brougham in the debate on the New Poor Law and the proposed Bastardy Clause, framed the patriarchal perspective in a potent rhetoric of blood discourse in which he claimed:

> common sense dictated that though want of chastity was a crime, a sin in man, it was still greater in a woman, whose error corrupted society at its very root ... Everybody knew that unmarried men did not lead a life of continency, and that one-twentieth part of crimes of this description committed by a man would be the utter ruin of a female. (*Hansard* 1834, p. 608)

The power of discourse to create and to reinforce nineteenth-century English society's patriarchal ideological perspective on the issue of illegitimacy is nowhere more apparent than in Brougham's 1834 parliamentary debate on the New Poor Law. Brougham, using *logos*, Aristotle's term for persuading by the use of reasoning, to reiterate society's patriarchal position on sex, told the nation that he felt it to be his duty 'at the expense of being denounced by his countrywomen, for the protection of whose honour and virtue he was as chivalrously devoted as any man in or out of that House' to put forward the proposed changes to the law that would deny mothers of illegitimate children parish relief. He reminded Parliament of the rules of society that proclaimed a fundamental difference in the treatment of women and men in terms of illegitimacy. Brougham drew upon the persuasive *logos* of common sense and ancient customs to argue that:

> want of chastity in woman was a much more grievous offence than want of chastity in man. How could any person deny this? Did not the practice of all ages – did not the common sense declare this to be the fact? Was it nothing for a woman to bring a spurious offspring to the bed of her husband; and would any noble Lord deny, that the sin of incontinence was not greater in an unmarried female than in an unmarried man? (*Hansard* 1834 p. 608)

Brougham's rhetoric reinforces how the power of bloodlines remained dominant in English society at a time in the nineteenth century when, Foucault argues, the notion of a society of blood was giving way to a society of sex. However, Foucault also acknowledges that this was not an abrupt transformation, but rather a seamless flow from one perspective into another which occurred over an extended period of time, and Brougham's parliamentary rhetoric, which articulates society's moral code in the 1830s, both reflects a society ruled by blood but also, through the proposed New Poor Law with its Bastardy Clause, reflects a society seeking to regulate female sexuality through legislation.

Brougham was an adept political debater and knew how to draw upon powerful rhetorical strategies in his addresses to Parliament, for example the use of phrases that created a 'them' and 'us' rhetorical binary, such as 'everybody knows' with its implication that anyone who disagrees is outside society's ideological square. By declaring 'Everybody knew, that unmarried men did not lead a life of continency, and that one-twentieth part of crimes of this description committed by a man would be the utter ruin of a female' (*Hansard* 1834, p. 608) Brougham framed his argument around the 'laws of society' and 'the law of the land' (Ibid., p. 608), inferring these unwritten laws were immutable. 'A virtuous woman', he claimed, 'was regarded as the bond of society, and when she once lost her virtue, "a pearl of great price," adieu to all decorum and decency in society; and if female chastity was once at a discount, not merely would the bonds of society be loosened, but actually burst asunder' (p. 608). The virtuous female, the Madonna of immaculate purity, was society's bulwark against depravity and as such, nineteenth-century English society looked to ways, both through parliamentary discourse and legislation, but also through cultural discourses, through news texts and the regular homilies in the popular family journals, and through novels, drama, poetry and the pulpit, to reinforce the virtuous woman as society's ideal female.

Brougham, and many of his parliamentary colleagues, along with the Poor Law Commissioners, embraced the Malthusian ideology that immoral women led to the multiplication of an impoverished population, and that bastardy could only be diminished by regulating female sexuality through legislative reforms. However, the Bishop of Exeter was a rare voice of dissent in the House of Lords; he told Parliament that he 'considered the part of the measure now under their Lordships' consideration to be pregnant with the rankest and foulest injustice. It obliged the mother solely to maintain her bastard child if she could, while the father was excused from all liability', something he 'charged as an act of the grossest injustice possible'. It was, he asserted, 'contrary to the law of God; and he did not hesitate to say, that the maintenance of his illegitimate child was a duty imposed upon the father as much by the divine law as it was by human legislation' (*Hansard* 1834, p. 610). The Bishop threw the argument back onto his fellow parliamentarians:

> If, for instance, any one of their Lordships had the misfortune of having an illegitimate child, could it be doubted that he would feel it as much his duty to maintain that child as if it had come into the world under the sanction of the law? And if that was the case, would not every man who heard him – every man in the country possessing the feelings of a man – shudder at the proposition now before them? (*Hansard* 1834, p. 610)

In the House of Commons Sir S. Whalley represented a small but determined minority who repudiated the Chancellor of the Exchequer, Lord Althorp's assertion 'that throwing the burden of illegitimacy on the mother would prevent bastardy' (Editorial, *Times* 19 April 1834, p. 5; 'House of Commons' *Times* 10 May 1834, p. 3). On the contrary, Whalley argued, it 'would operate as a premium on vice and immorality, by withdrawing all curb upon young men' and the 'burden upon the woman' would lead to 'still worse crimes', the rhetorical code for infanticide.

When 'The Poor Law Report' was tabled in Parliament much of its anecdotal evidence was published in *The Times* through parliamentary reports, reinforcing the public's view that the current law was the 'great political gangrene of England' (Martineau 1858, p. 378). The anecdote, with its direct appeal to personal experience, is one of the most influential forms of rhetorical discourse and as such is a feature of debating and is also found in news discourse where an anecdote acts as a powerful trope, effectively and efficiently representing a particular ideological position. The potent anecdotes embedded into the Poor Law Commissioners' Report and reported in *The Times* provided the explanatory framework that allowed middle and upper-class citizens to become outraged at the current law, which, the report argued, destroyed the morality of women. Multiple examples of female deception were provided as proof of the necessity to introduce new laws to fortify women's virtue. Personal stories, with binary oppositions – good and bad characters and good and bad actions and events – had direct appeal to readers, providing them with a 'common-sense' understanding of complex political and social processes. The public was persuaded by stories such as the one told by Mr Majendie of East Surrey of a woman of 'immoral habits' who had been 'collecting a number of payments from various men in respect of a train of bastards until she became a local heiress and could make an advantageous match' ('Evidence Mr Majendie, E. Surrey, Kent and Essex Poor Law Commissioners' Report 1834', p. 98). The Commissioners concluded that bastardy would never decline until a bastard was 'what Providence appears to have ordained that it should be, a burthern on its mother, where she cannot maintain it, on her parents' (ibid., p. 197). The rhetoric of the Commissioners' Report reflects Malthusian dogma, and while his polemic, *An Essay on the Principle of Population* (1798), was not cited in the document, its ideology forms the foundations of the Commissioners' Report.

The Times *editorial position*

The Times, along with other London newspapers, including its closest rival the *Morning Chronicle*, had advocated for a change to the law and accepted that something needed to be done about the numbers of immoral women abusing the system. Changes had to be made to ensure that poor relief was only available to the genuinely destitute. This view reflected the widespread fear amongst the middle class at the rising rate of illegitimacy and the fiscal burden to parishes. Through the charged rhetoric of an editorial in February 1834 *The Times* claimed 'relief of mothers of illegitimate children had reached a pitch extremely oppressive to the parishes and grievously detrimental to female morals throughout England' (Editorial 25 February 1834, p. 4). At the same time the editor, Thomas Barnes, was cautious about the proposed introduction of a bastardy clause and foresaw the problems with such a draconian measure:

> Our sapient Solons were duped into the belief that the surest way of diminishing female demoralization, is to encourage the seducer to spread his toils with greater care and skill, by promising him impunity if he succeed, – so leaving the weaker vessel, burdened with the maintenance of her helpless child, a prey to poverty as well as shame, and tempted to the commission of those crimes into which Irish women similarly circumstanced, are, as we have seen, commonly found to fall? (Editorial, *Times* 25 February 1834, p. 4)

Journalism represents 'opinion statements' (Richardson 2007) which are embedded in argumentation that makes them 'more or less defensible, reasonable, justifiable or legitimate as conclusions' (Van Dijk 1996, p. 24; Richardson 2007, pp. 64–5). The success of this argumentation often rests on the use of rhetorical tropes and here we have the editor of *The Times* creating rich rhetorical tropes and using metaphors and coded language which was readily understood by his educated upper and middle-class audience. The verbal metaphor 'spread his toils' enabled *The Times* to speak the unspeakable and the reader's imagination to do the rest;

the gendered metaphor framed women in the way society held them, as 'weaker vessels' who through poverty and shame could be tempted to commit infanticide. The racial slur speaks to England's racist opinion of the 'dissolute' Irish.

Two months later, in April, a *Times* editorial told readers the 'treatment of the poor law question by Parliament is to us a subject of the most unceasing and intense anxiety' (16 April 1834, p. 5). The editorial is cautious but supportive of the 'proposed alteration of the law of bastardy, whereby the support of the illegitimate child is henceforth to be cast upon the mother, the chief objection appears to be the probable increase in child murder. In other respects we think it an expedient and useful change'. The following day the Chancellor of the Exchequer, Lord Althorp, successfully brought the New Poor Law bill before Parliament and, according to Harriet Martineau (1858, p. 378), that night saw the members of Parliament go home 'feeling convinced that the evils of the old poor law system were virtually abolished'. When each of them 'took up the *Times* from the breakfast table, the next morning, [actually two days later] to gratify himself with the study of its advocacy of the measure – an advocacy sure to be more finely expressed than any that could be heard elsewhere – what was the amazement to find the thundering article against the measure!' (Martineau 1858, p. 378). To the surprise of the 'City' *The Times* editorial on Saturday 19 April 1834 criticized several sections of the bill. Its primary criticism was the centralization of power and what it saw as the 'formidable powers' of a 'central board', including the power of 'expenditure at its own discretion of enormous sums of public money'; a board 'which the jurisdiction, almost coextensive with that of Parliament itself, spreads from north to south of the kingdom'. The editorial asked: 'is this board of unconstitutional power necessary?' (Editorial, 19 April 1834, p. 5).

The public, especially the 'City', was stunned at this last-minute change of policy, remembering that the newspaper was regarded as 'the lungs of the British metropolis; the mouthpiece, oracle, and echo of the Stock Exchange; the representative of the mercantile interest' (Smith 1823, p. 363). The mercantile class had supported the proposed bill and were perplexed that *The Times*, which had also supported the need for changes to the old law, had now had such a dramatic last-minute change of opinion. *The Times* was not expected to take the line of the radical press and come out against the law, particularly as Thomas Barnes had so recently acknowledged the 'moral and fiscal outrage' of the current state of poor relief (*Times* Editorial 25 February 1834, p. 4).

However, while Barnes was critical of the centralizing of power in the new bill his position on the bastardy law remained supportive of the need for change. The language used in this editorial (25 February) in regards to the Bastardy Clause frames the mother of illegitimate children no longer as a 'weaker vessel' but now as 'the vicious mother' upon whom the new law threw the support of the 'illegitimate' child. Reflecting the Malthusian rhetoric he would later so vociferously reject, Barnes here argues that the current law gave 'facilities' to:

women to make a trade of swearing children to those men who can best pay
for their support, and who, under present law, must submit without redress
to the discredit as well as pecuniary punishment of a crime which they never
committed. This order of offences will be got rid of by the bill. Again, the
disastrous marriages which so frequently follow the birth of bastard children,
and which so soften end tragically for child, mother, or both, are henceforth less
likely to happen. (Editorial, *Times* 19 April 1834, p. 4)

This hard-edged rhetoric, which frames mothers as making a commercial enterprise
out of having children, picked up on the anecdotal evidence from magistrates
and overseers in the Poor Law Commissioners' Report. However, when the full
content of the new legislation was made available to the newspapers at the end of
April *The Times* overall opposition to the new law grew: 'The more we consider
the new system of poor laws the more (involuntarily and really against our wishes)
do our apprehensions increase respecting it' (Editorial, *Times* 30 April 1834, p. 5).
The *Times* continued to argue that the Poor Law Commissioners had far too many
powers while London's other influential newspaper, the *Morning Chronicle*,
pronounced 'the New Poor Law was '*the sheet-anchor of England*'; and that 'the
poor man must be *made to feel that pauperism is a disgrace*' (Oastler 1843, p. 62).
    While many were shocked at *The Times*'s opposition to the new law, it
reflected Barnes's overall humanitarian viewpoint. Roberts (2002, p. 267) writes
that Thomas Barnes, 'was an exuberant bohemian and one whose heart, it was
said, was "quickly touched by the pain of others". It was above all the pain of the
destitute, doomed either to starvation or the workhouse, that moved Barnes to
denounce the New Poor Law with an unrivaled fierceness and constancy'. Until
his death in 1841 Thomas Barnes would run a resolute campaign through the pages
of *The Times* against the New Poor Law and in particular against the Bastardy
Clause, drawing upon examples of infanticide from his newspaper's court reports
and coronial inquiries to argue that the rise in infanticide was as a direct result of
the new law.
    In a parliamentary report on 23 June 1834 *The Times* detailed what it saw as
the hard-heartedness of the Lord Chancellor and the Chancellor of the Exchequer,
Lord Althorp, who in his speech to the House of Lords had denounced the
'lazy, worthless, and ignominious class who pursued their self-gratification at
the expense of the earnings of the industrious part of the community' ('London
Monday', *Times* 23 June 1834, p. 4). Lord Althorp, drawing his position directly
from Malthus, argued that making the 'victims of the seducer's art maintain their
own bastard children is a "boon to the female population"' ('London Monday',
Times 23 June 1834, p. 4). He believed that to make illegitimacy 'burdensome and
disgraceful' to the mothers of bastards would eradicate illegitimacy.
    When in August the House of Lords rejected a proposal to drop the Bastardy
Clause from the New Poor Law Barnes could not contain his disappointment,
which is almost palpable in the leading article of 9 August 1834:

The defeat which we hoped the whole of the new Poor Law measure would have sustained by the rejection of the bastardy clause last night in the House of Lords has not occurred. After an able speech from the Bishop of Exeter, against the clause, and certainly an able one also for it by the Bishop of London, the clause, to the great regret of all feeling people, and we had almost said to the shame of manhood, was finally carried by a majority of 11 ... We look with heavy hearts to its future operation. The changes which it will produce in what may be termed social life – for the poor surely make a part of society – are of the most fearful and ominous kind ... It is with pain that we cease to hope that the House of Commons will reject so monstrous a bill. (Editorial, *Times* 9 August 1834, p. 5)

Barnes's persuasive rhetoric reflects his lifelong intent to bring the rigid strata of English society closer together. In an editorial three years earlier, in 1831, Barnes had reiterated his commitment to improving the conditions of the poor through the publication of leading articles in *The Times*:

We are too upright to be flatters of the wealthy, and what honest man will dare charge us with having ever abandoned or betrayed the poor? Who has pleaded more strenuously than we have done for the reform which has put power in the hands of so many of the working class? Who has pressed so vigorously against the landlords the wickedness of the tax upon the poor man's bread? Who raised and directed the public spirit in England against the vile massacre of the manufacturing poor at Peterloo in 1819? Who would now open the poor man's eyes to the snares and treacheries which his mock friends are practicing against him, who but this *Times* journal. (Editorial, *Times* 25 March 1831, p. 3)

Politicians were fearful of Barnes and the influence of his newspaper because he was inconsistent in supporting political leaders and parties. Many conservatives were shocked at *The Times*'s vociferous campaign against the New Poor Law. In 1858 Harriet Martineau (1858, p. 378) wrote of *The Times*'s campaign: 'The hostility had been so venomous, so unscrupulous, so mischievous in one direction, and so beneficial in others, so pertinacious, so vigilant ... that it could not be passed over in the history of a time when the press is admitted to be our fourth estate'.

With the implementation of the Bastardy Clause, and the removal of responsibility from the father, Barnes began to see the disastrous consequences for unmarried mothers left without relief and he argued that the Poor Law Act, what he called 'this execrable statute' (Editorial, *Times* 9 February 1835, p. 4), while a part of the law of the land, it was a '*bad* law' and that 'any but an [*sic*] heathen people should endure it long is utterly impossible, when cases like these occur, and the crime of infanticide, as the journals of each day demonstrate, is so fearfully on the increase' (Editorial, *Times* 9 February 1835, p. 4). The Poor Law Commissioners from the outset rejected the claims that the new law would lead to an increase in infanticide, arguing that any increase in infanticide was 'male-instigated' and that women, left to their own devices, would never kill their children from poverty alone:

> We do not believe that infanticide arises from any calculation as to expense. We believe that in no civilised country, and scarcely any barbarous country, has such a thing been heard of as a mother killing her own child in order to save the expense of feeding it. (1834 Poor Law Report 4/5 Will. 1V Ch. 76)

Such was the hegemonic view of the Poor Law Commissioners and Lord Althorp that maternity was the very essence of the female, that they could assert with certainty that mothers without a male provider, destitute, homeless, social pariahs, would never kill their newborn children. Barnes, disturbed by the growing evidence provided in the regular reports of infanticide in the pages of his newspaper, commissioned and authored stirring leading articles that cited the increase in infanticide as evidence of the need to reform the 'unchristian' New Poor Law. The familiar rhetoric argued: 'That this act must, in effect, be repealed, we have no doubt; but at the same time, the fact that such a law did once exist in this Christian and civilized land will for centuries to come be a deep and damning stain both upon the Ministers that proposed and the Parliament that passed it'. (Editorial, *Times* 5 February 1835, p. 2). This colonial discourse situates England as the civilized heart of the British Empire where infanticide was antithetical to its Christian values at a time when evidence of widespread infanticide was being reported from 'heathen' India and China.

In an editorial on 14 April 1837 Barnes acknowledged to his readers that he and members of his editorial staff had been gathering up infanticide news and infanticide court reports 'as happened to catch our eye in the newspapers of the day' and they had 'attempted to keep a sort of register of such authenticated cases of child-desertion and infanticide' as evidence of their predictions that the rates would increase with the introduction of the Bastardy Clause:

> Without laying claim to any extraordinary sagacity, we predicted years ago that one of the inevitable consequences of the new Poor Law would be an increased perpetration of these horrible crimes: nor was it till the instances of this had become multiplied to an extent deeply revolting to every humane observer that we began to keep the calamitous catalogue, the further prosecution of which we have at length been compelled to abandon, from the utter hopelessness of being able to overtake the vast accumulation of cases that daily pressed upon our attention. Almost all of them, at least of such as we have kept any note of, appear to be of the most affecting kind, accompanied by circumstances which occasionally dispose one to pity the criminals, who otherwise deserve execration. (Editorial, *Times* 14 April 1837, p. 4)

Through this intertextual discourse Barnes frames the infanticides as 'young females from 16 to 18 years of age, who had previously borne an innocent and irreproachable name' situating the problem squarely with the new law. Through his position as the editor of England's most influential newspaper desperate disaffected young women had a champion. At a time when there was little sympathy in Parliament or the pulpit for unmarried mothers Barnes was a powerful ally. He took up the cause sure of his position – he had reporters relaying to him not only the concerns of county justices and coroners at the impact of the new act, but also their support for his stance:

> Times without number have we protested against the bastardy clause of the New Poor Law, as being equally immoral and inhuman. How the educated gentlemen of the British Legislature should imagine that by throwing the burden of supporting an illegitimate child upon the frail creature who bears one, the arts of the seducer and the surrenders of his confiding victim would thereby be restrained, is to us wholly incomprehensible ... until we have a Parliamentary committee fairly and unexceptionably constituted to inquire into the whole question of the Poor Laws, with no preconcerted determination to prevent their modification or repeal, the *frightful havoc* which these laws are inflicting on the morals, peace, and lives of their victims, must obviously continue unabated. (Editorial, *Times* 14 April 1837, p. 4)

The infanticidal woman is represented in this editorial discourse as the stereotypical 'frail creature' who has fallen prey to a sexual predator, her 'seducer', who under current law was not held responsible for his actions or for the upkeep of his illegitimate offspring.

A month later *The Times* employs invective rhetoric to brand the Poor Law Commissioners, 'purple tetrarchs of Whiggery' (Editorial, *Times* 30 May 1837, p. 4), again drawing upon classical metaphors in a powerful model of argumentation. This editorial draws from a coronial inquiry in *The Times* to editorialize on a report from the paper's correspondent at Taunton on the verdict of a coroner's jury. The jury, in making their decision about the cause of death of a newborn child, found it had met its death by murder, and 'being persuaded that the crime of infanticide has been greatly increased by the operation of the bastardy clauses in the New Poor Law, the jurymen, acting with the concurrence of the coroner, embody in their deliverance an unequivocal expression of their opinion to that effect' (Editorial, *Times* 30 May 1837, p. 4). Barnes informed *Times* readers that when the Poor Law Commissioners heard of the jury's verdict:

> which both disturbs their tranquility and kindles their wrath ... now were the ancient Herods more disquieted by the remorseful remembrance of the butchered innocents, or by the rumoured reappearance of the beheaded Baptist, than are these purpled tetrarchs of Whiggery at the accumulating exposures of that dismal domain of theirs, whose spoils aggrandize their families, and whose atrocities condemn them to everlasting distinction? (Editorial, *Times* 30 May 1837, p. 4)

The editorial explicitly outlines how the 'honest jury' members were bullied into changing their findings by an officer of the local union who was appointed to 'frighten them into a retraction of the offensive portion of their verdict' and that the men:

> believing that they had got themselves in an alarming warfare with the high authorities of State, which, for aught they know, might involve them and their families in ruin, the poor men filled up the prescribed schedules precisely in the way which such circumstances were calculated to elicit ... in other words they allowed themselves to be intimidated into retracting their statement. (Editorial, *Times* 30 May 1837, p. 4).

Barnes is at his rhetorical best in this editorial where he directs his attack at Lord Althorp who continued to reject the claim that the new law would lead to an increase in infanticide because infanticide, Althorp argued, was 'male-instigated and women left to their own devices would never kill their child from poverty alone'. The infanticidal woman was now at the centre of *The Times*'s call to political action. Barnes claimed that 'every newspaper in the kingdom is teeming with instances wherein unhappy girls, depraved and disheartened by the want of those legitimate resources of which the Poor Law has cruelly deprived them, are driven, under the keenest pressure of anguish, to desert or destroy their offspring (Editorial, *Times* 30 May 1837, p. 4).

By December he was criticizing the citizens of England for their lack of commitment to legislative reform, charging that:

> Barons and beadles, thanes and tailors, magistrates and midwives, knights and nurses, chairmen and charwomen of all grades and descriptions, have been rummaged up and assorted, to attest in their several departments the extreme usefulness of this said Poor Law for diminishing their taxes, or for increasing their gin! (Editorial, *Times* 2 December 1837, p. 5)

The effective use of alliteration to encompass the breadth of citizens, the rhythmic syntax and collocations creates a potent discourse which argues that the police offices were daily crowded with 'workless wanderers', who, denied relief, were reduced in thousands 'to the most hopeless vagrancy'; they were 'apprehended under night either perishing on doorsteps or prowling for plunder'. The poetic cadence draws the reader into the dark details of infanticide and crime, feeding into the concerns of the middle and upper classes at the increasing threat of social disorder amongst the poor working class who were moving into the cities from agricultural districts in unprecedented numbers:

> The younger outcasts of the Poor Law Board are seen in every part of the country receiving their elementary education as prostitutes frightfully on the increase; and in proportion as men, not absolutely savages, are made cognisant

of the system, the louder is their cry, and the more resolute their efforts, for its
partial or total repeal. (Editorial, *Times* 2 December 1837, p. 5)

Just before Christmas Barnes wrote in a buoyant tone, that the 'progress of public
opinion' on the New Poor Law was 'satisfactory in the highest degree' and that 'for
some time past there has been, among various parties, a desperate combination of
effort to rescue it from the universal infamy to which it is inevitably hastening'
(Editorial, *Times* 22 December 1837, p. 5). The New Year arrived, however,
without any progress, and in February Barnes reminded readers in his usual
flamboyant rhetoric of the 'tyrannical and capricious stretch of power exercised
by [Poor Law] Commissioners, as well as the effect of the Bastardy Clause in
promoting infanticide and prostitution' (Editorial, *Times* 8 February 1838, p. 2).
An editorial on 8 February picked up on details from a news report on 6 February
1838, 'Numerous Meeting At Rochdale To Petition For A Repeal Of The New Poor
Law Act', in which Mr T. Livesey proposed a resolution that the Poor Law was
'unconstitutional, despotic, cruel, unchristian, and revolutionary'. Livesey argued
that 'the bastardy clause holds out inducements to seduction and infanticide and
is insulting and degrading to the female sex' ('Numerous Meeting at Rochdale',
Times 6 February 1838, p. 6). Barnes now lobbied for Londoners to take up the
example of citizens in the regions and form Anti-Poor-Law committees and was
happy to report that a public meeting had been called at the Crown and Anchor
in the Strand to form a society. *The Times* hoped that 'friends of humanity and
victims of oppression' would assemble in 'great force' on this 'exciting occasion'
(Editorial, *Times* 8 February 1838, p. 2). On 20 March a 2,329-word letter to the
editor from the honorary secretary to the Metropolitan Association for Repealing
the Poor Law, Mr Thomas Rodgers, contained several letters from supporters
and was given prominent coverage in the correspondence pages ('Poor Law
Commissioners', Letter *Times* 20 March 1838, p. 2). One letter from a country
supporter, signed 'Sheffielder', asked: 'are not our youthful innocent females,
even at this time, corrupted – our towns filling with bastards, and infanticide
encouraged? Are not families brought to misery, poverty, and mendacity, by men
driven from the agricultural unions to the railroads and towns, while this cursed
law has removed all restraints to such savage licentiousness?' (ibid.).

   Throughout the year *The Times* kept the New Poor Law on the news agenda,
publishing more than 300 articles, including leading articles, and parliamentary
reports on the topic. In August 1838 a correspondent who signed himself 'X' wrote
to the editor (with little hope that his letter would be published) about the 'frightful
increase in child murder since the enactment of the New Poor Law'. As the matter
had been 'so frequently brought to the public to no purpose' he doubted the paper
would publish his letter. He need not have worried. The letter was strategically
placed on the correspondence page under the bold capitalized headline: 'NEW
POOR LAW MURDERS' (*Times* 15 August 1838, p. 6). Drawing from 'two such
appalling events' of 'child-murder' reported in *The Times* the previous week the
letterwriter persuasively argued the devastating effects of the Bastardy Clause:

In one of these cases the wretched mother appears to have strangled her infant, an illegitimate child, at its birth. In the other case, a poor girl, who appears to have been a servant at a farmhouse, was convicted of having murdered her illegitimate child of 11 months of age. It came out in evidence that the infant was born in June 1837; that it was put to nurse when three weeks old, and that in May, 1838, the mother went to the house where the child was at nurse, and said 'she must take it away, as she could not afford to pay for it any longer; that she was very sorry to take it away, but could not help it; as she could not get any money from the father, and could not afford to pay for it herself. The child was taken away, found dead under a bridge, and the mother convicted, with a recommendation for mercy from the jury on account of her youth.' ('New Poor Law Murders', Letter, *Times* 15 August 1838, p. 6)

Using a measured tone and *logos* to argue his case, the anonymous correspondent first rejects the usual stereotype of the rural servant woman as immoral and untrustworthy, and in a paternalistic tone frames the 'poor girl' as 'laborious and frugal', which he infers 'from her being a farmhouse servant'. Careful not to be seen to be extenuating 'in the smallest degree', the 'guilt of these deeds of blood', he nevertheless avowed, 'that the death of this infant and its misguided mother are directly chargeable on the bastardy clauses of the new Poor Law'. In his view her youth positioned her as inexperienced in sexual matters and he placed the poor, inexperienced girl against the 'Whig Poor Law' that 'declares that she alone shall bear the whole consequences of her indiscretion, or her guilt, if you please, and that her partner in this guilt, perhaps a man of ample means and mature age, shall go unscathed by human laws to his grave'. Restraint leaves his prose when he argues that the:

atrocious enactments throw the whole responsibility and consequences of a culpable act on the weakest of the two offenders, Unable to support the consequences of her crime, and dreading that most detestable of all prisons, a workhouse, the poor girl is hurried on to the very gallows, while her partner in guilt may possibly be employed under the Poor Law Commissioners in administering that very law which indemnifies a criminal at the expense of his victim. I again say, Sir, that I will not extenuate the guilt of murder under any circumstances, but let our legislators ask themselves who, in such cases, are actually the murderers! ('New Poor Law Murders', Letter, *Times* 15 August 1838, p. 6)

Such persuasive argument, drawing specific cause and effect from infanticide and the Bastardy Clause by appropriating court reports from *The Times*, when published in the influential correspondence pages unintentionally but potently framed the actions of infanticidal women as political.

On Christmas Eve 1838 *The Times* published a 9,258-word news report on evidence taken before the Select Committee of the House of Lords Report on the

Poor Law Amendment Act. This Act was another attempt to amend the harshest aspects of the New Poor Law and the extensive report in the Christmas Eve edition of *The Times* filled the entire page two, providing comfortable middle-class *Times* readers with grim evidence of the disparity between the poor and the middle and upper classes. It told the tragic story of Susan Ling, 48, a widow with 12 children whose youngest children worked for 3d a day when they could gain work. The family were often without food, the children 'very nearly naked and they appeared very much distressed and the cottage very ill furnished; but what there was remarkably clean and decent'. This report, with its wealth of anecdotal evidence to move even the most hard-hearted pro-Malthusian reader at Christmas, nevertheless framed people according to their 'character'. The Relieving Officer admitted that he relieved the paupers according to their character and that he 'reduced the rates by encouraging the good and punishing the bad' ('The Poor law Amendment Act', *Times* 24 Dec. 1834, p. 2)

On Christmas Day the extensive coverage continued in a 10,393-word report, allowing a national platform for the dissenting voice of one woman, Jane Grayston, to be heard. Jane Grayston was a widow with 12 children, seven alive ranging in age from two to 18 with two older girls Susannah, 18, and Lydia, 15, in service. Jane's brother, the local blacksmith, noticed that Jane's daughter Hannah (aged 12) was in need of shoes and clothes and he offered to take her so that Jane could save money from her allowance for new clothes and shoes for the girl. However, the second week after Hannah was gone the Relieving Officer visited and reduced Jane's welfare successively over several weeks until by the end of the year she received nothing. In January her aged father who lived with her died and she was given two shillings. She complained that she could not feed her five children on that money and was told she would have to come into the workhouse. Her response, as recorded in the report, and published in *The Times*, was defiant:

> 'No, gentlemen, I shall not'. They then said they would have none of her sauce. 'Go out.' She said, 'I know what you all are, a pack of villains,' and tore their order all to atoms. Barclay said, 'Go out,' and 'Get out,' 'Go along with you.' Thus the poor woman was treated more like a dog than a Christian; and after she got out she staggered against the wall, and stood and cried for some time, and did not know what she was to do when she got home. If she had brought disgrace and trouble on herself or the parish she could have borne it, and felt she deserved it; but the losing her husband and her misfortunes altogether were brought on by Divine Providence, and she could not help it; and she is now left without any resource, and almost broken-hearted with grief, distress, and despair, and cannot tell what she is to do … She asked the guardians of her parish what she was to do – 'You will give nothing, and I must not rob or steal; what are we all to starve and perish?' Signed JANE GRAYSTON'. ('The Poor Law Amendment Act', *Times* 24 December 1838, p. 2)

This highly influential report from the Poor Law Commissioners was not readily accessible to members of the public, but through *The Times* newspaper and its publication of extensive extracts from the report middle and upper-class readers gained 'knowledge' of the lives of the poor and inadvertently through the publication of sections of the report, the newspaper provided a political voice to some of society's most disenfranchised citizens. Jane Grayston's story of defiance, when it was published in *The Times*, gave her the platform of the country's most influential newspaper.

The New Year brought no reforms to the law and by year's end Barnes was reflecting on lost opportunities when he published an editorial reflecting his frustration at the intransigence of the Government to repeal the law, writing with his usual rhetorical flourish: 'Nearly all England has now tasted the bitter fruits of this cruel experiment – such as infanticide, death by cold and hunger, workhouses depopulated by typhus fever, and the blood-stained introduction of the new tyranny into Bradford' (Editorial, *Times* 4 December 1838, p. 5). The report detailed at length empirical evidence garnered from its own pages.

The newspaper's campaign to amend the law continued throughout 1839 and 1840 and examples of the results of the Bastardy Clause continued to be regularly reported in the assizes columns. The New Year of 1841 was heralded in with a grim news report on the 'Infanticide and Mutilation of a Child' (*Times* 9 January 1841, p. 6). The body of a child wrapped in a brown paper parcel was found on the parapet of Waterloo Bridge, infamous as the place where young women threw themselves to their deaths into the fast flowing Thames. The body of the child was 'mutilated in a frightful manner'. This report forensically details the crime scene providing a grim narrative. A 'young gentleman' retrieved the parcel from the parapet and upon opening it found 'a coarse huckaback towel, and a new calico sheet'. He opened the sheet to find:

> The remains of a male child entirely dismembered. The head had been severed from the body, and the arms had been cut off above the wrists, and again divided above the elbows. The trunk was sawn in two, and the legs were separated from the body. The heart, lower part of the stomach, the lungs, and a portion of the legs were missing. In fact, the body was literally cut to pieces, though in a very clumsy manner. ('Infanticide and Mutilation of a Child', *Times* 9 January 1841, p. 6)

Because the parcel was not frozen it was deduced that the body had been there a short time. The suspected perpetrator, the stereotypical 'unnatural parent', was unknown but the report provided evidence which it was hoped would solve this murder-mystery: 'One of the wrappers is marked with the initials "W. H. No. 1" and this may probably give the policeman some clue to the discovery of the perpetrators of this horrible deed'.

A month later another sensationalized infanticide case was republished from the *Stirling Journal*. Laced with hyperbole and presented as hearsay it was closer to the gossip of the popular presses than the usual formality of *The Times*. The opening paragraph sets the tone: 'One of the most atrocious cases of child-murder that has ever come to our knowledge was discovered on Wednesday last' (*Times* 24 February 1841, p. 6). The language is imbued with the intonation of a Scotsman in conversation and tells readers: 'It appears that about 13 weeks ago, a young woman, residing with her mother and sister in a house in the Craigs of Stirling, was delivered of an illegitimate female child, but it had scarcely drawn the breath of life ere it was doomed to meet with a cruel death from the hands of the unnatural grandmother and aunt'. The grim narrative relates how no sooner had the child cried than the grandmother said 'she would soon stop its squalling' and 'procuring a piece of cloth, which she saturated in oil, and wrapping the infant within it, she placed the whole upon the fire, having first stirred it up in order to insure a speedy dissolution.' *The Times*'s readers were assured: 'these are the facts of the case, so far as they have reached us'. The grandmother, mother and aunt, readers were told, had been apprehended.

Thomas Barnes's important rhetorical strategy of using infanticide news to place the New Poor Law firmly on the public agenda also brought the influential role of the medical man to a mass audience. Medical men played a significant role in the administration and enactment of poor relief under the New Poor Law, being called upon to testify to the physical condition of people applying for relief. In a *Times* leader in January 1841 Barnes continued his dialogue of opposition to the 'iniquitous' law by quoting from a pamphlet written by a surgeon, Mr Roworth of Nottingham, which highlighted the influential role of the medical man in enacting the New Poor Law:

> A person called at my house to inform me (unknown to the persons he was come about) of a family in great want of food, the woman confined with twins, and there were four most afflicted creatures, with the loss of their limbs, and then, as I generally found is to be the case, some out-door-relief was given … .

> If there be one case in which more than another humanity is forward to provide for foreseen sorrow, it is surely that of a poor woman in childbirth.

> But humanity had no seat in that reformed house which framed the poor law, nor truth any honour in that committee. (Editorial, *Times* 4 January 1841, p. 5)

The Times privileged medical voices, particularly when doctors criticized the law, and elevated them to the status of primary definers of infanticide news. At the same time the newspaper created a highly popular news product in the form of sensational court reports on the inquests and trials of young women charged with infanticide.

In April 1841 Barnes was still doggedly championing the cause for reform in his last editorial on the evils of the 1834 New Poor Law:

Will they dare to tell us that the poor of this country have, through their means, been rendered one atom happier or better than they were five years ago? We trow not. A rod of terror without mercy would neither restrain vice nor create happiness … nor in their attempts to curb immorality, have been compelled to legitimate infanticide. Yet these are the undeniable effects of their system. (Editorial, *Times* 13 April 1841, p. 4)

Barnes, the voice of the middle-classes, again directly positions *The Times* as the champion of the poor and working class in his campaign to bring about reform. In his call to political action Barnes consistently looked to the young infanticidal female as the most potent evidence of the injustice of the law. Just a month later the editor who had been so 'unrelenting in his condemnation' of the New Poor Law (Roberts 1972, p. 18) was dead at 55.

Thomas Barnes's successor, John Delane, continued the tradition of lobbying for repeal of the New Poor Law using infanticide reports from *The Times* to inform his editorials. Unlike Barnes, Delane was not a literary man and did not write leading articles himself, however he maintained editorial control and he continued the tradition of using the newspaper to influence public opinion. Under Delane's editorship Abraham Lincoln told war correspondent William Russell that *The Times* was 'one of the greatest powers in the world' (Wilkerson 1970, p. 33). Delane held the editorship for more than 30 years from May 1841 to 1877. More pragmatic than Barnes, Delane's heart 'was less easily touched' (Roberts 2002, p. 267). Surrounded by Oxford and Cambridge men, he 'tempered Barnes's humanitarianism with High Church and Establishment orthodoxies' (Roberts 2002, p. 267) and while direct editorial criticism of the bastardy clause of the New Poor Law decreased under Delane's editorship, he was also a humanitarian and his editorial pages were strident in opposition to what he regarded as injustices in the treatment of the poor.

The Sevenoaks Workhouse Report

The inquiry into the Sevenoaks Workhouse in 1841 provided shocking evidence of the harsh reality of workhouse conditions and when John Delane provided extensive coverage of the inquiry he positioned himself as intending to continue Barnes's campaign to amend the poor laws. The report into the state of the workhouse at Sevenoaks was undertaken by two medical officers, Mr Adams and his assistant, Mr Jackson, and reflects Foucault's argument (1991a, p. 275) that medicine was understood and practiced as a 'service' and framed as assisting the 'sick poor', which allowed medicine to be interpreted primarily as a beneficial and valuable resource in society. Delane gave up nine leading articles between second November and 20 December 1841 to this report and in so doing privileged the medical voice of the report's authors. This medical discourse brought to the public shocking and compelling evidence of the brutal life of the workhouse, particularly for parturient women and their children:

> In February all of the children in the house (except two or three infants) had the itch; about a dozen had bad feet and chilblains, with the bones of their toes protruding, in consequence of neglect. On the 29th of April Mr Adams reported to the board that there were then in the house 78 boys and 94 girls and infant children; that all the 78 boys had enlargement of the neck and 42 had likewise goitres; that of the girls and infants 91 had enlarged glands at the back of the neck, and 63 also goitres. (Editorial, *Times* 29 November 1841, p. 4)

The rhetoric frames these anecdotal stories as empirical evidence, as quantifiable, and therefore authoritative and 'truthful'. *The Times*'s choice to allow the medical men to speak directly to their readers through the publication of the report, without editorial rhetoric cutting into the discourse, added a heightened sense of authority to the report and importantly turned the Poor Law Commissioners' Report back on the Commissioners through the most influential leading articles in the country. Delane's editorial framing in these stark, compelling nine leading articles strengthened the view that workhouses were designed to engender such fear and abhorrence that paupers would rather find labouring work than cross the threshold of a workhouse. The evidence also reinforced the inhumanity of the system and provided a greater understanding of the rationale of unmarried mothers who would rather kill their newborn babies than enter the workhouse. *The Times*'s editorials reported birthing women sharing fetid beds with fellow parturient women:

> There were two lying-in rooms only in the workhouse, one of them 7 feet long and 10 feet 9 inches wide, the other about 9 feet square. In each of these rooms were two beds, each of them 4 feet 6 inches wide, and 6 feet long. In each bed there were at one time two women at the least, either expecting labour or recently delivered. (Editorial, *Times* 29 November 1841, p. 4)

The medical rhetoric, with its use of precise measurements and forensic detail, reflected the diligence of scientific inquiry and provided an additional layer of authority to the stories of beds crawling with vermin which allowed no room for the 'nurse' to walk in between. 'Some beds had no change of linen for a week, others none for a fortnight; one stated that she left the house covered with vermin'. Beside her on the birthing bed lay a parturient woman's other children, suffering from goitre and 'the itch'. The report stated that at the time of the inquiry several of the women giving birth in shared beds died from puerperal fever.

As disturbing as the graphic reports of childbirth were to nineteenth-century readers, they were censored. Readers were told that *The Times* had 'abstained' from going into the 'disgusting details about the filthy state in which these poor women and others in the same situation were suffered to remain'. Certain evidence, it was determined, was unsuitable for female readers, again denying middle-class women the discursive knowledge about poor parturient women, and reinforcing the patriarchal power over knowledge and discourse. Nevertheless the exposure of some aspects of the appalling conditions in which poor women in English workhouses were forced to deliver their children, at a time when the child was being idealized by the middle classes, was a calculated strategy to gain sympathy from *Times*'s readers. The reports were confronting in their detail of the lived experience of individual women in the Sevenoaks workhouse and the acknowledgement of censorship created a space for imaginary horrors to amplify the abhorrent conditions. *The Times* editorials quantified the high rates of mortality amongst birthing women, and of children sleeping 15 in two beds. The *Times* rhetorical strategy of appropriating individual women's experiences and identifying these women and speaking to their bodily experiences, allowed the abstract misery of the workhouse poor to be realized:

> Fanny Giles was placed in the same bed with Sarah Watson on the 15th of December; on the 16th she was confined, being at the time alone in the bed, but two women being in the other bed with their children. The next night, within 10 hours of her confinement, she was removed, to make way for a new comer, into the bed already occupied by those two women and two children at the same time in one bed. From Sunday, the 13th of December, till a whole week after her confinement, she could not obtain clean linen of any kind, though she frequently applied for it. Shortly afterwards she was removed to the other lying-in room; and while there, on 25th December, a woman named Harriet Harborer was actually confined while in the bed with her. The next day Giles was again removed into the casual ward, and was there compelled to sleep in the same bed with a woman, who had a loathsome contagious disease, 'of a very bad character'. (Editorial, *Times* 29 November 1841, p. 4)

The hierarchy of deserving poor and undeserving poor is embedded into the discourse through the choice not to name the woman with the 'loathsome contagious disease' with whom Fanny Giles was forced to share a bed. The naming of individual women without honorifics denotes their low status in society, and created some distance from the middle-class readers of *The Times*, but the forensic detailing of their experiences through medical discourse appealed to their Christian humanity. Foucault's notion of the body's status as an economic unit is evident here, with the implicit understanding that these workhouse women who were producing sickly and often illegitimate children were not fulfilling their obligation to society to produce a healthy labour force. At a time when the essence of a working-class woman's existence was her ability to produce the next generation of workers for an increasingly industrialized society, *The Times*'s editorials reinforced the failure of a system to promote a healthy population.

The newspaper story created from the miserable lives of Rebecca Bignell and Mary Collins who were 'put into the delivery bed together about the same time, shortly before the 18th of December', had another layer of intention. This report on their birthing experience, provided by doctors Adams and Jackson and one of the workhouse's parturient women, Fanny Giles, retold through the influential leading articles in *The Times*, reiterated the quality medical care provided by workhouse doctors, and also fed neatly into the medical profession's campaign to take over the delivery room from midwifes and nurses:

> Collins was delivered on that day, in the daytime, Bignell not being then in bed. Collins remained in the same bed till the following day, and was only removed just before Bignell's labour, which then took place. At this time there were seven women in the two lying-in rooms, and only one nurse to attend them, who was unfit for the duty, and did not properly perform it. Bignell was seized with puerperal fever, and underwent medical treatment successfully for the first few days, so as to be apparently out of danger, and the medical officer thinks it probable that she would have recovered, if she had been properly nursed. She was neglected, however, and she died. All these facts were proved by the evidence of Fanny Giles and two of the medical officers of the union, Mr Adams and his assistant, Mr Jackson. (Editorial, *Times* 29 November 1841, p. 4)

The political rhetoric embedded into this discourse persuades readers of the professionalism of the medical doctor in opposition to the poor treatment from the 'nurse'. The women, reduced to objects of medical intervention by the use of their second names alone, 'underwent medical treatment' from the doctors while they were 'nursed' (poorly) by the midwife who was 'unfit for the duty' – code for a drunken midwife, a character who would be personified by Charles Dickens in the nurse Mrs Gamp in his serialized novel, *The Life and Adventures of Martin Chuzzlewit* (1843–44). The quantifiable evidence of the appalling conditions of these women in childbirth bolstered medicine's campaign to take over the care of the parturient woman from midwives.

Conclusion

Through an analysis of press discourses in *The Times* on illegitimacy, infanticide, poverty, the New Poor Law and the Sevenoaks Workhouse Inquiry this chapter has provided insight into some of the motivations for young woman to kill their babies in England after the introduction of the 1834 New Poor Law. An examination of Lord Brougham's parliamentary debate in 1834 exposed the patriarchal positioning on the issue of illegitimacy and how the 'rules of society' positioned and constrained women. The dominant view, reflected in the Lord Chancellor's speech to Parliament, was that when a young woman lost her virtue she became a threat to the 'decorum and decency in society'. Brougham told Parliament that the very 'bonds of society' would be 'burst asunder' if young women were allowed to cast aside their virtue. It was such positioning, along with the influential Poor Law Commissioners' Report into the State of the Current Poor Laws, with its potent anecdotal evidence about young women perjuring themselves, and duping innocent young men into marriage or into paying maintenance, that allowed for the passing of the 1834 New Poor Law and the Bastardy Clause. The analysis of the Thomas Barnes's campaigning editorials in *The Times* shows how *The Times* used infanticide as evidence and politicized the desperate actions of society's most disenfranchised citizens, unmarried mothers, in its campaign to repeal the New Poor Law. In Chapter 3 the disastrous consequences of the 1834 New Poor Law continue to be realized and through an analysis of the press discourse on the infanticide pronouncements of the influential coroner for central Middlesex, Dr Edwin Lankester, we see how his flawed statistics led to press claims that London in the 1860s was in the grip of an 'Infanticide Epidemic'.

Chapter 3
The 1860s Maternal Panic

Three decades after the introduction of the 1834 New Poor Law with its pernicious Bastardy Clause the disastrous effects of the law for unmarried mothers and their newborn babies were still apparent in the regular news reports of dead babies being found in the Thames and Regent's Canal, in the outhouses and rubbish heaps of London and in regional England. With no easing of the law and its harsh restrictions on parish relief for the mothers of illegitimate children, life for pregnant, unmarried women offered few viable options – the workhouse remained society's solution for destitute dishonourable woman. As the previous chapter showed the workhouse was a detested place where parturient women faced birth and death in fetid overcrowded conditions and babies' short, wretched lives ended in miserable deaths.

By the 1860s enterprising working-class women began establishing what became known as 'baby farms', in essence foster homes, which offered unmarried mothers a solution to their dilemma – at a cost. What seemed on the face of it a viable option, which allowed the unmarried mother to remain in employment, was soon exposed as a corrupt scheme, which encumbered poorly paid servant women with an unviable financial burden while their children were dying at rates as high and higher than the infant death rate in the workhouse. Several scandals, which will be discussed later in this chapter, uncovered the grim reality of many 'baby farms'. However, not all foster arrangements were poorly managed, and it could be argued that the wide press exposure of a number of appalling examples of foster care, which led to cries to abolish all 'baby farms', also reflected a patriarchal society that could not tolerate a system in which women themselves, outside the institutions of Family and Welfare, found ways to manage their situation. With the closure of numerous 'baby farms' in the 1860s infanticide remained the only option open to many destitute unmarried mothers.

The Coroner for Central Middlesex

In this chapter infanticide is analysed in the 1860s through *The Times* discourse on the pronouncements of the most influential voice on infanticide during the decade, the eloquent, campaigning medical coroner Dr Edwin Lankester. Through an analysis of Lankester's newsworthy pronouncements from the coroner's bench, and from press reports on his speeches delivered at the annual convention of the newly formed Social Science Association, the power of the press to shape public opinion becomes evident. The pronouncements of Lankester, who rose from humble origins in rural Suffolk to become a distinguished scientist, were inscribed with the dual authority of medicine and law. When his pronouncements were promoted by England's most influential newspaper it led to Lankester's designation as England's 'national oracle on infanticide' (Rose 1986, p. 62) and saw the infanticidal actions of desperate, unmarried mothers become the focus of prominent news discourses in a way that had not been seen since the 1830s and '40s. Foucault's notion of power challenges the binary model of power versus oppression and in this chapter my claim is not that there was a simple oppositional binary between the powerful voice of Lankester and the oppressed infanticidal women. Instead I will argue that the women who killed their newborn babies were part of a more complex power relationship, one that politicized their actions and reignited infanticide discourse in England.

Medical men, as Foucault tells us (1991a, p. 283), have a politico-medical hold on populations 'hedged by a whole series of prescriptions' relating not only to disease, but also to all forms of human behaviour. In the nineteenth century the rise of the medical coroner saw medicine become even more influential in regulating human behaviour through a politico-medical-legal hold on the population.

Dr Thomas Wakley

It was Dr Thomas Wakley, Edwin Lankester's predecessor as the coroner for central Middlesex, who as England's first medical coroner progressed medicine's role in controlling populations. Wakley was also a politician who first played a role in political debate on the issue of infanticide and the New Poor Law during the 1830s and 1840s. As an MP in the House of Commons for Finchley, and a medical authority, his pronouncements, reported in *The Times*, were influential in creating the environment in which society was receptive to the pronouncements of Lankester in the 1860s. In June 1847 in opposing the Poor Laws Administration Bill, *The Times* reported that Wakley 'announced his intention of dividing the house against' what he saw as 'a cruel, odious, obnoxious, and tyrannical bill' (*Times*, 25 June 1847, p. 4). His conviction of the evils of the law 'was so strong, that nothing should induce him to deviate from that resolution'. He 'horrified the house with an account of the great increase of infanticide which had taken place under the alteration of the law of Elizabeth' and 'maintained that the Bastardy Law has led to a great increase of the crime of infanticide' (*Times* 25 June 1847, p. 4). Wakley created multiple influential discourses through his dual roles as parliamentarian, coroner, medical scientist and as the founding editor of the medical journal, the *Lancet*. From its establishment in the 1840s the *Lancet* regularly called attention to the wide-spread 'evil of infanticide' creating powerful multi-layered discourses and reinforcing the fundamental role of medicine in controlling and managing infanticide. The *Lancet*, under his editorship claimed in 1861:

> In London alone within the last five years the bodies of 500 children have been
> found under such circumstances as could leave no doubt that their lives had been

intentionally sacrificed. Upwards of sixty were taken from the Thames, or from the neighbouring ponds or canals. More than 100 were discovered stowed away under railway arches, upon the door-steps of houses, or in cellars or other out of the way places, without exception in such cases as these, the children, if not dead when placed there, must have been deserted with the hope that death would speedily ensue. (*Lancet*, September 1861; Ryan 1862, p. 50)

Wakley drew upon his authoritative role as the medical coroner for central Middlesex to provide quantifiable statistics to argue the harmfulness of the 1834 New Poor Law and to urge for its abolition. In this scientific discourse Wakley does not moralize on the 'wanton wickedness' of the infanticidal woman, nor is he explicit in naming the act of infanticide, but rather he uses coded language such as 'intentionally sacrificed' and 'deserted with the hope that death would speedily ensue' as his explanatory framework for the act of infanticide. While deploring the act of infanticide he did so from the humane standpoint that the Bastardy Clause left desperate young mothers with few options and he argued that until the law was changed these abandoned young women would continue to turn to infanticide as a means of survival.

Dr Edwin Lankester

When Wakley died in 1862 Edwin Lankester stood for the coronership of central Middlesex and was elected by a majority of 47 votes over the legal candidate. Lankester, like Wakley, was a talented rhetor with the ability to influence audiences with his argument but, unlike Wakley, in Lankester's discourse there is an entrenched morality that frames 'the infanticide' as inherently wicked. In opposition to other social commentators of the day, and against *The Times*'s long-standing editorial policy, the newspaper reported Lankester in his first month on the bench as arguing that women who committed infanticide were not the victims of a heinous law, but rather wanton women who were a risk to the whole of society, thus putting them into the role of Stanley Cohen's (2002) classic 'folk devils' frame, casting them as deviant maternal figures. This perspective would become the dominant news frame for reporting stories about mothers who killed their babies in the 1860s and created the environment for a 'maternal panic'.

Edwin Lankester became an influential voice on the issue of infanticide in the 1860s because, like Wakley, he had multiple authoritarian positions from which to layer his infanticide discourse. As a member of the recently formed Social Science Association of England, founded in July 1857 by a group of prominent intellectuals who gathered at the home of Lord Brougham, 'to unite all those interested in social improvement' (Millman 1974, p. 122), Lankester had another platform upon which to broadcast his opinions on infanticide. The Social Science Association counted among its members such influential men as John Stuart Mill and Edwin Chadwick. Foucault found in his work on medical politics in eighteenth-century Europe that medicine had become a powerful influence over family life, and the family was the 'target for a great enterprise of medical acculturation' (Foucault 1991a, p. 280). The 'medico-administrative knowledge', which began to develop in the eighteenth century, 'concerning society, its health and sickness, its conditions of life, housing, and habits', served as the 'basic core for the social economy and sociology of the nineteenth century' (Foucault 1991a, p. 283) and created what Foucault (1991b) called 'docile bodies', a population that was managed through acculturation and self-control rather than directly through discipline and punishment. The education of the population through discourse is clearly evident in the speeches given and the papers produced by members of the Social Science Association. Edwin Chadwick was a British civil servant in the 1830s who produced a report on the *Sanitary Conditions of the Labouring Population*, which recommended a number of measures to improve public health among the working classes and led to the introduction of laws such as the Factory Act, improvements in water supplies, compulsory vaccinations and laws about child labour. Lankester, through the Association, championed the field of forensic science, and he also campaigned for an end to the high rate of infanticide in London through the better management of the parturient woman, and more coronial inquiries and better policing.

When Lankester took up the position of medical coroner for central Middlesex in 1862 he was already a man of influence. In 1849 he had obtained the post of Attending Physician at the Royal Pimlico Dispensary and Lying-In Institution in Belgrave Terrace, a position he kept for seven years. In 1854 when a cholera outbreak in St James's parish in Westminster killed 142 people in the first week and it was Lankester's research into the understanding of the water-borne nature of the spread of cholera that helped Dr John Snow to establish the causal link between the outbreak and the pumps at Broad and Campbell Streets. Lankester's contribution to stemming the cholera outbreak not only brought him to public attention, but also earned him a powerful role in the administration and control of the residents of Westminster through his appointment in 1856 as the first Medical Officer of Health for St James. In his new position Lankester aimed to halve the death rate in the parish and progress the health and welfare of the poor and infirm, and to this end he gathered statistics on weekly births and deaths and requested that all institutions, hospitals, doctors and parsons in the district report to him any incipient epidemics that came to their notice (English 1990, p. 95).

As well as his skill as a botanist, biologist, apothecary, surgeon and medical practitioner, Lankester was a distinguished lecturer in anatomy and physiology (Rose 1986, p. 62). He was an ambitious man who was shocked when his membership application to the Royal College of Physicians was refused 'because he was not of a sufficiently elevated social standing' (English 1990, p. *xv*). This rejection, according to his biographer, Mary English, made him 'not only shocked, but extremely angry' (p. 40), and he published a pamphlet stating forthrightly exactly what he thought about the College and its examiners. Although he had the support of influential friends, such as Charles Dickens, his London medical practice failed to attract wealthy clients because he was not considered their social equal and it was this life-long struggle for acceptance amongst his medical peers that fed into Lankester's reforming zeal and his campaign to reduce the number of infanticides in London. From August 1862 until his death in 1874 Edwin Lankester featured prominently in more than 400 coronial news stories in *The Times*, including infanticide reports of coronial inquiries in which his opinions invariably overtook the inquiry and dominated the press report. It was his inflamed 'scientific' opinions on the emotive issue of infanticide more than any other topic that saw Lankester privileged in news discourse over his coronial colleagues.

Lankester's statistics and an 'Infanticide Epidemic'
Lankester's coronial pronouncements started attracting press attention soon after his election and in September 1862 the reporter sitting in on an inquest into the death of a newly born male at Islington was so impressed by the pronouncements of the new medical coroner for Middlesex on the general state of infanticide that he shifted the focus of his news report away from the proceedings to Lankester's general pronouncements:

> INFANTICIDE IN THE METROPOLIS. – At an inquest held in Islington yesterday Dr Lankester, one of the coroners for Middlesex, took occasion to make some remarks on the very large number of cases of infanticide which occur in the metropolis, and on the failure of justice in instances where there is too much reason to suspect that actual murder has been committed. The inquiry into which the Coroner was presiding was one into the circumstances connected with the death of a newly born male child whose body was found on Thursday last in a mews at the rear of Compton-terrace, Islington. ('Infanticide in the Metropolis', *Times* 9 September 1862, p. 6)

While the reporter's narrative barely gives the dead child a mention, the provocative opinions of the new coroner were highly newsworthy, especially when he made claims that society was not generally aware that 'this was one of a class of cases which were exceedingly numerous at the present day' and that he 'regretted to state that such cases were constantly occurring in London. He believed he held nearly one inquest a day on the bodies of newly born infants ('Infanticide in the Metropolis', *Times* 9 September 1862, p. 6). The report concludes with Lankester's rhetoric framed in a spinous barb on the inefficiencies in police inquiries: 'So common was infanticide', he is reported as saying, that 'the police seemed to think no more of finding a dead child than they did of finding a dead cat or a dead dog. This was a blot on our civilization, and vigorous measures ought to be adopted with the view of removing so great an evil' ('Infanticide in the Metropolis', *Times* 9 September, 1862, p. 6). Such potent rhetoric encouraged reporters in the years ahead to frequently repeat Lankester's claims establishing a repetitive discourse that created a public and press perception that there was an epidemic of infanticide in the country.

A month later, in October 1862, Lankester fuelled the infanticide debate in a moral discourse that framed unmarried women who killed their babies as the epitome of female deviancy and as a direct threat to society:

> The crime of infanticide was likely to be attended with an even worse result than the death of the infant. It could not be doubted that after a woman killed her infant she would be less likely to look with abhorrence upon the crime of murder, and the blunting of her sensibility on that point was dangerous to society at large. ('Dr Lankester on Infanticide', *Times* 24 October 1862, p. 6)

While *The Times*, during its campaign to amend the Bastardy Clause, consistently branded the single infanticidal woman in reports on inquests and trials as 'unnatural' and her actions as 'atrocious' and 'wicked', in leading articles she was also framed as the victim of an unjust law. To Edwin Lankester, however, she was the personification of immorality and needed to be vigorously prosecuted for her actions.

Edwin Lankester's press persona was inextricably linked to his ability as a primary definer of infanticide news to consistently provide journalists with highly charged quotes on infanticide, especially his statistical data that added scientific authority to his claims. Lankester diligently collated data on infant deaths in the district of central Middlesex, along with national statistics from the Registrar-General's Reports, providing the quantifiable material upon which reporters created compelling and alarming infanticide news narratives in the 1860s. More than anything it was Lankester's ability to embed statistics into his discourse that saw his voice privileged in the press. Through the discourse of statistics Lankester created compelling fortnightly reports and a comprehensive annual report on the state of health in the district, a practice that would significantly influence his career as a medical coroner. Foucault's analysis of sex and his notions about how it gave rise 'to comprehensive measures, statistical assessment, and interventions aimed at the entire social body or at groups taken as a whole' (Foucault 2008a, p. 146) is a useful way of understanding the role of Lankester's infanticide statistics in the creation of an influential infanticide discourse and a maternal panic in 1860s London. Statistical discourse was seen as authoritative discourse, derived as it was from scientific calculation dealing with analysis and interpretation of numerical data, and was accepted uncritically by reporters and editors as a succinct and apparently unambiguous explanation for social situations.

Under John Delane's editorship *The Times* constructed a powerful leading article on 26 June 1863 headlined 'A Report from Dr Lankester', which appropriated Lankester's statistical report 'On the Sanitary State of the West-End Workrooms'. Lankester's report was the only source used in the editorial on the 'deplorable state of conditions for women within workrooms'. This influential editorial privileged the opinion of the newly appointed coroner for central Middlesex beginning with: 'Dr Lankester seems to think …' ('A Report from Dr Lankester', *Times* 26 June 1863, p. 8). This was the first of what would be a number of influential editorials over the decade in which *The Times* promoted Lankester under such headlines as: 'Dr

Lankester on Infanticide' (*Times* 24 October 1862, p. 6); 'Year's Work of a Coroner – Dr Lankester' (*Times* 12 June 1864, p. 9); 'Dr Lancester [*sic*] on Child Murder' (*Times* 15 August 1866, p. 7), 'A London Coroner's Work' (*Times* 16 April 1867, p. 11).

It was unusual for a coroner to publish coronial reports of the length and detail of Lankester's reports, but his need to have his opinions heard, together with his commitment to educating the population on matters of health, saw him driven to disseminate his data to as large an audience as possible, 'in order to draw attention to the social evils of the day and the means of remedying them' (English 1990, p. 142). He published his first two reports for 1862–63 and 1863–64 as supplements to the *Transactions of the National Association for the Promotion of Social Science*. The third and fourth were published in his own short-lived *Journal of Social Science*; the fifth to seventh again appeared as supplements to the *Transactions*, with the sixth also published as a booklet by Robert Hardwicke (English 1990, p. 142). Lionel Rose argues that it was Edwin Lankester's 'astounding proportions of "Murder and Manslaughter" verdicts allied no doubt to the man's own intellectual charisma', which made him 'an object of press attention' (Rose 1986, p. 65). In an introduction to Lankester's 'Third Report of the Coroner for the Central Middlesex' in 1866, the *Medical Times and Gazette* acknowledged the story-spinning potential of Lankester's statistics:

> Nothing can be more interesting than these serious histories of our own times, so short, so closely packed with the sins and sorrows of the very people among whom we live. Dr Lankester has the happy knack of making his reports readable, and yet so admirably arranged that they are as pocket dictionaries. ('Third Annual Report', *Medical Times and Gazette* 1 (1866): 369.)

In an earlier editorial in 1865 the same medical trade journal acknowledged Lankester's skill as a persuasive orator:

> Every inquest he holds is a practical lecture, and because practical more likely to be heeded by the class of persons who for the most part constitute coroners' juries. The doctrine taught, whether sanitary or ethical, comes home to the intelligence of the uneducated, and the repetition of the lesson must in time succeed in fixing it in the mind. From the inquest-room it goes to the public-house parlour, and there it is talked over, and into the shops, and there it is gossiped about, and into the family, and there the wife learns of it. Can it be believed that such work carried on earnestly and conscientiously, as Dr Lankester carries it on, shall fail in producing some impression upon those ranks in society which it is most important to teach and which it is otherwise so difficult to reach? ('Coroner's Court' *Medical Times and Gazette* 1 (1865): 2)

It was, however, the newspaper press – both the penny press with their lurid reports and the influential *Times* – that played the crucial role in disseminating Lankester's didactic courtroom pronouncements to a mass audience and lifting his public profile. An energetic self-promoter Lankester relied on *ethos*, a mode of proof that is linked explicitly to the rhetor's '"good character", someone with expertise or someone with firsthand experience' (Richardson 2007, pp. 159-60) to persuade his colleagues, the judiciary, the press and the public that his point of view was correct.

While Lankester's ability as an outspoken commentator assured he made news headlines, *The Times* abrogated its Fourth Estate role by neglecting to scrutinize the substance of Lankester's statements. Lankester's statistical pronouncements showed a remarkable inconsistency throughout his tenure as coroner for central Middlesex. This inconsistency was established in his first year as coroner with his sensational declaration on 9 September 1862 that infanticide was 'exceedingly numerous at the present day' and his claims of conducting 'nearly one inquest a day on the bodies of newly born infants' ('Infanticide in the Metropolis', *Times* 9 September 1862, p. 6). This inflammatory rhetoric actually contradicts Lankester's own statistics for 1862, which were published in *The Times* in January 1863, showing a *decrease* in infanticide in the central Middlesex district:

> MORTALITY OF INFANTS – In the course of some observations with reference to the death of two infants, Dr Lankester, the Coroner for Central Middlesex, stated on Saturday last that the crime of infanticide was on the decrease in the metropolis, or more artful means were being taken to hide the bodies of newly born infants. ('Mortality of Infants', *Times* 6 January 1863, p. 10)

Lankester's response, mediated through the journalist's prose, was to argue that it was the artifice of the murdering mothers that accounted for the drop in numbers. Lankester, a canny rhetor, also attributed the decrease in infanticide numbers to the power of the press as a social agent:

> Of the first 72 inquests held by him after his appointment, no less than 12 were inquiries into the circumstances under which deserted infants had come by their death. He called public attention to that state of things, and his remarks were made known to the press. Of the next 72 cases that case [*sic*] before him were of the class to which he had just referred; of the following 72 only four were of that description; and since then he had held 250 inquests, only six or eight of which were cases of infanticide. Unfortunately such cases were still numerous, but he thought that there was a marked decrease in their number, and that to the press we might attribute the improvement. ('Mortality of Infants', *Times* 6 January 1863, p. 10)

This discourse illustrates not only Lankester's ability to skilfully handle the press, but also his ability to avoid press scrutiny by praising the press for its role in the decrease of infanticide. It shows, too, his skill as a persuasive rhetor to capture press attention with flawed statistics delivered with the authoritative voice of an eminent scientist.

It was clear that the presence of the crusading coroner for central Middlesex ensured that more inquests were held on dead babies in that district than in the East End, thus creating the perception of a high number of infanticides in Lankester's district alone. However, *The Times* made no effort to investigative the apparent discrepancy in infanticide figures between central Middlesex and surrounding districts, although it implicitly challenged Lankester's statistics with a brief quote from the coroner for the eastern district of Middlesex, John Humphreys, in a letter published in October 1862. Humphreys acknowledged that although there were 'too many instances of infanticide and concealing the birth' in his district, and 'though this class of cases was at present attracting a great deal of public attention', the statistics he had collated for his district 'reflected credit on the Eastern district of Middlesex, which included a very large and densely populated portion of the metropolis' (Humphreys, Letter *Times* 18 October 1862, p. 12). Curiously he 'found it stated in an authenticated report of observations made by his colleague of the Central division, Dr Lankester held nearly one inquest a day in cases of this kind'. Using *logos* in his letter to the editor Humphreys argued that it was a 'striking anomaly that a larger and poorer population, the east end of London, should present such a favourable contrast with the Central Division, comprising neighbourhoods like Paddington, Hampstead, and Highgate' (ibid.).

As George Behlmer's 1979 study of infanticide in mid-Victorian England shows, Lankester almost tripled the number of inquests upon infants in his first year as coroner, with the number of inquests on the bodies of children in their first year rising from 121 in 1862 to 357 in 1863 (Behlmer 1979, p. 423). Lankester rejected the claim that his district was any more amoral than other districts of London and blamed the discrepancy on the lack of diligence of his coronial colleagues. Rather than directly respond to Humphreys's veiled criticism of his statistics through the letters pages of *The Times* Lankester took the opportunity four days later to appropriate the infanticide inquest into the death of a baby girl at the Marylebone workhouse to defend his claims of 'very large numbers of infanticide' in the district. In his rejoinder to Humphreys he even hinted that he had been misquoted in the press:

> He said it seemed to be supposed he had intended to convey the impression that the average number of inquests held in the central division of Middlesex concerning infants found dead was nearly one a day for the whole year. Now, he was not prepared to say that it was even as high as one every other day, from year's end to year's end; though there were times when he held an inquest of this kind nearly every day. He had held a very large number of them within a period of three months, and he feared that the return for the year would be very high ... He did not mean to say that there was a greater disposition towards the crime of infanticide in London than was to be found in other capitals but it had been stated to him, by persons who had made some inquiry into the subject, that this crime was of proportionately more frequent occurrence in London than in continental cities. ('Dr Lankester on Infanticide', *Times* 24 October 1862, p. 6)

Lankester's confused explanation of Humphreys's veiled criticism, without press scrutiny, was quickly forgotten, and Lankester's statistics continued to be privileged by *The Times*. When public interest in infanticide peaked during the mid 1860s with the press coverage of the case of Charlotte Winsor, Lankester was swept onto centre stage as the national oracle of infanticide.

The Torquay Infanticide

For more than 30 years *The Times* had been reporting on infanticide as an issue of national importance as part of its long-standing campaign to reform what it regarded as the 'iniquitous' 1834 New Poor Law. However, it was one particular infanticide case which captured national attention in 1865 that brought infanticide into the national media spotlight as one of *the* social issues of the day, and at the same time pushed Lankester into the national spotlight. The 'Torquay Infanticide' was not an infanticide in the legal sense of a mother murdering her newborn child; rather it was the case of a grandmother, Charlotte Winsor, murdering infants for profit. The 'Torquay Infanticide' was the first national news story to highlight the practice of baby-farming (although the term 'baby-farming' would not be coined until several years later), conflating the issues of illegitimacy, domestic servants, infanticide and child murder into a potent national news narrative which captured unprecedented press attention. John Delane set aside the entire *Times* editorial of 1 August 1865 to discuss the case, claiming the 'dreadful revelations' had 'over-excited the public mind on the subject of infanticide':

> The public mind has of late been more than usually horrified by cases of murder, and we might have hoped that it would have been for some time impossible to surpass the dreadful impression which had been made upon our minds. Yet a case has just been tried on the Western Circuit which not merely exceeds in horror the two recent cases, but, in all probability, transcends any instance within the resemblance of most of us. (Editorial, *Times* 1 August 1865, p. 6)

The body of a child had been found on a public road near Torquay wrapped in a newspaper sewn up with worsted. Inquiries led to a servant girl, Mary Jane Harris, who had placed the child with Charlotte Winsor and both women were arrested for the child's murder. News reports carried the sensational revelations of Charlotte Winsor's case to the public and reinforced public sympathy for young girls faced with unwanted pregnancies. Mary Jane Harris was jointly charged with Charlotte Winsor with the murder of her baby but from the beginning the public were sympathetic to the plight of the young servant girl forced to farm out her infant. The first jury could not reach a decision because of the lack of clarity in the evidence of the expert medical witness, Dr Stabb. After the abandoned first trial Mary Jane was offered and accepted as Queen's evidence (Editorial, *Times* 1 August 1865, p. 6) saving her from a second trial and allowing the shocking revelations of multiple child murder to unfold in sensational news narratives. At Charlotte Winsor's second trial *The Times* portrayed Mary Jane Harris in the victim role:

> Horrible as it is the story is not hard to understand. The girl is burdened with a child who is at once an expense and a disgrace to her, and the diabolical suggestion of the woman WINSOR ... tempts her with the chance of escape from further trouble. She is already sufficiently demoralized to listen, though with fear, to such a suggestion; she 'does not want the child to be done away with,' and yet she wants to be rid of it, and she will not ask too many questions if the bold bad woman, her accomplice, will cut the deadly knot for her. (Editorial, *Times* 1 August 1865, p. 6)

Upon the commission of the murder Mary Jane Harris was immediately remorseful 'the maternal instinct returns and rouses a loud remorse, and perhaps resentment against the woman who had pushed her so far'. Readers were told there was 'nothing extravagant in the mother's case. It is but the accident of a bold, vicious, accomplice which drives the criminal impulse to its utmost development' ('Editorial', *Times* 1 August 1865, p. 6). As if the facts of this case were not sensational enough, *The Times* inscribed an extra layer of hyperbole with the speculation:

> Is it likely that the crime can have been thus familiar, not only to her, but to the mothers of her victims, if it were so very unusual? She speaks of girls writing to her in anticipation of their requiring her infernal aid. How many more such agents of death are there in England? The statistics of infanticide compel us to believe that such crimes are by no means uncommon, and that, moreover, in the case of legitimate as well as illegitimate children. ('Editorial', *Times* 1 August 1865, p. 6)

Such inflamed rhetoric led to the claim the following day from a *Times* reader, who called himself 'Statist', that infanticide was the 'great crime of England' ('Statist' Letter *Times* 2 August 1865, p. 9). A few days later a Sussex parson reported that he had 'reason to fear that the crime of infanticide prevails to an extent as yet unknown in England' ('A Suffolk Parson' Letter *Times* 10 August 1865, p. 7) and another *Times* commentator claimed that the 'existing state of things was really a blot on the character of the nation' (Letter *Times* 17 August 1865, p. 6). Yet another correspondent, 'The Traveller', fuelling the public discourse, asserted that through his research infanticide was most common in countries where the interference of the government or the existence of charitable institutions provided for and afforded encouragement to the abandonment of children, and thus gave public sanction to the neglect of the maternal duties, and helped to loosen the natural claims of the babe upon the mother'. He argued that, as 'lamentably common' as infanticide was in Great Britain, 'there was no country in Europe in which child murder is more rare' ('The Traveller', Letter *Times* 8 August 1865, p. 7).

A week later, in the midst of the public outrage at the Winsor case, *The Times* backed away from its earlier speculations in an editorial calling for a calm and reasoned debate:

> We are told with utmost confidence, by persons who have not the slightest means more than ourselves of testing the truth of what they say, that Infanticide is the great and leading crime of England, that the case of Charlotte Winsor is only one of a very large class, and all manner of violent remedies are suggested to meet so dreadful a disease of the body politic. Now, in justice to our country, and above all to our countrywomen, we are bound, in the first instance, to state that the consideration of every subject is very much obscured and embroiled by rash assumptions and exaggerated assertions, and to demand that the question be considered in a calmer and more judicial spirit as to the facts, and from a larger point of view with regard to remedies. (Editorial *Times*, 10 Aug. 1865, p. 8)

What is of particular interest here is that this editorial appears to be rejecting the claims made by Dr Edwin Lankester of an infanticide epidemic, claims *The Times* had consistently promoted elsewhere in their news pages.

The 'Torquay Infanticide' discourse in *The Times* brought the plight of unmarried servant girls and their illegitimate babies to national attention, feeding into a public debate on the 'problem' of female domestic servants and infanticide, reflecting Lankester's view that the trouble lay with unmarried servant women. Not long after the public mind had been 'excited' by the Charlotte Winsor case, Lankester gave an influential and highly charged address to the annual general meeting of the Social Science Congress in Belfast in which he spoke authoritatively on the issue of infanticide. His timing was impeccable. The *Times*, so recently outraged by the 'Torquay Infanticide', was captivated by Lankester's pronouncements and his scientific figures. The lengthy report of Lankester's speech in *The Times* cemented Lankester in the public mind as the authoritative voice of infanticide. Since taking up the coroner's bench in August 1862 Lankester had been explicit in identifying the class of women he believed were responsible for the infanticide epidemic. He told the 1866 Social Science Congress's annual meeting:

> I would state my conviction, that in the majority of cases, they are women employed in domestic service; in fact, when the circumstances of the crime are inquired into, it seems almost impossible that any other class of women can be implicated. ('Social Science Congress – Dr Lankester's Report', *Times* 6 October 1866, p. 12)

The Stereotypical Infanticide

Stereotyping 'the infanticide' as an unmarried female domestic servant who was placed in moral peril when she moved away from the control and care of her own family, situated the blame for the crime on women at several levels: the mother who allowed her daughter to move away from her influence, the mistress who failed to control her female servants, and the woman herself. Lankester's rationale was that unmarried working-class women were naturally immoral and when a woman fell pregnant outside marriage she almost certainly would abrogate her maternal duties and turn murderously upon her offspring:

> Where girls are living at home or in lodgings, their condition is discovered long before the birth of the child, and where the existence of pregnancy is once known, there is seldom any attempt at the destruction of the child. It is almost essential to the perpetration of this crime that no one should be aware of the fact of the pregnancy, or the birth of the child. These conditions can only be generally secured when women are in domestic service. ('Social Science Congress – Dr Lankester's Report', *Times* 6 October 1866, p. 12)

Lankester's rhetoric is focused on the failings of middle-class women to control their servants and it is such rhetoric, broadcast through the mass media, that influenced the public opinion on infanticide. Evoking Bentham's panopticon and its self-surveillance and also surveillance by society, Lankester argued that secrecy, in this instance implicitly the household mistresses's lack of knowledge, led directly to the maidservant's actions. Lankester's statistical discourse claimed that it was in those districts of London where the largest number of servants lived that the greatest numbers of child murders were committed. Paddington he said had the highest rate of infant murder (one per 4,000 of population) because, he rationalized, servants 'in the West End of London … are more numerous, more independent of the mistress' and 'in the majority of cases these mothers were domestic servants, sleeping by themselves, and in almost all cases they had no one with them in the hour of nature's peril' ('Social Science Congress – Dr Lankester's Report', *Times* 6 October 1866, p. 12). Lankester blamed the upper middle-class mistresses, whose husbands were reading his pronouncements in *The Times*, for failing in their 'kindly and sisterly superintendence of female servants' ('Third Annual Report', *Medical Times and Gazette* 1866, p. 369). Rather than look to the male, or more specifically to those males of his own class, the husbands, sons and male guests who all too often impregnated the powerless young servant girls, Lankester, representative of patriarchal authority, chose to attack the women of the household, thus creating dual maternal folk devils:

> Infanticide and the domestic servant: Dr Lankester thought that the cause was to a great extent the distance maintained in families between mistresses and servants. He appealed to the women of England to cleanse their own households of this great crime, and they could do so by maintaining that superintendence of one woman over another by which the crime could be most effectually prevented. It had been proved that when the condition of a woman was once known she never murdered her child. ('Social Science Congress – Dr Lankester's Report', *Times* 6 October 1866, p. 12)

Lankester argued for the strict surveillance of female domestic servants, claiming that it: 'must be obvious to all that the extensive prevalence of such oversight in families would go far to prevent a crime which is most frequently perpetrated, not in the homes of the poor, but in those of the middle-and-upper classes of society in England' ('Social Science Congress – Dr Lankester's Report', *Times* 6 October 1866, p. 12).

The issue of surveillance of domestic servants, and young women in general, was a central point of discussion in infanticide court discourses. In the trial of 19-year-old domestic servant, Fanny Young, in service to Sir Arthur Baller of Kensington, her solicitor told the court 'the prisoner slept in a room by herself' ('Infanticide', *Times* 30 November 1863, p. 11). The inference was that the servant had not received adequate supervision, and that if she had she would not have killed her baby. One correspondent to *The Times*, Lord Sidney Godolphin Osborne ('S.G.O.'), praised the newspaper for drawing attention to the Harris and Winsor crime, and informed readers that he had 'conversed with the highest authorities about it [infanticide] 'but had never met with one single official who would deny that it was a crime fearfully on the increase' ('S.G.O.' Letter *Times* 5 August 1865, p. 7). He claimed that 'young women of the working class are, in the service of their employers, exposed to all conceivable temptation to the loss of character' ('S.G.O.' Letter *Times* 5 August 1865, p. 7). 'R. R' was also prompted by 'the circumstances connected with the horrific case of the women Harris and Winsor' to write to the editor of *The Times*, agreeing with Lord Sidney that the Harris/ Winsor case 'exhibits a state of things not at all uncommon' ('R.R.' Letter *Times* 10 August 1865, p. 7). This correspondent believed that:

> The main cause of female unchastity and all its consequences is the laxity of parents and masters, who are in the present day far too prone to abdicate the authority with which God has invested them. Witness in the class of domestic servants the 'Sunday out' (a source of endless immorality), the liberty to attend any place of worship without the presence of either master or mistress to see that the servants are there; in the labouring classes the daughters allowed full liberty after the age of 14 or 15 to be out 'on their own hook' at all hours, or, if they should return after the house is closed for the night, refusal of admission, the liberty to receive their 'young man' in the cottage after the rest of the family has retired to rest. I would add to these fruitful sources of mischief the practice of the worst of women being allowed to come *sages femmes* by profession, without licence or diploma of any kind, among whom I believe that there are many Winsors. ('R.R.' Letter *Times* 10 August 1865, p. 7).

Such epistolary arguments reflect a patriarchal society uncertain of the role of the women in a world of change, a world where industrialization and the rising middle class were bringing working-class people into the cities and towns and therefore more unmarried women into their homes as servants, and a society in which women were finding new and enterprising ways to live. These debates invariably failed to acknowledge sexual harassment within the workplace, believing that young women 'should be taught the sinfulness of unchastity' (*Times* 'Social Science Congress', 6 October 1866, p. 12) rather than be protected by law from unwelcome sexual advances in the workplace.

Statistics and the Social Science Congress

The dominant voice in *The Times* report of the 1866 Social Science Congress, reflecting the dominant voice in the infanticide news discourse throughout the 1860s, remained that of the eminent scientist, Dr Edwin Lankester. The accomplished *rhetor* told the Congress that punishment would have 'a salutary effect in the way of prevention' and that the way to facilitate this was to 'offer a reward in every case of an unknown child found dead' ('Social Science Congress', *Times* 6 October 1866, p. 12). Against vociferous criticism, Lankester argued for the establishment of foundling hospitals, maintaining that although the rate of infant deaths in these hospitals was high, 'it is probably better that the child should be lost in the attempt to secure its life, than that a large number of women should be living with the consciousness of having sacrificed their offspring' ('Third Annual Report of the Coroner for Central Middlesex', *British Medical Journal* 1 (1866): 448–50). John Delane, in a rare show of disagreement with Lankester's point of view, argued in a *Times* editorial that foundling hospitals furnished a 'most dangerous argument against female virtue' by 'providing a means of disposing of children without the guilt of actual murder and without the expense of supporting them' ('The cause of good sense and humanity', *Times* 10 August 1865, p. 8).

In his address to the Social Science Congress in 1866 Lankester finally fell in line with *The Times* long-running campaign against the New Poor Law and argued against the inequities of the Bastardy Laws:

> The difficulties of making the father legally responsible for his offspring are so great that, practically, few women avail themselves of these laws. Such a change in the law as should compel men more generally to support their children would not only remove one great temptation to infanticide, but would save the life of both the woman and of the child. ('Social Science Congress – Dr Lankester's Report', *Times* 6 October 1866, p. 12)

In an early example of Marcus Felson's routine activities theory, which maintains that crimes occur where three necessary elements converge: a motivated offender, a suitable target, and an absence of capable guardians (Ward 1999, p. 254), Lankester believed the answer was to keep women under surveillance throughout every stage of their pregnancy and birth. He advocated for the registration of pregnancies, births and stillbirths, claiming such a system would go a long way to ridding England of the infanticide problem. He told *The Times* that he once spoke to the Registrar-General upon the subject of registration, and the Registrar-

General had said "'it would be very disagreeable to ladies in high life to have their abortions recorded'".. This, he claimed, 'was at the bottom of the dislike of the House of Commons to deal with the question, but this is not the spirit on which we should legislate' (Lankester 1870, pp. 205–17).

Lankester's charismatic 1866 address to the Social Science Congress in Belfast, laden with his inflammatory statistics, fed into the public debate and was taken up and promoted not only by *The Times*, but also by prominent social commentators such as Henry Humble, Harold King and the Reverend Shipley, further endorsing Lankester's position as *the* authority on infanticide. Henry Humble opened an essay, 'Infanticide: its Cause and Cure' in 1866 with the words: 'Dr Lankester has been sounding in the ears of the public, for many years, his warnings on the terrible increase of child-murder' (Humble 1866, p. 169). Humble, a great admirer of Lankester, was so disturbed by the medical coroner's statistics that in his sanguinary infanticide paper he claimed that 'the land is becoming defiled by the blood of her innocents':

> Bundles are left lying about the streets, which people will not touch, lest the too familiar object – a dead body – should be revealed, perchance with a pitch-plaster over its mouth, or a woman's garter round its throat. Thus, too, the metropolitan canal boats are impeded, as they are tracked along, by the number of drowned infants with which they come in contact. (Humble 1866, p. 169)

The powerful imagery of bundles containing dead babies, woman's garters round their throats, lying in great numbers throughout the streets of London, created from Lankester's potent statistical discourse, was, however, based on false statistics. Lankester's statistics make it difficult to obtain an accurate picture of the rates of infanticide for the whole Middlesex division, and bring into question his claims of an alarming overall rise in infanticide, which fuelled claims of an infanticide epidemic in the 1860s. As his biographer, Mary English, acknowledges, Lankester's methodology was not without its problems:

> Lankester used statistics frequently and forcefully throughout his tenure of the post of Medical Officer of Health, though inevitably he handled figures in a far less sophisticated manner than would be the case today. He compared averages, and sometimes 'cases per thousand', but he never used percentages. (English 1990, p. 98)

Statistics, because they represent logic derived from sound reasoning founded on scientific data, are often read as the ultimate reflection of a reality; however, statistics are also just one alternative discourse – they offer one other way of looking at knowledge. Statistical discourse has a powerful influence through the combination of scientific imprimatur and the narratives humans extract from the data. When Dr Edwin Lankester created his potent statistics *The Times* accepted his data as the benchmark measure of reality fashioning Lankester into their primary definer of infanticide news and privileging his scientific voice above all others on the issue of infanticide and, without scrutiny, embellishing news stories with his emotive statistics.

At an inquest held at the Elephant and Castle in Camden Town on the body of an infant in August 1866 Lankester appropriated the troubles of a 'well nourished' and 'neatly dressed' deceased two-month-old infant and its absent mother to energetically defend himself against recent criticism that he 'had been blamed in many quarters for the statements he had made respecting the prevalence of child-murder, and was charged by some of the journals as a libeler of his countrywomen' ('Dr Lancester [sic] on Child Murder', Times 15 August 1866, p. 7). After suggesting that the inquest upon which he was presiding should be adjourned, and that 'the vestry of the parish be requested to issue placards offering a reward for the discovery of the perpetrators of the crime' (ibid.), Lankester addressed the issue of the recent public opposition to his infanticide statistics.

Lankester's Statistics under Scrutiny

In a bold and provocative move, using *ethos* bolstered by his statistics, he answered his critics by reporting his most recent calculations on the number of infanticides in central London:

> In one year he held inquests on 80 children found dead in the streets, and he believed he would be justified in assuming that there was an equal number of children hidden and their corpses not discovered. This would be 160 murders in his own district; while there were two other districts in the metropolis, each probably bearing an equal proportion as regarded infanticide. This would make 480 child-murders in London in one year; but, in order to be on the lowest side, he would take it for granted that the number would be 400 only. The mothers who were discovered to be guilty of the murders of their children were found to be on an average 20 years of age; and, as the expectancy of life of a young woman of that age was 60 years, or 40 years of additional life, he multiplied the 400 by 40, and the startling deduction was that there were in London alone 16,000 women who had murdered their offspring. This was based on the assumption that the same woman only once imbued her hands in the blood of the child. ('Dr Lancester [sic] on Child Murder', Times 15 August 1866, p. 7)

Pall Mall Gazette

When a man of influential standing in the community, like Lankester, applied logic derived from scientific reasoning, founded on scientific data, general readers accepted such discourse as the 'truth'. However, there were others, men of science, who looked at his highly charged claim that 16,000 women in London were guilty of murdering their children, and openly questioned Lankester's calculations.

Finally, the statistics of the coroner for central Middlesex came under press scrutiny, but it was not the 'newspaper of record' that scrutinized Lankester's statistics, but the recently launched national newspaper, the *Pall Mall Gazette*, who took him to task. The *Pall Mall Gazette* had been launched in February 1865 by Frederick Greenwood and George Smith with the idea of running a newspaper which, rather than breaking news, analysed news gleaned from the morning papers. In response to Lankester's claims published in *The Times* on 15 August 1866, a week later the *Pall Mall Gazette* published a cutting commentary questioning Dr Edwin Lankester's methodology for calculating such 'startling' statistics. The *Gazette* begins its report with a note of praise for the honourable character of Dr Lankester, before quickly exposing Lankester's faulty arithmetic:

> Dr Lankester is an energetic and valuable public officer, but he can hardly be congratulated on his management of figures. The defence which he had just made of his very startling theory as to the number of child-murderesses in London only brings out more clearly the fallacy of his calculations. ('Dr Lankester', *Pall Mall Gazette* 22 August 1866 p. 6)

The *Pall Mall Gazette* argued that Lankester's calculations were 'pure hypothesis', nothing more than 'a guess', and that his assumptions were 'extraordinary' and that on the whole, Lankester's calculations break down 'at every step, and whatever be the real frequency of the crime, it never can be ascertained by these haphazard guesses, which serve only a sensational end, and terrify people into imagining that the evil is too gigantic to be arrested' ('Dr Lankester', *Pall Mall Gazette* 22 August 1866 p. 6).

The *Times*, however, still refused to openly scrutinize their primary definer of infanticide and John Delane's response to the *Pall Mall Gazette* story was not an incisive editorial, nor was it a news story generated by one of his own journalists, rather he made the choice to republish the *Pall Mall Gazette* article the following day without editorial comment under the heading 'A Coroner's Arithmetic – Dr Lankester' (*Times* 23 August 1866, p. 8).

Two months later in the report on the annual meeting of the Social Science Congress ('Social Science Congress – Dr Lankester's Report', *Times* 6 October 1866, p. 12) Lankester is reported as testily declaring that he was 'quite disgusted with a paragraph which never ought to have appeared in a respectable paper, entitled "Coroner's Arithmetic"'. Mediated through *The Times*'s reporter, Lankester responds to the *Pall Mall Gazette* article explaining his contentious methodology using a shaky logic:

> When it was remembered that the cases that came before the Coroner's Court were only those that had been clumsily put away – thrown into some neighbouring street or pond – it had always appeared to him that a very large number of infants were successfully put away and concealed. It was not improbable that for every body discovered another was successfully concealed. Adopting that calculation

he had endeavoured to show to what extent the crime of infanticide prevailed in this country. ('Social Science Congress – Dr Lankester's Report', *Times* 6 October 1866, p. 12)

With a tone of self-righteous indignation Lankester acknowledges that his figures might 'perhaps, be too high or too low, but his theories ought not to be laughed at upon that account'. His calculation was that in England and Wales 'there could not be fewer than 1,000 cases of infanticide annually' (ibid.). Significantly, the *British Medical Journal* had in September 1866 also republished the *Pall Mall Gazette* article, 'A Coroner's Arithmetic'.[1] The medical trade journal, the *Medical Times and Gazette*, which had long been an outspoken supporter of Lankester's reports, also challenged the coroner's statistics in an editorial, 'Asserted Increase in Infanticide' (1867, p. 455). A century before Stanley Cohen created the theory of moral panic, the medical trade journal claimed that Lankester, and the coverage of his inquests and reports in the 'cheap press', was 'largely responsible for what is considered a "panic" over the supposed increase of infanticide' (1867, p. 455).

Undaunted by the public criticism, Lankester continued to apply his statistical methodology to cases of infanticide that came to his attention. Middlesex, he claimed a year later in 1867, was still responsible for 'over half of all "infanticides"' throughout England and Wales (Rose, p. 65). In 1867, in another paper presented to the Social Science Association titled 'The Repression of Infanticide', the irrepressible Lankester pondered on the question of 'how large a figure we should put down for those undiscovered cases of infanticide':

> Some writers have suggested that for every body discovered there is another securely concealed, and adopting this calculation as not altogether improbable, I have endeavoured to show, in my annual report, to what extent the crime of infanticide probably prevails in this country. (Lankester 1868b, p. 220)

He was wise enough to concede that 'of course all such calculations are liable to correction by accurate observation, and it may happen that the deduction errs in too high or too low an estimate of unobserved probabilities' (Lankester 1868b, p. 220). Using his calculations for central Middlesex he reached a national figure for infanticide in England and Wales in 1867 as no 'fewer than 1,000 cases of infanticide annually' (ibid., p. 221). He refrained from putting these figures in other forms, confident that 'those accustomed to work out probabilities by a deductive

---

[1] The decision by the prestigious medical journal to criticize Lankester's mathematics would have remarkable resonances more than a century later when the same journal criticized another high-profile medical expert, Professor Sir Roy Meadow, for his use of inflated infant death statistics in giving evidence at the 1999 murder trial of English woman Sally Clark who was subsequently convicted of the murder of her two infant sons (and later fully exonerated when Meadow's evidence and the false evidence of other medical expert witnesses, and other evidence, was deemed to be flawed (see Goc 2007).

process when observed data are insufficient, will see in these calculations sufficient to alarm and awaken interest in the question before us' (ibid., p. 221). Having made his qualifications, Lankester then went on to create a highly charged rhetoric that reinforced his data of probabilities:

> In the first place it seems to me that the attention of the moralist and philanthropist should be drawn to the fearful picture of immorality which this crime brings before us. Put the case as you may, the suspected destruction of 1,000 infant lives annually by their mothers, in a country boasting of its civilisation and Christianity, is a fearful blot. (Lankester 1868b, p. 219)

According to Lankester's calculations central Middlesex alone accounted for an average of over one third of the nation's inquest murder verdicts on infants between 1864 and the early 1870s (Rose 1986, p. 65). Lionel Rose found in his study of infanticide in nineteenth-century London that the slum district of Stepney, which in 1861 had half the population of Marylebone, also had a high proportion of infanticide. As Rose argues, 'plenty of infanticide was going on here as well without the glare of publicity' (Rose p. 66). Rose also found that distortions in the official illegitimacy rates in the 1860s 'would have us believe that London's West End was far more immoral than the slum denizens of East End', but he argues that the slums were 'better able to conceal their bastardy', and 'better able to hide their infanticide in an environment where an inordinate infant death rate did not arouse suspicion and there were few doctors to inspect the dead children' (Rose pp. 66–7). The West End parishes, Rose says, 'came in for attention because the infanticide was taking the more conspicuous form of "dropping", literally on the upper classes' own doorsteps', (Rose p. 68). Ironically, Lankester's claim of an increase in infanticide in London in the 1860s could also have been due to the modernization of the sanitation system and the introduction of closed drains in the West End parishes, a progressive initiative for which Lankester, as Medical Officer of Health, was responsible. It may have been, then, that it was Lankester's own initiatives which brought about the changes that led him to argue that dead babies were now found daily in the gutters and streets of Central London.

Lancet

In 1869 another prestigious medical journal, the *Lancet*, established by Lankester's predecessor, Dr Thomas Wakley, felt obliged to criticize Lankester's recent infanticide statistics that claimed that 12,000 London women had murdered their babies. Reporting on Lankester's public address to a large audience at the Freemason's Tavern on the subject of infanticide, the journal told its readers that it had 'all sympathy with Dr Lankester in his desire to put an end to infanticide', and supported Lankester's call for social remedies including the 'alteration to the bastardy law, the substitution of some other than capital punishment for infanticide, a compulsory registration of births (still-born included), and the enactment of punishments for the concealment of pregnancy' (Editorial, *Lancet* 12 June 1869, p. 824). However, the *Lancet* then proceeded to take Lankester to task for his use of statistics:

> The only point upon which we cannot go with him is his assertion about the 12000 murderesses living amongst us. Such an idea is much too horrible to find ready acceptance, and we cannot help thinking that there must be some fallacy in the statistical reasoning which leads to so startling a result. The condensed report of Dr Lankester's lecture from which we write is not explicit enough to warrant us in discussing this theory at present, but we do not hesitate to avow our conviction that it does considerably exaggerate the extent to which the crime of infanticide prevails in the metropolis. (Editorial *Lancet* 12 June 1869, p. 824)

This criticism of Lankester's creative use of statistics by the *Lancet* still did not stop *The Times* from continuing to support his worthy campaign to reduce the number of infanticides in London. The *Times* did not report the public meeting at the Freemason's Hall, or the *Lancet*'s subsequent criticism of Lankester's address, and continued to promote Lankester's opinions. Just three months after the *Lancet*'s criticism of Lankester's statistics John Delane devoted another leading article to his pronouncements, recommending 'Dr Lankester's Annual Coronial Report' as 'an appropriate holyday topic' which should be 'taken as the bitter which, as children, we were all taught possesses such valuable corrective properties after a liberal indulgence in sweets' ('Dr Lankester's Annual Coronial Report' Editorial, *Times* 7 September 1869, p. 7). 'Dr Lankester's catalogue', Delane declared, 'bears witness to a sum of crime, vice, ignorance, and carelessness which is far from creditable to the metropolis':

> Dr LANKESTER is not merely giving the reins to his fancy when he warns us of the ease with which the sentiment of the inconvenience of life to an illegitimate child sooth the way to neglecting it, and thus assists the imputed tenderness of PROVIDENCE in granting it a 'happy release.' The terrible proportion of the Inquests held on illegitimate children to those on children born in wedlock proves the need of this official intervention on the part of society. ('Dr Lankester's Annual Coronial Report as an appropriate holyday topic', Editorial *Times* 7 September 1869, p. 7)

For more than 40 years the newspaper of record had been campaigning to have the gross inequities of the 1834 New Poor Law and the Bastardy Clause changed, but the Parliament of England had been resistant to repealing or reforming the law. This inflexible stance was not only reflective of an economic rationalist argument, but also of the belief that the law was a deterrent to licentiousness and illegitimacy through the denial of easily accessible parish relief to bastards and their mothers. The decades of campaigning finally brought results in the first years of the 1870s with the introduction of the Infant Life Protection Act in 1871 and a clause in

1872 which saw the amendment of the Bastardy Law to make the putative father equally liable for the support of the illegitimate child until the age of 16. The 1871 law, which was to serve as the basis for dealing with the financial management of illegitimate children in England until 1957 (Haller 1989, p. 9) finally brought about a decrease in infanticide.

In 1874, some weeks after sitting on an inquiry into the death of a cabman who died through the excitement occasioned by proceedings being taken against him by the Duke of Bedford ('Duke of Bedford and the Cabman' *Times* 11 August 1874, p. 3), Dr Edwin Lankester died. The *Times* paid tribute to their primary definer of infanticide news, reporting: 'DR LANKESTER. – We regret to record the death yesterday morning, at Margate, in his 61st year, of Edwin Lankester, M.D., coroner for Middlesex' ('Dr Lankester – We regret', *Times* 31 October 1874, p. 5). The report outlined Lankester's medical career, acknowledging his skill as a medical communicator: 'He was a very prolific writer on science ... and also published ... voluminous reports on various sanitary subjects'. The *Times* obituary, however, made no mention of the significant part Lankester played as a coroner in bringing to public attention the issue of infanticide. After his death there was a significant decrease in infanticide news in *The Times*. This, it could be argued, was because infanticide had lost its currency with the changes to the law and the decrease in the crime, although substantial decreases were not recorded for another decade. It could also be argued that with Lankester's death *The Times* lost its most eloquent voice on infanticide.

Conclusion

By privileging the pronouncements of Edwin Lankester *The Times*, as the newspaper of record in nineteenth-century England, created a potent infanticide news discourse in which murdering mothers were placed in polar opposition to the crusading medical coroner. Because Edwin Lankester was an eminent scientist in a position of power and authority, who used *ethos* to create highly newsworthy stories about profligate young female servants murdering their babies and dropping them in the gutters of London, and he was able to quantify his stories with alarming statistics, *The Times* privileged Lankester's voice. His alarming claims that the streets of London were strewn with the bodies of dead babies and that 12,000–16,000 murderesses lived amongst the populace, with the exception of the republishing of the *Pall Mall Gazette* report, went unquestioned by England's most powerful newspaper. The fact that adjoining districts did not reflect high infanticide rates was eloquently argued away by Lankester as due to the lack of thoroughness by his coronial colleagues. When Lankester's statistics were questioned by the *Pall Mall Gazette*, and then by his peers in the influential medical journals, *The Times* ignored Lankester's problematic mathematics and continued to privilege his voice in infanticide news. After Lankester's death the *Medical Times and Gazette* in a barbed obituary, reported that Lankester, 'without a profundity of knowledge ... by a happy readiness of expression, a good delivery and a fine presence [succeeded] to obtain a great reputation as a popular lecturer' ('The Late Dr Lankester', *Medical Times and Gazette* 1875, p. 320).

During the years of *The Times* sustained campaign to bring about a reduction in the numbers of infanticides through legislative reform (1834–70) the middle class was becoming more conscious of the poverty and suffering around them. This new awareness helped to improve standards of the workhouses in the 1840s and led to the 1848 Public Health Act. Two Criminal Law Commissions, one in 1834 and another in 1848, did not, however, recommend legal reforms to infanticide with the exception of the concealment of birth. In the wake of Edwin Lankester's pronouncements infanticide was included in the 1866–67 the Law of Capital Punishment Amendment Bills, however, the influence of Baron Bramwell, and others, in casting doubt on the 'desirability and the practicability of reform' (Davies 1938, p. 269) saw the infanticide clauses fail. Through the 1870s there were several attempts to reform the Infanticide Act including the 1874 and 1874 Infanticide Amendment Bills, both of which failed. The promoters of these bills reintroduced a similar measure in 1875, which also failed, and in 1876 another unsuccessful Homicide Law Amendment Bill was introduced by Sir Eardley Wilmot which provided for the killing by a mother of her infant within seven days of the birth as second category murder. The Capital Punishments Bills of 1877, 1878, and 1881, 'did not refer specifically to child-killing but were relevant inasmuch as they proposed that the punishment for all murders should be a life sentence' (Davies 1938, p. 274). According to D. Seaborne Davies in his review of child-killing laws in 1938, the Home Office had a 'perennial tendency to avoid reforms of the substantive law by relying upon recourse to judicial or executive discretion' (Davies 1938, p. 270). *The Times*, through its sustained discourse on the rise in infanticide, kept the issue on its news agenda until the introduction of the Infant Life Protection Bill 1871. This bill was introduced to protect the lives of bastard children and called for the registration and supervision of nurses who cared for children on a daily basis and led not only to a decrease in the deaths of children in care, but also to a sharp decline in reported infanticides. This bill was the direct result of the reporting of the notorious Brixton horror baby-farming story in the press and the story of Mrs Harnett in Greenwich who, for a fee, took a newborn baby from the lying-in house of Mr Stevens and fed it watered down sour milk, arrowroot and corn flour until it succumbed to starvation (Haller 1989). However, it would not be until the introduction of the 1922 Infanticide Act in the wake of Edith Roberts's case (Chapter 6) that infanticide was dealt with differently by the courts.

In London in the 1860s Dr Edwin Lankester's infanticide pronouncements, reported in the influential London *Times*, placed infanticide and the infanticidal woman back on the political agenda for the first time since the campaigning editorials of the 1830s and '40s. With Lankester's alarming pronouncements of dead babies littering the streets of London *The Times*'s editor, John Delane, put the issue of infanticide back on the political agenda creating an influential political discourse that reinforced the moral shame ascribed to the 'fallen woman'. By bringing the intensely personal stories of young infanticidal women into the glare of public scrutiny, *The Times*'s coverage placed them at the centre of political discourse. At a time when the ideal woman was a silent, submissive being, the 'angel in the house' who submitted to her husband's will, the most disenfranchised woman in mid-Victorian society, the unwed mother who killed her own baby, was politicized through her actions, reported prominently in the press through Dr Edwin Lankester's pronouncements.

This chapter ends Part I of this study and the analysis of infanticide and the infanticidal women in press discourse in the London *Times*. In Part II the focus shifts to five case studies in regional newspapers first in colonial Australia and finally returning to England to regional Hinkley in Leicester and the 1922 press campaign that played a major role in finally bringing about legislative change to the infanticide law.

PART II
Infanticide News in the Regional Press: 1830–1922

Part II shifts the analysis of infanticide and the infanticidal woman in news discourse to regional newspapers and a case-study approach. Using Critical Discourse Analysis and close textual analysis this section provides a counterpoint to Part I through an analysis of five infanticide cases from the 1830s to the 1920s, all of which were the focus of significant news coverage in small, but influential, regional newspapers in Australia and England. It begins with the cases of convict servant Mary McLauchlan and married woman Sarah Masters in colonial Australia then looks at two women living in the Tasmanian bush, Harriet Lovell and Lilian Wakefield, before returning to England and Edith Roberts's infanticide in the rural village of Hinkley.

Infanticide was part of news discourse across the British Empire in the nineteenth century. In colonial Australia the explanatory frame for understanding infanticide when the perpetrator was a British woman, rather than an aboriginal woman, was the same predictable trope – she was the perpetrator of an unnatural crime motivated by shame. When the focus of infanticide news discourse was an aboriginal woman her actions were reported in the racist imperial frame used by The Times in its reports of infanticide in India and China – that is the individual woman's actions were emblematic of a barbarous, heathen nation. In colonial Australia there was not the same consistency and regularity of infanticide news in court and coronial reports, and when infanticide was the subject of court reports, not unsurprisingly, the style and format mirrored the English press, providing little new insight into the representation of infanticide and the infanticidal woman in press discourse. With the exception of reports on infanticide in the aboriginal population, my work on infanticide and the press in colonial Australia has not found evidence in colonial newspapers where infanticide was part of a broader political discourse or was instrumental in the creation of a press campaign, or a maternal panic, as it was in the national English newspaper *The Times*. There were, however, particular moments when infanticide and the infanticidal woman did become enmeshed in political discourse in colonial newspapers, as in the case of Mary McLauchlan, and to a lesser extent in the case of Sarah Masters, women who both feature in Chapter 4. As mentioned earlier, regional newspapers, with their focus on local news, provided extensive coverage of individual local infanticide cases that captured the press and public imagination at particular moments in time and this coverage provided me in Part II of this study with the opportunity to study in depth the coverage of particular cases and to expose similarities and differences in the way regional newspapers represented infanticide and the infanticidal woman.

In regional Australia at the end of the century infanticide was brought into the ideological frame of madness, feeding into the romantic Australian trope of 'great bush loneliness', personified in the fictional writings of Henry Lawson and Barbara Baynton. By framing infanticide in rural Australia as madness it allowed female failure to be understood within the broader discourse on nationhood, as evidenced in the two infanticide cases of Harriet Lovell and Lilian Wakefield featured in Chapter 5. The final case-study analyses the press discourse in the *Leicester Mercury* and the infanticidal actions of a young factory worker, Edith Roberts, and how this regional newspaper campaign to spare the young woman from the ignominy of a death sentence catapulted infanticide back onto the national political agenda in England in 1921–22, almost a century after *The Times* campaign to amend the 1834 New Poor Law. This important moment in the history of infanticide closes this study of infanticide and the infanticidal women in press discourse.

Chapter 4
Infanticide in the Van Diemen's Land Press

'Neutral words, such as place-names, can be made to symbolize complex ideas and emotions' (Cohen 2002, p. 27), reflecting the power of language to infuse disparate and conflicting beliefs and values. In nineteenth-century England 'Van Diemen's Land'[1] came to connote a dark place of brutal punishment half a world away from 'home'. In 1830 both the editor of the *Hobart Town Courier*, James Ross, and the editor of the *Colonial Times*, Henry Melville, argued:

> However unpalatable the term may be, still the fact cannot be controverted, that Van Diemen's Land is a jail upon a large scale for English criminals – that the Governor is the head Custos – the Officers of State or Government are next in rank to him as keepers or Custodes, and every Settler throughout the Colony, who has an assigned servant, is *de ipso facto*, only one other link of the same chain. ('Editorial', *Colonial Times* 7 May 1830, p. 2)

In 1834 Henry Walter Parker reported that people in Britain, upon hearing the name Van Diemen's Land, thought of 'a receptacle for the expatriated thieves of England' of a 'spot exclusively and especially appropriated to crime and immorality, contaminated and disgraced throughout in all its relations, a sink of impurity, and not to be thought of as a place of abode for any honest man' (Parker 1834, p. 65). A popular street ballad performed in the streets of England at the time encapsulates the dread associated with the name Van Diemen's Land:

> Every night when I lay down I wet my straw with tears,
> While wind upon that horrid shore did whistle in our ears,
> Those dreadful beasts upon that land around our cots do roar,
> Most dismal is our doom upon Van Diemen's shore.
> (Cited Murray 1991, p. 18)

Van Diemen's Land was one of the few places in the world where large numbers of women (12,500) were sent as convicts.

This chapter provides two case studies on infanticide press discourse 11,000 miles from England in the British penal colony of Van Diemen's Land, where a young convict, Mary McLauchlan, was tried and executed for infanticide in

---

[1] Now known as Tasmania. Such was the shame of the name Van Diemen's Land that upon the cessation of transportation in 1853 the British colony's name was changed to remove the 'convict stain'.

1830, and a free woman, Sarah Masters, the wife of a petty bureaucrat, killed her newborn child at a jailhouse in 1835. In this chapter I analyse how politics played a role in the colonial press's coverage in both of these disparate infanticide cases. I examine how race factored into the way Sarah Masters's case was extensively reported (almost 8,000 words) in the colonial press and how in the case of Mary McLauchlan a newspaper editor found a creative way to expose corruption amongst the elite in the penal colony while preventing himself from being the respondent in a libel action.

Infanticide in the Colonial Press

The cases of Mary McLauchlan and Sarah Masters stand out because they were the most prominent cases covered by the press in the colony's first 40 years. A keyword search of the National Library of Australia's Trove database on the word 'infanticide' in three Hobart Town newspapers, the *Hobart Town Courier*, the *Colonial Times* and the *Hobart Town Gazette* (the Trove database does not include the *Tasmanian Austral Asiatic Review*, which reported Mary McLauchlan's case) in the period from first European settlement, February 1803 to December 1840, found only three headlined local cases of infanticide: Mary McLauchlan's case in 1830 (*Hobart Town Courier* and *Colonial Times*), another in 1837, which briefly mentions the inquest on the body of a dead infant found 'wrapped in a white calico wrapper and cap lying on the pathway opposite No. 6 Liverpool Street' ('Infanticide', *Hobart Town Courier* 7 April 1837; p. 3); and the trial of a free servant, Sarah Coffee, who was charged with smothering her newborn infant in her master's house at Bellerive in 1837 ('Coroner's Inquest – Infanticide', *Hobart Town Courier* 8 December 1837, 3; *Colonial Times* 8 December 1837, p. 3).

A keyword search using the phrase 'child-murder' for the same time period, February 1803 to December 1840, in the same newspapers found four reports. One was not an infanticide and another was republished in the *Colonial Times* from the *Sydney Herald* and was a story on the discovery of child murder 'committed by the natives' in which a 'woman near the time of delivery was found missing'. This colonial discourse introduced the trope of heathen savages in binary opposition to the civilized Europeans into the news discourse. According to the report a search was made and the cries of an infant led the European party to a spot where a 'new-born female child was found thrown on the fire'. The 'wise' and 'humanitarian' Europeans 'immediately rescued' the child. When it died the next day it was considered 'another proof of the affinity that exists between the Aborigines of New Holland and the islanders of the Pacific Ocean' (*Colonial Times* 10 September 1833, p. 5) who also practised infanticide. The fourth 'child murder' report was republished from the recently arrived English presses:

> The head of the unfortunate woman who was lately executed at the Old Bailey
> for child murder, was submitted, it is said, to the examination of a celebrated

Phrenologist, who announced that the organ of destructiveness was very imperfectly developed, and that of *philopregetiveness* (love of offspring) very strong! ('Latest English News', *Colonial Times* 10 July 1829, p. 3)

This ideological discourse speaks directly to earlier discussions on medicine's influential role in the management of the infanticidal woman and how medical discourse was used as the explanatory frame to make sense of the 'unnatural' act of infanticide.

The third case, reported in the *Hobart Town Courier* (4 September 1830, p. 2), was that of Ann Edwards, who was charged with killing her newborn infant. The verdict was that the child 'died through carelessness and neglect of the mother, whereby, it became smothered and choked', but there was no follow-up report of a trial. The fourth report and the only infanticide report in the Van Diemen's Land press under the headline 'child-murder', was a story on the discovery of the body of a newborn infant found in a bandbox in a stone quarry above Providence Valley (now Lenah Valley, a suburb of Hobart). An inquest was held at Mr Tilley's Sawyer's Arms, but a publishing deadline meant that the reporter was unable to provide readers with the coroner's verdict: 'no result had transpired when we went to press' (*Hobart Town Courier* 9 October 1840, p. 4). The outcome of the inquest was not subsequently reported.

It would seem that in the penal colony newspaper proprietors were not interested in the crime of infanticide, or were loath to admit in a place with a paucity of females that the crime of infanticide was part of the lived experience. As mentioned earlier, the returns for crimes committed in the period tell us that there were convictions for the crime but infanticide may not have been considered worthy of coverage in court reports due to a lack of public interest in this female specific crime in a penal colony where bushrangers, escaped convicts, murder and robbery under arms were the common crimes that threatened the welfare and safety of settlers. The gross shortage of females in the colony meant that female convicts were much sought after to provide free domestic labour in the settler's houses and this shortage may also have had an impact on how colonial society generally treated women who committed infanticide. Whatever the reason, the crime of infanticide remained low in terms of news values – until two cases of infanticide involving prominent individuals created scandals in the colony.

Mary McLauchlan

Mary McLauchlan was one of more than 12,500 women, and 74,000 convicts in total, transported from Britain to the island of Van Diemen's Land between 1803 and 1853. For the first half of the nineteenth century the island was in effect a giant jail, governed by rules specific to a penal colony with a closed port and restrictions on entry and trade and the authority to enslave prisoners. Under the rule of the authoritarian and much-hated Lieutenant Governor George Arthur (1823–37), the island gained a reputation for being notoriously harsh and one of the most dreaded penal colonies in the world.

In 1830 of the 10,195 convicts in the island colony only 1,318 were female (Martin 1839, p. 443) and this gender imbalance created particular problems as there was an overall shortage of free females (4,623 women to 8,351 men) in the colony, which meant female convict servants were at a premium. The total population of Van Diemen's Land in 1830, including military and aborigines, was calculated at 24,504 with only 6,276 of those female, There was no official policy mandating the reformation of female convicts transported to the island, other than assigning them to free settlers to work as convict servants. The majority of convicts in the colony were assigned to free settlers as free or slave labour for the cost of feeding, accommodating and clothing. Artist and writer Louisa Anne Meredith, who settled with her husband Charles on the east coast of Van Diemen's Land in 1840, wrote of the many challenges she faced in securing reliable female servants. Her diary offers an insight into how female convicts were regarded by free settlers:

> My first prisoner nurse girl was taken at random by our agent in Hobarton, from among the herd of incorrigibles in the female house of correction, or 'Factory' as it is termed; and was indeed a notable example: – dirty beyond all imagining! She drank rum, smoked tobacco, swore awfully, and was in all respects the lowest specimen of woman-kind I ever had the sorrow to behold. Before I had time to procure another, she drank herself into violent fits, so that four men could not hold her from knocking herself against the walls and floor, then went to hospital, and, finally, got married! (Meredith 1852, p. 153)

Marriage was indeed the ultimate ambition of most convict women for they knew that if they found a husband they would be assigned to him and in effect be free from the institutionalized slavery of the convict system. It also freed convict women from the harsh discipline attached to a pregnancy.

When a female convict became pregnant her value in the labour force of the colony was significantly diminished. With the shortage of free labour in the colony there was a high demand on the assignment system and the loss of labour attached to pregnancy, and the unproductive cost of housing the pregnant convict woman and her infant, was considered an unacceptable economic burden. Pregnancy for female convicts was a 'public taboo' (Marousi 1997, p. 125) and the punishment was particularly harsh. Once a woman's pregnancy was discovered she was sentenced to six months imprisonment in the crime class at the Female Factory at Cascades[2] in Hobart Town (also known as the Female House of Correction).

---

[2]   Although much of the structure has been demolished, the convict walls and some of the outbuildings still exist today. The site was granted World Heritage Status in 2010. A visit to the site provides a poignant experience of what life must have been like for the convict women and their babies.

Crime class was the worst class of prisoner and meant six months' hard labour at the overcrowded, poorly ventilated Female Factory where yet to be assigned or unassignable convict women, and those who were pregnant, infirm or undergoing punishment, were housed. After delivery convict women were kept housed in the Factory under hard labour until their children were weaned, generally at six months, at which time they were reassigned, leaving their babies behind in the overcrowded nursery. Not unlike the unmarried mothers in England who looked to infanticide to avoid the deprivation and misery of the workhouse, convict women in Van Diemen's Land had a strong motivation to kill their newborn babies to avoid consignment to the Female House of Correction.

In the same week in January 1829 that Mary McLauchlan disembarked from the convict ship *Harmony* onto the Hobart Town docks the editor of the *Hobart Town Courier*, Dr James Ross, was extolling the advantages of the 'new House of Correction' in a leading article. Ross told his readers that the new facility was 'likely to be attended with much advantage, an instance of which already sensibly appears in the disposal of the female prisoners by the *Harmony*'. The new facility, with its children's nursery, meant that female convicts with children were no longer unassignable as the infants could be left in the nursery while the mothers were assigned. 'By this means a large proportion of the prisoners by the *Harmony*, who had children with them, and who on the former system must have remained a charge on the public, have been assigned to service' (Editorial *HTC*[3] 31 January 1829, p. 3). Ross writes glowingly of the 'improved discipline which this building enables the Superintendent to exercise. Farewell now to idleness and impudence, love-letter writing, throwing of packets etc over the wall, and all the concomitants of clandestine taking and receiving'.

However, just six months later when Mary McLauchlan entered the Female Factory, Robert Lathrop Murray, as caretaker editor at the *Colonial Times,* was demanding Governor Arthur look into the high number of infant deaths in the Factory nursery:

> We have to call the attention of the Authorities to a letter signed 'Humanity' inserted in another part of our paper, pointing out the great number of deaths which constantly occur in the *new* Female Factory ... We have made this enquiry, and we find them more than corroborated; for we learn from the most respectable sources that so many as six or seven children have laid dead there at the same time. We have not only heard these facts from respectable sources, but even some Government Officers have stated in our hearing that Dr Secombe, before he left the Colony, admitted that a great number of deaths occurred in this Establishment, among the infant children. (Editorial, *Colonial Times* 7 August 1829, p. 3)

---

[3]   In this part of the analysis for easy of reading I have abbreviated in text the names of the newspapers: the *Hobart Town Courier – HTC*; the *Colonial Times – CT*; the *Tasmanian Austral Asiatic Review – TAAR*.

In this feeling editorial Murray, reflecting the tone of *The Times*'s editors during their campaign against the New Poor Law, held that the idea that 'poor helpless babes, just ushered into the world' would 'perish from the cold and damp of this dreary place,' was 'revolting to humanity'. Murray drew upon rhetorical *logos* to argue that the deaths were preventable, as evidenced by the fact that 'so very few infants born in the Colony at large die' and that 'in fact, the death of an infant is a rare occurrence'. The matter was of such 'serious import', he told his readers, that it 'ought to be brought under the notice of His Excellency the Lieutenant Governor' (Editorial, *CT* 7 August 1829, p. 3). The death rate for infants housed in the nursery remained for the next decade 'exceedingly great' (Marousi 1997, p. 125). The 'nurses', according to a report by the medical officer in 1834, 'had no incentive or inducement for constant care' and when children were weaned from their mothers and placed in the nursery 'their deaths are very numerous' (cited Marousi, p. 125). These children were afflicted with diseases, which, the report determined, were caused by 'impoverished living and want of exercise'.

When Mary McLauchlan disembarked from the convict ship *Harmony* in Hobart Town on a mild summer's day in January 1829 her convict record painted a picture of a young woman with an oval visage, a dark complexion, hazel eyes and brown hair (CON 18/24 TAHO). At the time of her infanticide trial (April 1830) it was reported that 'when in health she must have been an interesting woman, with rather a pleasing countenance' (*HTC* 24 April 1830, p. 3). Mary was born in 1801 in Saltcoats, a seaside village in Ayrshire, on the coast of the Frith of Clyde, 32 miles from Glasgow. The village had been a centre for salt harvesting, using seawater, but by the early nineteenth century when Mary was growing up in the village, fishing, coal mining and handloom weaving were the main industries. The population in the 1830s was about 4,000, a considerable number of who were sailors, colliers and weavers ('Saltcoats', *The Penny Cyclopædia* 1842, p. 369). In July 1837 there were 'above 450 looms in the Ardrossan side of the town, chiefly kept in the work by the Glasgow and Paisley manufacturers, producing gauzes, shawls, trimmings, silks, and so on'. Many women were employed in sewing and flowering muslin. Mary most likely learned her weaving skills from her parents, as there is a long lineage of McLauchlans from Saltcoats who were either weavers or coalminers.

By the 1820s the collapsing handloom weaving industry was suffering from a continual inrush of soldiers returning from the Napoleonic Wars and out-of-work journeymen. Mary's husband, William Sutherland, from Glasgow, was an out-of-work weaver at the time of Mary's arrest. With two young children aged five and eight and no income one can only imagine the dire straits they were in, with the fear of the dreaded workhouse looming over their lives. In 1828 Mary McLauchlan was brought before the West Circuit of the High Court of Justiciary in Glasgow charged with housebreaking and theft. At her trial she admitted to having received stolen goods, but rejected the more serious charge of breaking into a dwelling house. She was found guilty of theft and sentenced to 14 years transportation – in effect transportation for life as few convicts having served their sentence had the resources to return to Britain. Historian Helen MacDonald believes Mary was the victim of a harsh judgment by a magistrate who, during the same Assizes, sentenced half of the 14 women who came before him to either life or 14 years' transportation (MacDonald 2005, p. 55). MacDonald also conjectures Mary may have received a harsh sentence because she refused to co-operate by naming the person or persons from whom she had received the stolen goods. 'In the records relating to her trial, it seems clear that William Sutherland, not his wife, was the chief suspect' (MacDonald p. 55). Mary railed against the sentence that would separate her from her husband and children forever and her jail records report her behaviour in the Tolbooth jail as 'troublesome' (MacDonald, p. 55). Despite her unruly behaviour the jailer acknowledged in her prison report that Mary was previously a respectable woman: 'Connexions respectable and former course of life good' (MacDonald, p. 55).

The course of Mary's life in Van Diemen's Land was determined by the assignment system which saw her placed with Scotsman Charles Ross Nairne. Nairne was a wealthy Paisley merchant who immigrated to the colony with his wife, Katherine Stirling, and a young son in 1822. The Nairne family settled on the fertile plains of the Coal River valley northeast of Hobart Town calling their property 'Glen Nairne'. When news of the arrival of a female convict ship reached the Coal River in the summer of 1829 Nairne travelled down to Hobart Town with the hope of obtaining a female convict to assist his wife, Katherine, who was eight months pregnant. The good-looking Scots woman caught Nairne's eye from amongst the women of the *Harmony* mustered on the Hobart docks. The official paperwork completed, Nairne, breaking protocol, travelled back to his property 'Glen Nairne' alone with Mary. It was considered improper for a free man to travel alone for any distance with a female convict. Whether anything untoward happened on the journey through the hinterland was never determined, but what is known is that within two months of disembarking in Hobart Town and being assigned to Charles Ross Nairne Mary McLauchlan was pregnant.

The power in all convict/master relationships was always heavily in favour of the master, but for convict women that power relationship was grossly distorted against the woman. Female convict servants were more vulnerable to the sexual advances of their masters in the colonies than free female servants working for the middle and upper classes in England. In Van Diemen's Land female convicts, assigned to settlers in the hinterland out of view of the moderating influences of the society and the authorities, were particularly vulnerable to abuse. In Van Diemen's Land a female convict who rejected her master's sexual advances faced arbitrary discipline. At the very least she could be denied certain supplies, such as tea or tobacco, which were considered luxuries, but more often she would find herself sent back to one of the female factories as a troublesome convict and there be subjected to harsh punishment. Although the Superintendent of Convicts was required to listen to a woman's point of view, and convict women did often make complaints against their masters regarding the failure to provide adequate food or clothing, few convict women in Van Diemen's Land complained about sexual impropriety. Perhaps experience told the women that accusations of sexual misconduct would not be taken seriously because there was an implicit assumption that all female convicts were immoral. The wife of one influential settler, Elizabeth Fenton, regarded female convicts as an 'immoral physical force' (MacDonald 2005, p. 64). John West believed the system of female assignment in Van Diemen's Land, even for the 'better disposed has been one of great hazard and temptation'. He argued that the 'last state of female degradation' – prostitution – was 'their inevitable lot':

> They were surrendered to solicitations and even violence: a convict constable conducted them to the houses of their master; they lodged on the road, wherever they could obtain shelter; convict servants were usually their companions – or when their manners were superior to their class, corrupters of a higher rung were always at hand to betray or destroy them. Reformation has been commonly deemed unattainable, and precautions useless. (West 1852, p. 320)

Convict women, framed as irredeemable, were thus seen as disposable sexual commodities. Marriage, as mentioned above, was the ultimate ambition of most convict women for they knew that if they found a husband they would be assigned to him and in effect be free from the institutionalized slavery of the convict system. However, for Mary McLauchlan marriage was not going to save her from domestic slavery or the unwanted sexual advances of her master. While many canny convict women realized that a marital status of 'single' on the muster roll on arrival in Hobart Town would allow them the opportunity for a new life in the colony, when the Superintendent of Convicts, Josiah Spode, asked Mary her marital status, she had responded 'married'.

Once Mary's pregnancy became obvious Charles Nairne was anxious to be rid of her. In August 1829, when Mary was five months pregnant, Nairne returned her to Hobart Town and had her brought before Josiah Spode on a charge of misconduct. When the charge was read to Mary her feisty rejoinder was that she had not received the correct quantity of clothing from Mrs Nairne. Mary's charge was found 'to be without foundation' and she was charged with leaving her master's house without permission and sentenced to six days' solitary confinement at the Cascades Female Factory on bread and water, 'Crime Class', and when she was next assigned she was to be sent as a worst offender further into the interior of Van Diemen's Land. This was an unusually harsh sentence for a first offender, particularly as Mary had no charges against her.

The Cascades Female Factory sat under the looming shadow of Mount Wellington on the floor of a steep, heavily wooded valley. The cold, airless buildings were prone to flooding from the adjacent rivulet and even at the height of summer the Factory remained damp and cold. As a Crime Class convict Mary, on entering the Female Factory, was subjected to having her long dark hair cut off as an additional punishment, and was forced to wear coarse prison dress that prominently distinguished her from the other first and second class prisoners. Her dress had a large 'C' in the centre of the back, on the right sleeve and on the back part of the petticoat. She was also assigned to the most arduous labour – to wash for the factory, the orphan schools and the penitentiary – and also to carding and spinning wool. Four months after her arrival at the Female Factory, on an early December day, Mary gave birth to a male child in the privy at the Female Factory and there she allegedly strangled her child shortly after birth. She was soon after charged with murder and on Thursday 15 April 1830 Mary was put on trial at the Hobart Town Supreme Court. The military jury consisted of seven men from the 63rd Regiment. At the time Robert William Lathrop Murray was conducting a press campaign to pressure Arthur to introduce civil juries due to the alleged corruption in military juries. Five of the jurists at Mary's trial were influential colonists connected to key players in the case – two of the men were business partners of Charles Ross Nairne. The presiding judge was Chief Justice John Pedder. Mary did not have legal counsel.

The Newspaper Reports

Three colonial newspapers, the *Hobart Town Courier*, the *Tasmanian Austral Asiatic Review* and the *Colonial Times*, brought Mary McLauchlan's tragic infanticide to the residents of Van Diemen's Land. One newspaper alone, Robert Lathrop Murray's *Tasmanian Austral Asiatic Review* would later transform this infanticide story into a sensational piece of political journalism.

Each of the newspapers reported the trial with a brevity not found in infanticide newspaper reports in the English press at the time. The anti-Arthur and anti-establishment newspaper proprietors, Henry Melville and Robert Lathrop Murray, as well as the conservative pro-Arthur and pro-Government proprietor, Dr James Ross, saw infanticide by a female convict as having little news value. News values, as discussed earlier, are dictated by the environment in which the journalism is being practiced, and in the British penal colony of Van Diemen's Land in 1830 the newspaper readership was predominantly drawn from the relatively small literate section of the free settler class.

In the reports of Mary McLauchlan's trial there is little deviation in the facts recorded in each of the newspapers. It is possible that the same report may have been provided to all three newspapers by the same law clerk, as was the practice in England. However, each newspaper provided a different spelling for 'McLauchlan', and this point of difference may speak to different newspapermen attending the trial. Henry Melville and James Ross were both known to report on trials but it is impossible to be certain whether they attended Mary McLauchlan's trial. Whether the decision not to include certain details was determined by the primary gatekeeper, the court reporter, who as a Government bureaucrat may have considered it not in the public interest to provide a full account of the trial of a convict woman charged with infanticide, or whether each of the newspaper editors reporting the trial themselves determined not to report particulars of the trial, cannot be determined.

The brutal brevity of Robert Lathrop Murray's 26-word single sentence report in the *Tasmanian Austral Asiatic Review* ('Supreme Court – Criminal Side', 16 April 1830, p. 3) is shocking even today. Sandwiched between reports of the other trials from the previous week, Murray's report simply states: 'April 15 – Mary McLauchlin [*sic*] alias Sutherland, for the murder of her infant child, was found Guilty, and sentenced at the bar to be executed to-morrow'. It is the significance of the final words with their specific temporal meaning that create a connotation which even at the time was antithetical to the concept of due process and justice, and speaks to an unpalatably swift judicial process. Coupled with the misspelling of Mary's name, this report of Mary McLauchlan's trial is on all journalistic criteria, inadequate. This single sentence report of barely three lines reflects a rejection of the notion of news values in the daylong trial of a convict woman charged with the murder of her bastard child. Murray was, in his defence, probably of the opinion that the death sentence would be commuted, as was almost always the case in England. Within a few short days Murray's positioning of this story and its newsworthiness would change dramatically.

Ross's report in the *Hobart Town Courier* on Saturday 17 April ('Mary M'Laughland' *HTC* 17 April 1830, p.2) likewise relegated Mary McLauchlan's lengthy trial to a crude footnote, and an incorrect spelling of her name. In this case the report consists of two equally brutal sentences: 'Mary M'Laughland [*sic*] was arraigned for the wilful murder of a male bastard child. She was found guilty and sentence [*sic*] to be executed this morning' (ibid.). Again the final clause and the coupling of 'execution' and 'morning' create a connotation antithetical to the concept of due process, although again Ross may have expected her sentence to be commuted. As it was, by the time Ross's report was read Mary McLauchlan was dead. The style, tone and syntax of Ross's report speak of his distaste at the whole sordid affair. James Ross was a schoolmaster to the Governor's children and a deeply religious man who regularly utilized editorial space in his newspaper to provide homilies and morality tales to his readers. His clipped, pejorative wording 'male bastard child', as opposed to Murray's softer 'infant child' reflects the high moral tone Ross imbued in his newspaper discourse. Mary's guilty verdict and imminent execution are again compressed, this time into less than a dozen words. The grammatical error, in the word 'sentence' would have annoyed the schoolmaster.

Melville's report in the *Colonial Times* ('Criminal Court 15 April 1830', *CT* 16 April 1830, p. 3) is the longest of the three reports and the one that provides key information about the trial itself. No records of the trial have survived making Melville's account significant. Melville reported that 'a vast number of witnesses were examined' and that there was a 'most and [*sic*] patient investigation, lasting from morning until late in the evening'. Frustratingly none of the newspapers provide any discourse on this evidence, there is no elaboration beyond the most cursory details and therefore there is none of the usual journalistic court-reporting style recreating the events as told by the witnesses. Who said what and how they said it inside the courtroom when published in newspapers, as discussed earlier, says much about the individual voices, including the mediating voice of the court reporter and the newspaper editor. While Melville's account is verbose in comparison to the reports of Ross and Murray, it adheres to a truncated style which fails to inform and therefore negates its role as 'news reporting', leaving the reader with many unanswered questions. Melville's version does, however, provide some details of the alleged crime: 'it appeared that the prisoner had been privately delivered of a child whilst confined in the female house of correction, and had caused its death by strangulation and afterwards concealed it in the water closet'. The use of the word 'appeared' creates a less definitive tone than that found in the other reports. In Melville's account the tone is not dogmatic and there is an absence of any hard-edged certainty. It is in Melville's report that Mary McLauchlan's name is finally spelled correctly (or as recorded in her colonial convict records). In concert with the other two reports, Melville's account also creates the sense of a disconcerting haste. In a final garbled two-sentence paragraph the reader is told of the 'vast evidence from witnesses' that 'was put before the court'. Without any further elaboration on this evidence the reader is informed that: 'the prisoner was found Guilty, and sentenced to be executed on Saturday morning, and her body to be dissected'. The final phrase is chilling, speaking to an ignominious punishment that was only imposed on the dead bodies of the worst criminals. The knowledge that this final act of corporeal punishment would be imposed on the body of a woman, even if purely hypothetical (the expectation being that the sentence would be commuted) would have been confronting to the inhabitants of the penal colony.

It is in the final sentence of Melville's report that the high news-values of this trial finally become apparent: 'This is only the second instance of a female being tried for murder, in this Colony and the first convicted of the offence' ('Criminal Court 15 April 1830', *CT* 16 April 1830, p. 3). Melville's acknowledgement of the significance of the trial, however, sits in opposition to the brevity of all three reports.

While the newspaper editors may have been slow to realize that all was not as it should be in Mary McLauchlan's trial, two members of the Executive Council (the executive arm of colonial government), the Colonial Secretary, John Burnett, and the Colonial Treasurer, Jocelyn Thomas, immediately the guilty verdict was brought down and a sentence of death recorded, requested the Executive Council (made up of the Colonial Secretary John Burnett, the Colonial Treasurer Mr Jocelyn Thomas, the Chief Justice John Pedder,[4] and the Lieutenant Governor George Arthur) delay their meeting to determine Mary McLauchlan's sentence while certain 'suspicions were investigated' ('Executive Council Minutes', Friday 16 April 1830, TAHO). The use of such a loaded phrase spoke of this appeal being something far more significant than the usual letter of appeal for a commutation of a death sentence.

---

[4]   Two years later Thomas and Burnett would face allegations of corruption. Thomas was said to be in collusion with the Collector of Customs in embezzling Government funds and Burnett was allegedly involved in corrupt land dealings.

Thomas and Burnett picked up on certain things that did not sit right if justice was to be seen to be done. The men were uncomfortable that at least two of the jurors were business partners of Charles Nairne, Mary McLauchlan's former master. They were also aware, as surely the newspaper editors would have been, of certain rumours sweeping through the settlement that Mary McLauchlan was being sacrificed to save Nairne's reputation. When the Executive Council met the following day, Friday 16 April, Burnett and Thomas told the meeting:

> As the crime was not one of frequent occurrence and in the present case appeared to have been committed without any known adequate motive, and as there were some grounds for suspicion that she might have been incited to its commission by the father of the child, who was supposed to be a person of better education and higher rank in society than herself it was desirable that a reprieve of a few days might be granted to ascertain whether these suspicions had any foundation in truth and in the hope that something might come to light extenuating the enormity of the first public execution of a female in this Colony. (Executive Council Minutes, 16 Friday April 1830, TAHO)

This is not the usual proforma letter requesting the commutation of the death sentence in the crime of infanticide. Such letters invariably spoke to the good character of the defendant, her level of contrition and the impact on her family if the death penalty was carried out. This formal legal document, after acknowledging that infanticide was not a crime in the colony in need of such a harsh deterrent, goes on to explicitly point to coercion and the immoral actions of the unnamed father of the child, a man of 'better education and higher rank in society'. Without identifying the father, he was nevertheless known to everyone at the Executive Council meeting. The attempt by Thomas and Burnett to save Mary McLauchlan from the gallows was admirable, but vested interests were determined to silence her and save the reputation of one of their own.

By the time the next newspaper reports were published a week later in the three Hobart Town newspapers Mary McLauchlan's dissected body has been disposed of in an unmarked grave in the government cemetery. Through these news reports Mary's last hours can be pieced together. On Monday 19 April 1835 Henry Melville reported that she walked from the condemned cell 'dressed in a white garment with a black ribbon round her waist, and a very large concourse assembled to witness her ignominious end. On the falling of the drop, the instant before her mortal scene was closed, she had just time to utter Oh! My God!' ('Executed', *CT* 23 April 1830, p. 3). The potent symbolism of the white dress and black waist ribbon brings a poignancy to the narrative. Each of the press reports described the clothes Mary wore to her death in the same way, creating a romantic trope of the young convict woman clothed in a white dress, the marker of purity symbolizing the fallen women returning to her original pure status at the moment of her death, and the black ribbon, connoting death and mourning.

The first execution of a woman in the colony was on all criteria 'breaking news'; however, each of the three newspapers covered the execution in quite diverse ways. While 'the gloomy festival of punishment was dying out' (Foucault 2008b, p. 8) in the early nineteenth century in England and Europe, it was a focus of the regime of discipline and punishment in the island penal colony of Van Diemen's Land. At a time when punishment had 'gradually ceased to be a spectacle' (Foucault 2008b, pp. 9–10) in England, and 'whatever theatrical elements it still retained were now downgraded'(ibid., pp. 9–10) public executions were still a focus of life in the penal colony. Indeed Lieutenant Governor George Arthur was so committed to the application of the rope as a deterrent that in the two years from 1826 to 1827 103 men were executed in the colony. In Arthur's term of office (1824–36) there were more than 260 executions, nearly half the total number of executions in Tasmanian history (Davis 1974). On one day alone in September 1826 eight men had been hanged in unison at the Hobart Town gallows before a crowd of assembled free and emancipated settlers and convicts in chains.

Dr James Ross's reports
Newspaper editor Dr James Ross was a strident supporter of capital punishment and he made a point of attending every execution in the colony. However, he now confessed to his readers through the editorial 'we', to distance himself from his lack of conviction, that 'the present case was too painful for our feelings, and we were not present' ('On Monday', *HTC* 24 April 1830, p. 3). The underlying message is clear, for all 'feeling' men the witnessing of the execution of a female would be all 'too painful' to their feelings.

Ross through his newspaper report supports Arthur's decision not to intervene in the case and to let justice take its course. He explicitly places the blame for the distressing execution of the first woman in the colony with Mary McLauchlan alone. As the author of her own demise she not only sacrificed her own life, but placed all men in the colony in the invidious position of having to witness her execution. Ross, as a vocal supporter of Arthur's regime, was emphatic about her motive and refused to countenance political interference. He reported the case as a distasteful example of the immorality of female convicts. He was, however, able to reassure his readers that through the 'assiduous ministry' of Rev. Mr Bedford, 'a certain hope of forgiveness supported her at the last hour, and she died contrite and resigned'. He continued:

> How awful, and we trust impressive, the dreadful lesson thus held forth to both
> sexes in this peculiarly situated colony. Well has the first step to error been
> compared to the burning spark, which when once lighted, may carry destruction
> in inconceivable bounds. But will mankind take a lesson? Cannot the horrible
> tenacity be broken with which the devil keeps his hold, when once he has put his
> finger on his victim? ('On Monday', *Hobart Town Courier* 23 April 1830, p. 3)

At the same time as Ross's didactic discourse was moralizing about the inadequacies of female convicts and their dissolute behaviour, several of Mary's convict shipmates from the *Harmony* were ensconced in his household as unpaid domestic servants.

Henry Melville's report

Henry Melville's report in the *Colonial Times* is a rather strange discursive opinion piece on the topic of male versus female execution. Melville poses the question that 'naturally arises to all thinking persons': 'why is it that so many more of the latter [men] should suffer [execution]?' Pointing to Mary McLauchlan as the first woman to be 'brought to the scaffold' he asks his readers why it has taken so long? Melville contrasts the public outcry over Mary's public execution with 'the many and frequent executions which take place of the male community' ('Execution' *CT* 23 April 1830, p. 3). This rambling news discourse with its convoluted rhetoric goes on to philosophize on the virtue or not of women:

> It is sometimes said that there is no medium with respect to the female character, that either they are all that's good and virtuous, or that they are depraved and abandoned in the extreme; how then is it that in a place like this, where the most profligate and wicked of the female sex are to be found – how is it, we say, that the proportionate number of females suffering the severe penalty of the law, should be so comparatively small, when compared with the number of male malefactor? ('Execution', *Colonial Times* 23 April 1830, p. 3)

As discussed earlier in this study, words get meaning from their collocates, and in Melville's report on Mary McLauchlan's execution he uses collocation to emphasize meaning. By positioning binary collocates in his discourse: 'barbarously murdered' with 'innocent infant', and 'unspeakable horror' with 'hapless victim', and adding the collocate 'unnatural parent', his rhetoric provides a stereotypical reading of the infanticidal woman and reinforces society's abhorrence at Mary McLauchlan's actions. He further layers this meaning with his positioning of women as being at either end of two polarities, 'good and virtuous' or 'depraved and abandoned' and 'profligate and wicked' reinforcing the dominant patriarchal view of women. Melville sermonizes to the residents of the penal colony, a standard rhetorical strategy used by all of the newspaper editors in the penal colony. Through the use of the phrases such as 'a place like this', a code the readers of the *Colonial Times* would readily understand, he appeals to the women of the colony to be something other than 'the most profligate and wicked' of females. In answer to his own question he situates the illegitimate child killed by its mother as united with her, her property alone, reflecting the English poor laws after 1834. No matter how 'depraved', 'abandoned', 'profligate' or 'wicked' the woman she 'is only herself the sufferer'; while on the other hand 'unfortunately, the wicked man generally causes others to suffer by his depravity'.

He then returns to the news topic of the day, the execution of the first woman in the colony, and his focus now shifts to the absent male in the Mary McLauchlan infanticide discourse:

> the reports that have been circulated since her death appear to us almost incredible. We pitied the woman that could be guilty of such a crime – we now pity much more the originator of her sufferings; she has left the world penitent – may her seducer on his death-bed do the same. ('Execution', *Colonial Times* 23 April 1830, p. 3)

Despite this rhetoric Melville, adhering to the rules of a deeply patriarchal society of blood, did not name the 'originator' of Mary's suffering. While Melville placed the woman as 'only herself the sufferer' and the male as the 'originator of her suffering' he acknowledges that 'it is at all times distressing to hear of the depriving of a female of life – but blood for blood – the awful voice of justice must be heard'. 'Blood for blood' reinforces the nineteenth-century Western Christian view as ordained in the Bible: 'Whoso sheddeth man's blood, by man shall his blood be shed' (Genesis 11:6 King James Bible). As Foucault tells us, 'nothing was more on the side of the law, death, transgression, the symbolic and sovereignty than blood' (1991a, p. 269). While Foucault talked about blood and a 'society of blood' in a gender-neutral way, in this study 'a society of blood' is read from a gendered perspective. In nineteenth-century infanticide discourse the female body and the concept of the female in society, as I discussed earlier, is at the centre of 'a society of blood'.

Directly below Henry Melville's report on Mary McLauchlan's execution, under the 'Supreme Court' headline, is to be found, buried in another report, information of particular interest to this case:

> The following prisoners were discharged by Proclamation: George Boot, for perjury; Mary Rice and Charles Wood, for stealing tea; Richard Barnes and Bryant Kane, for cattle stealing; Robert Weare, for cutting and maiming; James Jackson, Eliza Murtaugh, and Catherine Jackson, for feloniously entering a dwelling; Mary Cameron, for the murder of a male child; and Mayhew Meek and James Murtaugh for sheep stealing. ('Supreme Court', *Colonial Times* 23 April 1830, p. 3)

Mary Cameron according to the Executive Council records, was with Mary McLauchlan the night she gave birth, and was also charged with the murder of Mary's child. At her trial and in her last hours Mary McLauchlan refused to 'give up' Mary Cameron. Details of Mary Cameron's appearance before the Supreme Court were not reported in the colonial newspapers and her acquittal was reported in a mere nine words.

Robert Lathrop Murray's report

It is through a close reading of Robert Lathrop Murray's press reports and the Executive Minutes that Mary McLauchlan's last hours come into focus. We learn that Mary McLauchlan had given up the name of her child's father before her death: 'in the presence of all those in the prison lobby; and she then went forth and submitted to her fate, with calmness and resignation' ('The First Woman Executed', *TAAR* 23 April 1830, p. 533). Mary had been persuaded by Reverend William Bedford not to shout out the name of her 'seducer' to the gathering crowd as she stepped onto the gallows (as she had said she wanted to). Perhaps Bedford had assured her that her progress into the afterlife would be smoother if she forgave her enemy. Bedford was Colonial Chaplain and held a seat on the Legislative Council. He was known for his assiduous work in building churches throughout the colony and for his work with prisoners, and in particular with those who were condemned to die on the gallows, who dubbed him 'Holy Willie'. A man full of self-confidence he was also known to have a combative nature and was headstrong, indiscreet and vain according to Bishop Nixon. Bedford was a man of 'uncertain principles' who had involved himself in 'many controversies in his long colonial service' (*ADB* 1966). Colonial diarist George Boyes portrayed Bedford as a 'liar, mischief-maker and back-biter' (*ADB* 1966). From Murray's press report we learn (no doubt from Bedford's account of the events) that when he administered the consolation of the Sacrament to Mary just before she stepped onto the gallows she:

> related her melancholy tale, and the cold-hearted treatment she received from the author of her destruction. She was most desirous to denounce him on the scaffold to the assembled multitude, with her dying words. Mr Bedford, with a kindness and consideration, most undeserved by him upon whom it was bestowed, dissuaded her from this, which she consented to, only upon the condition of declaring it to the sheriff. ('First Woman Executed', *Tasmanian Austral Asiatic Review* 23 April 1830, p. 533)

The meaning was clear to those who understood colonial politics: Reverend William Bedford had entered into a gallows bargain with Mary McLauchlan and a faction of the Hobart Town elite had closed ranks to keep the name of Mary's 'seducer' out of the public domain. Bedford and the Hobart Town cabal were no doubt grimly satisfied, feeling certain at the drop of the gallows door that the 'good name' of one of the patriarchal elite had been saved from ignominy. But no one had factored in the ingenuity of Lathrop Murray.

It was from Murray's report that the public were also made aware of the behind the scenes negotiations going on over the life of the young Scotswoman. According to Murray's report Colonial Secretary, John Burnett and the Colonial Treasurer, Mr Jocelyn Thomas, had appealed to Arthur to reprieve Mary McLauchlan's death sentence, and that the Governor, reluctant to interfere, had requested advice from the Chief Justice, John Pedder. Pedder was adamant that the sentence should stand

and when the Executive Council finally broke up at six o'clock on the Friday evening Thomas was still in favour of a reprieve, Burnett was wavering, and Governor Arthur was yet to make up his mind. The press statement issued by the Council, and published by Murray alone, reported that the 'Chief Justice, in the case of McLauchlan, could not advise the Lieutenant Governor to interfere with the course of the law'. Readers learnt from Murray's report that the Lieutenant Governor had 'stated that he was not aware of the practice in England with regard to interfering with the course of the law in similar cases'. The absurdity of Arthur's mealy mouthed response was now exposed for all to see, as rarely at this time in the British Empire were women found guilty of infanticide executed. The wording of the Chief Justice's statement and the use of the word 'anxious' and the phrase 'before coming to a decision' aimed to create a sense of a considered response and due processes, and may have allayed the concerns of most of the Hobart Town populous reading Murray's report.

Murray's report draws upon well-known rhetorical tropes to explain the events that led up to the execution of the first woman in the colony. The minister is all 'kindness and consideration' while Nairne is 'the most underserved', 'the author of her destruction' and Mary the 'poor unfortunate woman'. Through the use of collocation in phrases such as 'melancholy tale' and 'cold-hearted treatment' readers began to understand the level of political interference in Mary McLauchlan's execution.

While Bedford had entered into his gallows bargain with Mary, Murray had not and he made it clear to his readers that Mary McLauchlan had given up the name of her child's father 'in the presence of all those in the prison lobby; and she then went forth and submitted to her fate, with calmness and resignation' ('First Woman Executed', *TAAR* 23 April 1830, p. 533). Although Murray may have felt it his duty as a newspaper editor to expose the name of the father of Mary McLauchlan's dead child to his readers, he was all too aware of the consequences of a libel charge – at the time his friend and colleague Andrew Bent, former editor of the *Colonial Times*, languished in the Hobart Town jail thanks to the libel action of Governor Arthur. But suppressing the name of a man at the centre of this corrupt affair must have played on Murray's conscience. The only words attributed directly to Mary McLauchlan in all of the newspaper reports of her trial and execution, were the hastily uttered words: 'Oh! My God!' Through the typeface of Murray's report, however, Mary's voice rings clear. In a display of typographical brilliance Murray published the name of the man responsible for Mary McLauchlan's execution in a way that left no doubt as to the 'author of her fate', but saved Murray from a costly libel suit. It is perhaps fanciful but tempting to picture the newspaper editor standing over the compositor, directing him to place the damning typeface into the printer's block. With the use of capitalized type and the careful placement of the text, Murray exposed the father of Mary's child for all in the colony to see:

> The circumstances of the case, as they appeared at the trial, were shortly these – She had been in the service of Mr C.R. NAIRNE. Having there become pregnant, she was returned to the Female House of Correction, where she was delivered of a child, which was soon afterwards found dead, in a particular place, under circumstances which induced the Jury to find her guilty of murder. ('First Woman Executed', *Tasmanian Austral Asiatic Review* 23 April 1830, p. 533)

Nairne's name amplified in capitals exposed him to the colonial world of Van Diemen's Land as the metaphorical 'author' of Mary's 'destruction'. Murray had turned to a well-used typographical discursive practice in the use of capitalized letters for emphasis, and significantly, this strategy was understood by newspaper readers as connoting special significance. Typographically buttressed between the phrases 'in the service of' and 'having there become pregnant' the connotation of the capitalized 'Mr C.R. NAIRNE' became apparent. Murray had used the stylistic typesetting device of the compositor to amplify meaning in a way that placed him at no risk of libellous action, leaving Nairne with no legal recourse.

No one in the penal colony was now in any doubt as to who was responsible for Mary McLauchlan's fate. Murray's invective against Nairne framed Mary as a victim of a callous and immoral colonial master and also as the victim of an unjust judicial decision. Her execution, he argued, was a gross injustice carried out with the assent of a corrupt government under Governor Arthur. He reminded readers that in England 'in most cases Juries return a verdict for the minor offence, that of concealing pregnancy'. Taking the view of many of the juries sitting on infanticide trials in England at the time, Murray argued that all human beings were 'aware of the suffering of every woman during parturition' and if ever there was a 'shadow of apology for the crime of murder' then surely it was 'under the agony of mind which every unhappy creature must experience who is giving birth to an infant under the miserable circumstances of imprisonment'. He then draws Nairne into the moment of parturition to argue that Mary:

> under the additional misery of owing it to a man (it is profaning the name to call him one,) whose heart urged him not, to place the wretched woman in a situation where not only the previous necessaries might be provided, but also where she could have all possible consolation in that extremity at which the bosom of every father softens with tenderness, and compassion. ('First Woman Executed', *Tasmanian Austral Asiatic Review* 23 April 1830, p. 533)

Mary McLauchlan was the victim of a patriarchal penal society that treated female convicts as tenured slaves and allowed a young woman to be put to death to save a man's reputation. Her execution was such a gross injustice that one member of the patriarchal press, Robert Lathrop Murray, felt it was his duty as a newspaperman to not only acknowledge the injustice, but also to posthumously give the powerless convict woman her voice and it was through Murray's press discourse that Mary's albeit mediated voice was brought to the people of Hobart Town.

Murray's rhetoric continued through the use of what would have been a familiar trope of deathbed accountability: 'And what must be the feelings of him who brought her to it! Can he have any? – Impossible! Can he sleep? At the midnight hour the fearful image of his expiring victim would strike upon his affrighted imagination in the dreadful agony of death, and awaken him in all the horrors of recollection'. But Murray reminds his readers in a biting aside, 'we have forgotten. His "respectability" may probably render him callous to conscience'. Murray is relentless with his blaming rhetoric, providing further evidence of Nairne's callous behaviour, as the metaphorical 'author of her misfortune' not only did he not 'furnish her with legal assistance' but 'left her without comfort, consolation, or even any – the slightest – addition to the gaol allowance of her food' and as a final affront to Mary McLauchlan, nor did he 'provide for her appropriate apparel to die in!'

Did Robert Lathrop Murray, in creating his potent news discourse, have another motivation beyond the obvious intent to expose a gross injustice? He was (at this stage) anti-Arthur and wrote scathingly in opposition to his regime. He was also a businessman who would have been familiar with Charles Nairne and his business dealings in the small community of Hobart Town. Whatever Murray's motive, through his innovative use of typography Mary McLauchlan's last wishes to name the man who was the 'author of her demise' was realized. In death she had the voice she was denied in life.

Henry Melville's editorial
The manner in which Murray alone exposed the father of Mary McLauchlan's child must have preyed on the mind of Henry Melville, who in May wrote a turgid editorial in the *Colonial Times* lauding 'the legitimate power of the [colonial] press'. He informed readers that it was 'a source of gratification to us that we belong to a ... Public press which is in so well ordered and temperate a state as to have more than once drawn forth the commendations of our sister Colonists in New South Wales'. Into this eulogising editorial he explicitly introduces the reporting by the colonial press of Mary McLauchlan's infanticide:

> Although, however, we would thus avoid personality in combating points with public writers, we are not of the number of those who would like to see the Public Press shorn of part of its powers and control upon the morals of the people, by letting it be silent to the faults and vices of private individuals; for, on the contrary to instance a case, we consider that the heartlessness and cold blooded inhumanity of the seducer of the unfortunate Mary McLauchlan, who latterly expiated her crime of infanticide, upon the scaffold, deserves nothing better than that his name should have been held up by the Press to the scorn, contempt, and hatred of all classes ... ('Editorial', *Colonial Times* 7 May 1830, p. 2)

Those colonists reading this editorial, anticipating the explicit naming of Mary McLauchlan's seducer, were unfortunately to be disappointed by the mealy mouthed editorial response: 'nor should we shrink even from doing this, had we not reason to believe that he is already sufficiently punished by the manner in which his society is universally evaded'. A young woman was dead, unjustly silenced on the colonial gallows, while Charles Nairne, her master and her 'seducer' (or perhaps rapist) is deemed to have suffered enough because society in the penal colony spurned him. Melville's editorial, his opinion statement, is representative of the patriarchal mindset that dominated the nineteenth-century press across the Western world. No matter how openly he discursively threw invective at Mary's seducer, so long as Nairne remained unnamed in public discourse, despite Melville's claims that he had been sufficiently punished by Hobart Town society, with justice not seen to be done, the anonymous male, representative of his sex, escaped unqualified censure.

But it does appear that life for Charles Nairne was never quite the same after Mary McLauchlan's execution and his position as an elite member of Hobart Town society was over. His marriage never recovered from the scandal and by the end of the year Nairne had left Hobart Town, alone, to live in Victoria where he died 12 years later in 1842.

Sarah Masters – Infanticide at the Oatlands Jail

In the early autumn of 1835, five years after Mary McLauchlan was executed for infanticide in the penal colony, another infanticide created a sensation when it was reported in Henry Melville's *Colonial Times*. This extraordinary 7,991-word report was the most extensive infanticide report I have found published in the colonial press in Van Diemen's Land during the nineteenth century. The *Colonial Times* coverage extended to almost five full-page columns of the four-page newspaper on 12 May 1835, despite the case lacking high news-values – the defendant was a married woman who was acquitted of the crime. Nineteenth-century newspapers rarely reported infanticide within marriage at length – without an understandable motive the infanticidal woman was invariably declared insane and dealt with medically. Neither James Ross or Robert Lathrop Murray was interested in the trial – Ross ran a short two-paragraph routine report while Murray's *Tasmanian Austral Asiatic Review*, now part-owned by Melville, made no mention of the trial. James Ross's conservative pro-Arthurian *Hobart Town Courier* acknowledged that the court was occupied with the judicial proceedings for two days, but the prudish Ross censored the evidence. In his report the jury's verdict to acquit was followed by a final sentence, 'the evidence was not of a nature to lay before our readers; though it excited intense interest among the numerous auditory' ('Supreme Court', *HTC* 15 May 1835, p. 3).

Henry Melville's Report

Sarah Masters was a free woman therefore her pregnancy and infanticide were not dealt with by the convict bureaucracy, and there was no imperative to report her case extensively through the court columns as an example to the convict population or as a warning to the free settlers of the licentious and criminal behaviour of convict women. So why did Sarah Masters's infanticide trial receive such extensive publicity in Henry Melville's press? An analysis of Melville's news report of Sarah Masters's trial exposes an uncommon infanticide narrative where infidelity and race factored in a free woman's infanticidal actions. Sarah's husband, Joseph, was a government bureaucrat, the jailer at Oatlands, an important satellite penal settlement that housed the chain gangs that were building the Hobart to Launceston road. Melville had a fundamental dislike of Arthur's regime and had been running a press campaign against what he saw as the corrupt and despotic government of Governor George Arthur for some time and on a weekly basis his newspaper ran stories about rorting or corruption amongst petty bureaucrats. Perhaps Melville saw Sarah Masters's trial, with its disclosures of infidelity, as another example of a bad regime.

The fact that Sarah Masters's case even reached the courts is unusual as at this time in England and the other Australian colonies married women were usually declared unfit to stand trial and secreted away to an asylum. It is also unusual that the case went to trial from the fact that there was no definitive medical evidence. At the coronial inquiry (not reported by the press) the medical evidence was unclear as to whether the child had been born alive or dead, or whether it had died from smothering or from loss of blood soon after birth because the umbilical cord was not tied. Nevertheless Sarah Masters was put on trial for the capital crime of murdering her infant son. She endured a lengthy two-day trial which was prosecuted by the Attorney General, Joseph Tice Gellibrand. A retinue of witnesses from the Oatlands settlement provided salacious evidence and there was also extensive evidence from three medical expert witnesses including the Surgeon General, Dr James Scott. The Attorney General in prosecuting the case said 'the mother being a married woman, would perhaps, repudiate the idea of becoming the murderer of her own child, but this he thought, would act against her' ('LAW INTELLIGENCE – Supreme Court – Criminal Side; Friday 8 May', *CT* 12 May 1835, pp. 150–51).

Henry Melville had no qualms about the nature of the evidence and either Melville or Henry Savery,[5] a colonial novelist who often wrote court reports for Melville, proceeded to merge constructed dialogue, editorial commentary and legal discourse in a comprehensive report that lay out the salacious evidence in the 7,991-word report (ibid.). Melville's newspaper report is the only historical evidence of Sarah Masters's infanticide trial, reinforcing the power of news texts to be read and accepted as 'true stories of everyday history' (Foucault 2008b, p. 90). Without other reports or court documents Melville's version offers the only information on Sarah Masters's infanticide and trial.

---

[5] Melville had published Savery's novel, *Quintus Servinton*, the first Australian novel published in Australia, two years previously, and since that time Savery had written at times for Melville's newspaper and had reported on criminal trials.

The report begins with no indication of the length or importance of the account to follow, and is embedded within the weekly 'LAW INTELLIGENCE – Supreme Court – Criminal Side' report, placed half way down the page, under the nondescript sub-heading 'May 8'. The narrative begins in legal language, laying out the charges:

> Sarah Masters pleaded not guilty to an indictment, which contained three counts: the first charged her with, on the 10th of March, bringing forth a male child alive, and afterwards making an assault upon the body of the said child, by smothering it in a blanket, by which act of the mother, the child instantly died; and 'charging her with procuring the death of the child by pressing or squeezing with both her hands, and thereby suffocating or strangling the said child. ('LAW INTELLIGENCE – Supreme Court – Criminal Side; Friday 8 May', *Colonial Times* 12 May 1835, pp. 150–51)

The constructed dialogue then places the prosecuting counsel, the Attorney General, Joseph Tice Gellibrand, as the narrator of the court discourse. In addressing the jury 'in a most feeling and pathetic manner' Gellibrand frames this case as one in which medical evidence and legal argument are crucial to a conviction or acquittal and refers the military jury to several sections of the pertinent acts including 'Lord Lansdowne's Act. The section in question provides, that if the mother, by *secret burying*, or other *disposition of the dead body, endeavoured to conceal the birth*, the Jury may specially find such facts upon indictment for *murder*, such concealment being punishable in itself as a substantial misdemeanour'. The inference here is that the jury could still find against Sarah Masters, but on the lesser charge of concealment. However, in the report of the judge's lengthy summation his instruction to the jury provides a different opinion: 'The Judge decided, firstly that the "burying or disposition must be the act of the *mother herself*, and consequently, that in this present case the disposition of the dead body in the lagoon being the act of either an accomplice, or an innocent agent, it was not within the statute".' The report informs readers that on a second point the depositing by the mother of the body in 'the *box*' was also not within the statute; and thirdly 'the endeavour to conceal, intended by the statute, is a concealment from all the world, and that, consequently her confession to the witness Catherine Fenwick, was the actual agent in the disposition of the body, prevented the statute from operating'.

Catherine Fenwick's evidence

Catherine Fenwick's evidence, crucial to the case, spans two and a half columns and through constructed dialogue allows the voice of a convict woman to be privileged in this judicial discourse. Catherine Fenwick is represented as a feisty 25-year-old Irish woman from County Cork who had been at the Oatlands jail 'in solitary confinement four days, for punishment'. She was there under sentence for drunkenness and was called upon to assist fellow convict Mary Mullins, who 'was about a fortnight in labour'. In the birthing room Catherine frequently saw

Sarah Masters who 'appeared very large in the family way'. The précis narrative style stops abruptly with the reporter overtly entering the discourse to establish the witnesses' credentials as an 'expert' witness in a maternal discourse: 'witness was married at home; has herself had one child'. Her testimony continues, mediated by the court reporter, to relate an intimate and detailed account of the dramatic domestic scene. After attending to Mary Mullins and her stillborn child with the surgeon Mr Park, 'the witness' went to sleep for about two hours then 'Mrs Masters came in and said she was very bad; said she had the cold shivers. Witness then accompanied her to the kitchen fire; she gave her some warm gruel'.

The voice of Sarah Masters, the 'prisoner', enters the narrative through transformed indirect quotations and the constructed dialogue of Catherine Fenwick:

> Prisoner said there was no need of any assistance; she knelt down by the fire as if in pain; witness again asked if she would have any assistance; she said no. She sat on a chair a short time, as if recovered, only she still had the cold shivers. She then told her (witness) to go to rest, and she (prisoner) would go to her own bed. (LAW INTELLIGENCE – Supreme Court – Criminal Side; Friday 8 May', *Colonial Times* 12 May 1835, pp. 150–51)

The hearsay evidence of Catherine Fenwick continues to bring the voice of Sarah Masters, the defendant sitting mute in the dock, and her actions, into the courtroom and into newspaper discourse, presenting a damning picture of Sarah Masters who had steadfastly maintained that she 'was not ill' as she laboured throughout the day. The picture of a pregnant woman hiding the fact from her husband that she was in the last stages of labour astounded nineteenth-century readers (and still astounds readers today), and speaks to Sarah Masters's desperation and determination to protect her marriage and her family life. According to Catherine's evidence, mediated through the news report, some hours past when Catherine did not see her mistress. When she did see Sarah again Catherine Fenwick asked her how she was: 'she said she was much better, and had had a good sleep, and should like to have some gruel'. Near teatime Catherine 'went into her again; prisoner said she was better' and ordered 'half a pint of brandy'. Henry Soby, the cook at the Oatlands jail, was sent to fetch brandy from the local inn and when it arrived Catherine returned to the bedroom where Sarah gave her some brandy before telling her 'she had something particular to tell her, if she might trust her'. Catherine said she might. Sarah, her voice overtly mediated in the press discourse then confesses to Catherine that she had been delivered of 'a still-born child' creating the astounding imagery of Sarah Masters lying in the marital bed beside her husband secretly enduring the final stages of labour in agonized silence. She told Catherine: 'if Mr Masters had remained in the room five minutes longer last time, he must have known the secret'. According to the *Colonial Times* Catherine next asked Sarah where the infant was and Sarah pulled a box out from under the bed.

Catherine's mediated voice, under cross-examination from the Attorney General, Joseph Tice Gellibrand, now retraces the evidence she has already given. The Attorney General , challenges her on her evidence regarding the baby. The reporter, précising Catherine Fenwick's testimony, informs readers that she said that she did not look 'too closely' at the body of the baby lying in the box. Her frustration at the Attorney General's questioning comes through the press report with her exasperated response: 'considered it still-born because Mrs Masters told her so'. Catherine Fenwick's sensational testimony continues, through the reporter's clumsy prose, to bring Sarah Masters's voice into the discourse. The reporter, while reconstructing the dialogue, has kept the intonation and colloquial language of the speakers, allowing readers to form impressions of the 'characters' in this judicial drama as distinct individuals. Catherine relates how, sitting by the bedside, Sarah Masters made a confession:

> She laughed and said, she (witness) was a poor creature, and not fit for trouble; and told her (witness) it was not Mr Master's child, that she had it when he had been absent from her six months, by a man she had been acquainted with before; witness asked her if he was on the settlement (Oatlands.) She said no – she said he had cost her many a pound; she said, if her husband knew she went her full time, it would be the cause of their parting, and she loved her husband and two children, as she loved her life; it was the first time she had been guilty of such a crime since her marriage; she did not wish her husband to know it was any thing more than a miscarriage; she then sent for more brandy, to have it in the house for the night. (LAW INTELLIGENCE – Supreme Court – Criminal Side; Friday 8 May', *Colonial Times* 12 May 1835, pp. 150–51)

This sensational, intimate, confessional discourse, published in the colonial press, brought the most intimate details of an infanticidal woman's experience into the public domain and provides us today with an insight into the complex lives of individual nineteenth-century infanticidal women.

Catherine Fenwick's testimony continues for another half a column and includes details of a bizarre conversation she had with Sarah and Joseph Masters as they lay in their marital bed:

> Mr Masters asked why I did not tell him Mrs Masters was over her trouble. I told him, it was a miscarriage; Mr and Mrs Masters were in bed. Mr Masters wished to know, particularly, as he had been away some time; his wife then accused him of jealousy; he said he was not; and if it was a miscarriage, he was satisfied. (LAW INTELLIGENCE – Supreme Court – Criminal Side; Friday 8 May', *Colonial Times* 12 May 1835, pp. 150–51)

Catherine Fenwick's testimony completed, Henry Soby, the cook at the Oatlands jail, takes the stand and through his statement the dead baby becomes the central focus of the discourse, its corporeal presence being modified from 'something in a bucket' which Soby was told was 'Mrs Master's miscarriage' and 'to throw it in the lagoon' to a 'fully grown child'. Through the crucial medical evidence of the surgeon who conducted the autopsy, Mr F. J. Park, the news report shifts to the medical gaze and the dead child is brought into full focus, transforming the news narrative:

> the child was perfect; should say the child was not entirely of European origin; has no doubt of it, from the general appearance of face, with width of nostrils, and the thickness of the nose and lips; the hair was jet black, and thick; much thicker than children's hair usually is; the face was very dark; there was a woolly appearance on both sides of the face; the colour of the body was not much darker than children generally are when born; he did not remark that the skin was unusually dark; knows Mr Masters – he is not a black. (LAW INTELLIGENCE – Supreme Court – Criminal Side; Friday 8 May', *Colonial Times* 12 May 1835, pp. 150–51)

'Not Entirely European' – Dr Park's evidence
This colonial trope with its coded meanings, to the residents of an island where the 'Black War' had so recently been fought to dislocate the indigenous population, ensured that anyone in the colony reading this court news discourse would have understood the implications of Sarah Masters's transgression. Through news discourse the colonial gaze reinforced the rules of British society. The explicit framing of the physical characteristics of the child as 'not entirely of European origin', and the forensic measuring and recording of the child's 'not entirely European' physical characteristics reinforced the dominant cultural specifications of a British citizen. Foucault's 'society of blood' takes on a racial perspective in this infanticide discourse and Sarah Masters, as a British subject, as well as a married woman, is represented not only as having broken the marriage laws and as having committed the capital crime of infanticide, but she is also represented as a woman whose overriding transgression is to have broken the racial laws of the Empire. Having a sexual relationship with a man who was not European, in a penal colony where the 'hostile' indigenous population was at the time being suppressed, placed her deviancy in another realm. Sarah Masters's sexual connection with a 'man of colour' was a taboo in a 'society of blood' where blood 'purity' was regarded as crucial to the maintaining of British dominance. (It is quite possible that Sarah Masters's lover was an African American sailor rather than a Tasmanian aborigine, as records show that African American sailors did visit the colony and some stayed for extended periods of time.)

Dr Park's important medical forensic evidence, second only in length to Catherine Fenwick's testimony in the newspaper report, extends for a full column and concludes with the doctor partly imputing 'the death of this child to the naval string not having been tied, and partly from respiration having been checked'. The husband and wife are then brought into his scientific discourse to answer to questions about their sex life, but the Attorney General interjects to tell the court (and the reporter sitting on the press bench): 'it was not necessary to publish this part of the evidence. This witness [Dr Park] was examined and cross-examined at considerable length, the nature of the evidence will not allow of its publication'. Censorship, whether imposed by the journalist or editor, or explicitly by the court, manipulated the public discourse to ensure that the details about the sexual life of a husband and his wife remained out of the public domain, and as discussed in Part One, was a political device used to control knowledge, and to suppress and exclude women from particular discourses.

According to the report on the second day of the trial Dr Park was re-examined in the witness box. Under cross-examination from the Attorney General he continued his sanguinary account of the autopsy, the focus of the questioning was on whether the child had breathed. A second medical doctor, Dr Edward Bedford (the son of Reverend William Bedford), enters the discourse to provide an alternative perspective on the scientific evidence: 'Has known cases where respiration has commenced before the birth of a child – fainting is a possible effect on a woman after being delivered without assistance in a bed, and the life of the child may thereby be endangered.' Finally a third medical doctor brought in by the prosecution, Colonial Surgeon, Dr James Scott, admitted he could not, from the evidence, form an opinion as to the remote cause of the child's death. He explained at length the multiple probable causes of the infant's death, concluding that the probable cause of death was strangulation. Then Sarah Masters momentarily becomes the focus of the *Colonial Times* judicial discourse: 'Sarah Masters, when called upon for her defence, said she was innocent of it'. And finally, after almost 8,000 words the abrupt ending: 'His Honor summed up, and the Jury returned a verdict of Not Guilty'.

By the time Melville's newspaper report of Sarah Masters's trial was being read by the settlers of Hobart Town Sarah Masters was back at her Oatlands home with Joseph and her children and, despite Sarah's fears that her husband would reject her, they remained together and in the years to come Sarah was occasionally mentioned in government reports. It seems Sarah took a liking to drink and was on occasion accused of being 'too lax with the female convicts in allowing them to bring drink into her house' (Colonial Secretary's Office, CSO1, TAHO). Rather than fading into anonymity after the humiliation of the very public exposure of his marriage and his wife's disgrace, Joseph felt no enmity towards the *Colonial Times* or Henry Melville and in fact he took up the pen as a journalist of sorts writing as the 'Oatlands Correspondent' for the *Colonial Times*, reporting on corruption and rorting between stock inspectors, the Chief District Constable of Oatlands, Mr Whiteford, and other settlers in the district. When Joseph Masters's report turned to moral censure, his journalism is laced with unintended irony: 'I will give you a word or two in my next, about the convict constables, and tell you of the shameful way they are living in open adultery – but this is enough for the present' ('Domestic Intelligence', *Colonial Times* 20 December 1835, p. 434).

Ten years later Sarah was dead and Joseph left the colony with his children to live in New Zealand where he married another Sarah and became a respected pioneer and community leader. The township of Masterton was named after him.

Conclusion

Through the analysis of the press reporting of the infanticide trials of two women in colonial Australia, Mary McLauchlan and Sarah Masters, in this chapter I have examined the ways in which infanticidal women's actions were exposed and politicized through press discourse in the nascent penal colony of Van Diemen's Land. The young convict mother, Mary McLauchlan, was executed as a direct result of a corrupt colonial society. But one of the colonial elite, a representative of the patriarchal press, Robert Lathrop Murray, gave Mary McLauchlan a (mediated) voice in death through the columns of his newspaper, naming the man who was the 'author' of Mary's destruction. Sarah Masters was found not guilty of infanticide by the judicial system, but was shamed in the most comprehensive way through Henry Melville's extensive report of her infanticide trial in the *Colonial Times*. His report which transformed a domestic tragedy into a potent scandal with racial overtones. In the 1830s in the most patriarchal environment in the British Empire, a penal colony where men outnumbered women four to one, two women through their infanticidal actions placed the maternal figure at the centre of public discourse. Mary McLauchlan and Sarah Masters became public figures in the penal colony through press reporting that captured the imagination of the citizens. In neither of these cases was madness used explicitly to either explain or to mitigate the actions of the infanticidal mothers. In the next chapter we will see how madness became the way of understanding infanticide.

Chapter 5
'Bush Madness' in the *Mercury*

From the first years of colonization women who settled in the remote bush of Australia were represented in newspapers and literature as the personification of self-sacrifice and endurance. The Australian press played a significant role in the creation of the 'Madonna of the bush' mythology through a grand national narrative of bush heroism and endurance, epitomized in countless news stories of heroic survival from natural disasters. The Australian bush was mythologized in discourse as a place where 'failure kills, or success is writ large; where weak women are made strong and courage finds birth in a single day of struggle' (Ackermann 1913, pp. 60–61). In 1902 a journalist from the Melbourne *Argus* created a rare example of public praise for the bush woman in a eulogy that framed the bush housemother who:

> began work before the sun rose. She milked, fed calves, pigs, fowls, got breakfast ... washed up, sent children to school, carried water in kerosene tins from the dam for the day's use, set the house in order, made bread, scrubbed or washed, for washing-day must be frequent when the supply of clothes is small. The washing, too, must be done outside in the broiling sun, the clothes boiling in ever-useful kerosene tins. Dinner must be prepared – mutton, potatoes, or with finding the pigs that have escaped into the scrub. Then milking time, then tea time – cold beef, merely bread, dripping, and tea. After tea, clothes to make, or maize to shell, or potatoes to cut for the morrow's planting ... Is it any wonder they grow lean and bronzed and hard, prematurely old, and sad? Where there is little or no capital to begin with, the struggle to make both ends meet continues throughout their lives. They cannot afford to pay labour. If they cannot manage all their domestic duties, and assist their husbands as well, their farms must fall. ('Women Who Work: Hard Lot of Farmer's Wives – Lino', *Argus* 13 January 1902, pp. 5–6)

Such eulogizing rhetoric, however, came from outsiders, the city journalists and overseas visitors who from a distance could acknowledge the work of bush women, because, as Jessie Ackermann, a peripatetic American journalist who toured outback Australia from 1900 to 1912 wrote, the names of these pioneering bush women should be 'written large in the history of their country', but 'they never will be. *It is not the custom*' (Ackermann 1913, pp. 60–61). The exaggerated patriarchy of the Australian bush ordained that women should triumph and suffer in silence. Bush women were, as the *Argus* journalist asserts, central to the success or failure of a selection, but their contribution was rarely acknowledged, and, as Ackermann's eulogizing rhetoric told readers, 'Women have burnt, beaten and hammered their imprint upon this country in a manner that only Eternity will reveal. While men cleared the bush, women wrought to the extreme of their strength' (Ackermann 1913, pp. 60–61).

Women in Australia, as in England and elsewhere, were socialized from a young age into being docile female bodies who knew well how to 'suffer and be still' (Vicinus 1973). The power of discourse to create and to reinforce Australian society's patriarchal ideological perspective was forever present in Australian press discourse throughout the nineteenth and twentieth centuries when journalism was preoccupied with contributing to, reinforcing and even creating (as in the national magazine *The Bulletin*) a grand masculine national narrative. This master narrative ordained that Australian women were hardworking but silent and submissive to their fathers, husbands and sons who were credited with creating a nation built on 'mateship'. Failure, by both bush women and bush men, was shameful and rarely entered the national discourse unless the failure was spectacular. This ingrained reluctance to acknowledge personal hardship and failure had very real consequences for women and men who lived in remote districts, as will become evident in this chapter in the analysis of the cases of Lilian Wakefield and Harriet Lovell. When an Australian woman living in the bush no longer lived up to the ideal, when 'Hope' died and a woman lost the spirit to chase 'the shadows of Despair that lower and settle upon the heavy grind of daily toil' (Ackermann 1913, p. 59) her 'failure' was rarely recorded, except when she transgressed in such a significant manner that her story became the focus of news discourse.

It is from the perspective of heroic bush narratives that in this chapter I analyse two disparate bush infanticide discourses from the same newspaper, the Hobart *Mercury*, in 1912. The infanticides of Harriet Lovell and Lilian Wakefield were reported within two months of each other and occurred in the same remote district in southern Tasmania. In the first case 32-year-old Harriet Lovell premeditatedly killed her young daughter, Dorothy, after years of abuse and was also suspected of killing her four infant children in similar circumstances over the previous decade. In the second case 22-year-old Lilian Wakefield (allegedly) killed her three children and then herself in one brief frenzied moment. The press made sense of the actions of both women through the explanatory framework of 'bush madness'. 'Psychiatric discourse,' as Foucault tells us (2002a, p. 46), 'finds a way of limiting its domain, of defining what it is talking about, of giving it the status of an object – and therefore of making it manifest, nameable, and describable' (Foucault 2002a, p. 46). 'Bush madness' provided an understandable rationale for the murderous actions of these two mothers and removed the imperative for the community or the state to examine the living conditions that limited and oppressed women living in remote bush settlements.

The *Mercury* is a conservative newspaper established in 1854 by ex-convict John Davies when Hobart had a vibrant and competitive newspaper industry. Over the next half century the Davies family bought up all the competition, including the *Colonial Times* and the *Hobart Town Courier*, until by 1912 it was Hobart's only daily newspaper. The newspaper had correspondents around the island sending in reports including a correspondent in the Huon district on the southwest side of the towering Mount Wellington that overshadows the capital city of Hobart and separates the Huon from the metropolis. In 1912 the close-knit Huon community lived off the land, mainly fruit orchards – Tasmania was known as the 'Apple Isle' predominantly through the extensive apple orchards in the Huon district. Settlers also established small berry farms and raised dairy cattle in the district. The poorest of the settlers worked under contract felling the timber in the towering impenetrable forests of the South West. Both Harriet Lovell and Lilian Wakefield lived in remote, roughly hewn timber-getters' cottages.

The *Mercury* journalist – 'Our Huon Correspondent' – lived in the district and regularly telegraphed his prosaic copy, consisting of agricultural news, community, social and sporting events and obituaries on notable citizens, to the *Mercury* newspaper office in Hobart. But in the late autumn and winter of 1912 news that two local women living a few miles apart in remote bush cottages had murdered their children brought the tranquil rural district into the national spotlight. At a time when news from the island rarely made it into newspapers outside the state, newspapers across Australia, from remote Cairns in far north Queensland to the far west in Western Australia, published stories on these two sensational Tasmanian infanticide cases.

Harriet Lovell

In this case study infanticide is read through the news reports of the death of nine-year-old Dorothy Lovell and the inquest and the murder trial of the mother. Harriet Lovell was never charged with infanticide, however, embedded within this murder discourse is a wretched infanticide narrative with accusations that Harriet Lovell was responsible for the infanticidal deaths of her four other infant children over a period of some 10 years. Harriet Lovell was the 32-year-old wife of timber-getter and farm labourer, Benjamin Lovell, and the mother of 9-year-old Dorothy and 11–year-old adopted daughter Ida. She lived in a remote bush cottage at Mountain River in the foothills of the Mount Wellington ranges in southern Tasmania. The Lovell's cottage was in a densely forested bush setting where the tree canopy was so thick that even in summer the daylight only penetrated the forest briefly at midday when the sun was high in the sky, and in winter the diffused light rarely fell on the bush cottage. The nearest neighbour, Harriet's cousin, Rosina Banks, was a mile away through a narrow bush track.

Harriet Lovell first became the focus of press attention on 10 May 1912 when the Huon correspondent of the Hobart *Mercury* filed a brief report on the tragic death of nine-year-old Dorothy Mary Catherine Lovell under the headline: 'SHOCKING ACCIDENT: Child Burnt to Death at Longley' (*Mercury* 10 May 1912, p. 5). This brief account begins in a speculative tone:

> It appears that there was a bonfire in the yard adjoining Mr Lovell's house and the
> unfortunate child was playing near it when, by some means, her clothing caught

alight, and immediately she was enveloped in flames. The mother, who was close by, rushed to her child's assistance, and bravely endeavoured to extinguish the flames, but failed to do so before the child had received shocking injuries. ('SHOCKING ACCIDENT: Child Burnt to Death at Longley', *Mercury* 10 May 1912, p. 5)

Note the patriarchal framing of the bush home. Here we have the schema of Jessie Ackermann's heroine of the bush, with Harriet valiantly trying to extinguish the flames that engulfed her daughter. The tragic death of a child in such horrific circumstances would have struck a chord with *Mercury* readers all too aware of the dangers of open laundry fires. In the report's concluding sentence, however, doubt cuts across the discourse to reframe the entire narrative as something less clear-cut: 'A painful circumstance in connection with this fatality is the fact that the unfortunate little child was the last survivor of three [it was actually four] children belonging to the same family, who have all died violent deaths.' The collocation of the last two words transform this not unusual 'shocking accident' into a narrative of maternal deviancy so extreme that it was broadcast across the nation.

The Mercury's Report

A week later the *Mercury*'s correspondent created a surprisingly brief 140-word story from the day-long inquest at the Upper Mountain River community hall, which heard sensational evidence from Harriet and Benjamin Lovell, the local trooper, the doctor and neighbours. Why Tasmania's capital-city daily newspaper, the *Mercury*, the closest newspaper geographically to this highly newsworthy inquest, provided such an inadequate report of the inquest is unclear. Newspapers are competitive by nature, news is a saleable commodity and newspapers compete to be the first to bring the news to the public, so it is inexplicable as to why the *Mercury*, with its resident Huon correspondent, failed to grasp the newsworthiness of this inquest and to provide its readers with a full report of the proceedings, particularly as the story was acknowledged from the start as a story worthy of national press coverage. Such was the newsworthiness of the evidence heard at the inquest that newspapers across Australia carried detailed reports that were strikingly varied from the *Mercury*'s cursory account. The only clue comes in the absence of the Huon correspondent's by-line, which may speak to his physical absence from the coronial inquiry, although his comprehensive report of the inquest published a day later, on 17 May, points to this not being the case.

   The *Mercury*'s report of the inquest, headlined 'Child's Death by Burning' (*Mercury* 16 May 1912, p. 4), adopted the customary constructed dialogue format to focus on Dorothy Lovell, providing graphic imagery of the dead child who was 'burnt from head to foot'. The *Mercury*'s pithy report did, however, allow Dr Harold Cummings to cast doubt on the mother's version of events:

If the clothing of the deceased caught fire, and she immediately ran as far as she could through the open air, the direction of the flames would be behind her. The front of the child was as extensively burnt as the back part of the body. ('Child's Death by Burning', *Mercury* 16 May 1912, p. 4)

The lexical placement of the conjunction 'if' indicates the modification of the sentence sequence and even without a 'but' to introduce the opposing proposition the following sentence places Harriet directly into a frame of suspicion. Criminal action was introduced into the next sentence: 'Harriet Lovell, mother of the child, after being cautioned by the Coroner that she need not give evidence that might incriminate herself, stated that she was washing outside where there was a fire, and the child's clothes caught alight'. Harriett Lovell's voice, mediated through constructed dialogue and transformed indirect quotation in the evidence of 'Trooper Crosswell' explains her actions: 'she said the child ran away. She chased her with a bath of water, but, being unable to overtake her, put the bath down, and on catching the child rolled her over' ('Child's Death by Burning', *Mercury* 16 May 1912, p. 4). The final sentence in this 140-word report points to, but provides no details, of the 'evidence of several other witnesses' and simply informs readers of the jury's verdict that the child died from 'shock caused by extreme burns'. Importantly, in the *Mercury*'s report there is no mention of the jury's 'open verdict'. Why the state's only capital-city newspaper neglected most of the highly newsworthy details in their brief report is hard to know without fully understanding the production processes. Technical difficulties, illness – or a deliberate editorial decision, it is impossible to speculate in any meaningful way.

National Newspaper Coverage

As mentioned earlier, reports of Dorothy Lovell's death would appear in newspapers across the nation, as far away as Cairns in far north Queensland and also in West Australia, South Australia, New South Wales and Victoria. Each of the newspapers selected particular testimony from the coronial inquiry dictated by what they regarded as the news values of the case. The Adelaide *Advertiser* created a potent, but brief, 120-line report that focused on the 'open verdict', missed by the *Mercury*, and the allegations against the mother. Here Harriet Lovell is framed unambiguously as a deviant mother, with readers being told that not only was the father away at the time of the child's death, but that when he was informed, he remarked, 'The big murdering – ; she has succeeded at last' ('A Child's Death', *Advertiser* 16 May 1912, p. 10). This sensational dialogue is presented in direct quotes, adding agency to Benjamin Lovell's utterance. The constructed dialogue which follows further layers the blaming discourse of Benjamin Lovell: 'The father, in evidence, said his wife treated the deceased cruelly' … 'and at one time [she] tried to smother the little one with a pillowcase' (ibid.).

The northern Tasmanian newspaper, the Launceston *Examiner*, brought infanticide into the coronial discourse with a brief but startling story which revealed further details of the deaths of Dorothy's infant siblings: 'from other evidence it transpired that four other children of the same family had died violent deaths. Two passed away in convulsions, one was found drowned in a bath, and another was burned to death' ('Little Girl's Fate', *Examiner* 16 May 1912, p. 6). Such evidence, in any configuration of news values, is highly newsworthy, although speculative. Adopting the standard constructed dialogue format the northern newspaper provides further damning evidence against Harriet Lovell through the mediated voice of Benjamin Lovell: 'that on one occasion he took the child to a neighbour's because its mother had threatened to drown it'.

The Mercury Amends Earlier Report

As if to make amends for the neglect in their previous report, the following day the *Mercury* published an all-embracing report that took up 90 per cent of the editorial space in the broadsheet's page seven under a multi-layered headline:

HUON BURNING FATALITY.
YOUNG GIRL'S DREADFUL DEATH.
SOME EXTRAORDINARY EVIDENCE.
(From Our Huon reporter)
(*Mercury* 17 May 1912, p. 7)

In comparison to the previous truncated account this comprehensive 1,184-word coronial report on Dorothy Lovell's death now exposes the multiple damning discourses of the witnesses and their portrayal of Harriet Lovell as a cruel brutalizing mother. Multiple subheadings separate the evidence of each witness providing readers with the preferred reading of the text that follows:

THE MOTHER'S EVIDENCE
LITTLE GIRL'S STORY
EVIDENCE OF A NEIGHBOUR
THE FATHER'S PATHETIC STORY
FARMER'S SENSATIONAL STATEMENT
THE MEDICAL EVIDENCE
EVIDENCE OF THE LOCAL TROOPER

The headlines, telling a highly compressed version of the narrative, also establish the ideological criteria by which readers make sense of the text and influences the way readers interpret the discourse. The choice of nouns used in framing the testimony of each witness is of interest: the evidentiary discourses of the mother, neighbour Rosina Banks, and the local policeman are framed as 'evidence' with the discursive connotation of factuality; the farmer's evidentiary discourse is presented as a 'sensational statement' connoting astounding facts; the doctor's evidence is framed as 'medical evidence' reminding readers that the doctor speaks on behalf of medicine and therefore his evidence is scientific and 'factual'; while the evidentiary discourse of Harriet's adopted daughter, Ida, and that of her husband, Joseph, are presented as 'stories' with the dual connotation of fact and fiction, connoting an emotionality not evident in the other witnesses' 'evidence'. The strength of their testimony is further softened by the use of the collocation adjectives: 'little girl' and 'pathetic story'.

The report begins with the newspaper unintentionally acknowledging its own untimely news practice:

> An inquest was held on Wednesday at Upper Mountain River on the body of the unfortunate little girl, Dorothy Mabel Catherine Lovell, who was burned to death on Thursday last, under circumstances already reported in 'The Mercury'. ('HUON BURNING FATALITY', *Mercury* 17 May 1912, p. 7)

From here on in the report, framed in a formal legal lexical structure, is littered with pejorative language embedded within the constructed dialogue format. For the first time *Mercury* readers are made aware that Dorothy Lovell was the 'last of a family of five, who have all come to an untimely end, and the death of three of them has been due to other than natural causes'.

Deviant mother frame

This report, with its comprehensive evidentiary discourse of neighbours and expert witnesses, frames Harriet Lovell as a violent, abusive mother and wife, but it is Harriet Lovell herself who presents the damning details of the deaths of her other children and puts herself in the frame as an infanticidal woman by providing a disturbing litany of death:

> Deceased was the eldest of them. The first, Joseph, died in convulsions at one month old; the second, Benjamin, died at three years and three months old, being drowned in a bath of water; the third, Mary, died in convulsions at four months and three weeks old; while the fourth, William, met his death at three years of age by burning, his clothes catching fire. Witness had also been burnt out once and a couple of times her clothes had been on fire. She was also in hospital for a fortnight after Willie met his death by burning. Deceased, added witness was a real good little girl, but witness smacked her on the hand the night before, and the child cried a little. ('HUON BURNING FATALITY', *Mercury* 17 May 1912, p. 7)

Next the shocking and compelling narrative of maternal deviance and the terrible death of Dorothy is reconstructed and placed before the readers of the *Mercury*. Readers learn that Harriet Lovell was alone with Dorothy on the day of the child's death, having sent her 11-year-old adopted daughter Ida to Lower Longley for some meat. Harriet had been preparing a large laundry pot of water on an outdoor fire about 20 yards from the house when, according to her evidence, Dorothy asked her 'if she might go and put some boughs and bark upon the fire outside', with Harriet asserting that she replied: '"Yes, dear, you may; but mind your clothes don't catch on fire"'. According to Harriet's testimony about three minutes later the child shouted: '"Mummy I am on fire – put me out"' and then ran past her mother and down into the orchard. Harriet claimed she tried to catch the deceased child, but the latter was too quick for her, and she also failed in an attempt to throw water over the child. When she caught up with Dorothy she rolled her 'over and over on the ground to try to extinguish the flames, but did not succeed in doing so'. She 'then ripped the burning clothes off the child's body, and wrapped her own skirts round her' saying to the child, '"Oh. Dorothy – why did you run?"' discursively shifting the blame onto the child herself. And then the pathos is heightened by the introduction of religion into the discourse: 'When she put Dorothy on the bed she said to her, '"Oh, my God, my little daughter." When deceased said, "God is good mamma," and started to pray. She could not remember whether the deceased said anything further about the fire or not' (ibid.).

'Evidence of a neighbour'

The evidence of Harriet Lovell's cousin, Rosina Banks, framed under the sub-heading, 'Evidence of a Neighbour', provides a contradicting discourse. When she arrived at the house she told the inquest she heard Dorothy say to her mother: 'You are cruel,' or 'They are cruel.' Shortly after she heard Dorothy 'ask God to take her as she was suffering great pain. She also heard her calling for her daddy as well as she could' (ibid.).

Rosina Banks's poignant reconstituted evidence also provides readers with insight into the Lovell's family life. She told the inquiry that Harriet had admitted to her that the night before she had had a 'row' with her husband over Dorothy. When Benjamin Lovell arrived at the house she said she heard him say to Harriet, '"You murdering big –"' and Harriet had replied, '"Oh, dad, I never laid a finger on her"', adding, '"Dorothy was outside making a fire under the washpot, and caught fire"'. Rosina Banks further explained that this was 'the third time Dorothy has almost met her death, her life has been in danger ever since her little brother, Willie, was burned'. She also recalled further hearsay evidence that during the quarrel between Harriet and Benjamin Lovell he had reminded his wife of the time she was:

> walking up and down the passage at the time you were trying to smother Dorothy, looking to see if anyone was coming. The deceased child had told her about a year ago that Mrs Lovell had attempted to smother her with a pillow. She also heard Lovell say to his wife, 'You will be easy now you have got that little thing under.' ('HUON BURNING FATALITY', *Mercury* 17 May 1912, p. 7)

Rosina Banks's damning testimony was only the first of multiple testimonies that were at odds with Harriet Lovell's version of events.

The father's evidence

Benjamin Lovell's testimony, presented under the 'pathetic story' sub-heading, shows the husband to be the antithesis of the Australian bushman. He is portrayed as a man who failed to control his wife, to manage his home, and to protect his children. In the judicial forum his weakness is amplified when he is discursively framed as the loyal 'pathetic' husband of a monstrous wife, the 'pathetic' husband of a woman who denied him of his progeny, who humiliated him, who beat and bloodied him, and of whom he was afraid. Bush patriarchy required Benjamin Lovell, up until this moment, to maintain at least the appearance of a man in control of his affairs, but now, in the judicial process, that same patriarchy expected him to disclose what he had tried to keep out of sight for more than a decade. Benjamin Lovell's voice, mediated through the reporter has been distanced from the events of that May day when he arrived home to find 'his child' 'burnt up' and asked his wife what had happened. Occasionally through a vernacular word or phrase his voice surfaces: 'He said he was fond of his children' and that 'this was a great shock to him. He had had a nasty feeling hanging over him all that day, and when he got the news he thought that that was what had caused the feeling'. He was, however, reluctant to place blame upon his wife, telling the inquiry that he could not recall saying to anyone, 'I thought so when I left home this morning.' But he did remember that the night previous to Dorothy's death when he came home from work she seemed 'a little fretful' and now the dead child's voice enters the discourse:

> He said, 'What is the matter, dear?' She replied, 'Nothing, daddy.' And he said, 'Come here, my dears,' and she got on to his lap. She started on her last night, and gave her a beating, and the child was sobbing on the sofa when I went in. ('HUON BURNING FATALITY', *Mercury* 17 May 1912, p. 7).

Through Benjamin Lovell's mediated testimony he shifts from being the loyal husband refusing to incriminate his wife in the death of his daughter, to representing her as a violent mother through such chilling phrases as: 'She started on her last night.' He explained his 'anger with his wife' because 'there had been so many accidents in the family that she could not be too careful, but he could not remember what he called her. This was the fifth child he had lost through them meeting with violent deaths'. Through his own words Benjamin Lovell is portrayed as a weak, cowardly man unwilling to stand up to his violent wife and to protect his children. In a deeply patriarchal society the parental roles of men and women were strictly defined and Benjamin Lovell was expected to leave the family home for long days in the bush felling trees to support his family, and to labour on neighbouring farms. However, it does appear that he did make some futile attempts to protect his daughter. He told the inquiry he had been 'anxious about the child before and had taken her away from her home twice' because 'she used to get into trouble with her mother'. But as the loyal husband, he also told the inquiry he 'could not recall accusing his wife of having ever harmed his daughter'. His evidence, diluted and mediated through constructed dialogue, exposes his failure as the patriarch of his family and his inability to protect his children.

'Farmer's Sensational Statement'

Neighbouring farmer George Manning's reconstructed evidence, given legitimacy through the sub-heading 'Farmer's Sensational Statement', creates a picture of Harriet Lovell as a violent woman who frequently attacked her children and her husband in fits of hysteria and fury. Benjamin Lovell's pathetic voice, mediated through his neighbour, presents a husband cowered and unable to cope with his domestic situation, but also a man compelled to disclose his dysfunctional life to a confidant, demonstrating that the lived experience of individuals is always more nuanced, less clear-cut and more complex than it may appear. According to George Manning's evidence, when Ida ran down the hill to tell Benjamin Lovell that Dorothy had been burned, he said:

> 'My God, I expected this this morning. The mother gave her a beating last night,
> and I found her on the sofa sobbing when I got home.' He also said, 'My God, I
> don't know what's to be done with the damned woman. She will be satisfied now
> they are all done.' And tapping himself on the chest, said, 'I shall be the next,
> if I don't look out.' He then left with the little girl, and went home. ('HUON
> BURNING FATALITY', *Mercury* 17 May 1912, p. 7)

This pathetic disclosure drains the stereotypical masculinity from the Australian bushman's persona, and his weakness is reinforced by further evidence from George Manning that some time in May of the previous year when Benjamin Lovell brought his daughter Dorothy to his house, 'he had blood on his face'. At that time Benjamin Lovell explained: 'his wife had struck him with a piece of wood because he wanted to take the child away, adding that he was afraid to leave her at home, as the mother was too cruel and severe upon her'. Manning told the inquest that on this occasion Lovell wanted to leave Dorothy at his house, 'but afterwards he came back, and said that he was afraid to leave her there as the mother might come and take her away in his absence'. The picture is created of a society where men and women are so deeply rooted in a patriarchy that dictates family problems are dealt with inside the family home that they are unable to conceive of a viable way forward.

Maurice Fleming's evidence

Another neighbouring farmer, Maurice Fleming, also deposed that he remembered 'Lovell and his deceased daughter, Dorothy, coming to his home about the end of April 1911, the former telling him that he had brought the child for protection', and that Harriet Lovell 'had threatened to drown her'. Fleming said Lovell's face was:

> covered with blood at the time, and when witness asked him how he came to be
> in that state he replied that he did not like to say. Witness then said, 'It is no use,

Ben, in hiding it. How did it happen?' Lovell then replied that his wife had struck him with a stick for taking the part of the child and removing it by force from her neighbourhood because of her threat to drown it. Witness offered to take the child, but the latter did not wish to leave her father, and Lovell then said that he would take her to his mother's which he did. ('HUON BURNING FATALITY', *Mercury* 17 May 1912, p. 7)

Despite Benjamin Lovell voicing his fears and disclosing his wife's violent and dysfunctional behaviour, no one felt able to act. The Lovells were part of a rural society where child-beating was still a common form of punishment and despite the suspicions and rumours that Harriet Lovell's dead children spoke of something more sinister than harsh physical discipline, the Huon district was a closed society, far away from the bureaucracy of the Hobart Bureau of Child Welfare. It was a society where Harriet Lovell's behaviour was an open secret. The neighbours and family knew her only living birth child was vulnerable, and yet people were unwilling or felt powerless to interfere in the Lovell's domestic affairs. Even Trooper Crosswell was aware of Harriet's propensity to violence – in the news discourse he is reported as having asked Benjamin Lovell when he arrived at the scene of Dorothy's death, if he was 'having more trouble?' to which Lovell had replied 'Yes'. It was the Launceston *Examiner* alone that brought bureaucratic welfare into the discourse on 28 May with a report that the 'child Ida Helmer, who had been adopted by Joseph Lovell and his wife ... had been committed to the care of the Neglected Children's Department at Huonville Court' ('Care of A Child', *Examiner* 28 May 1912, p. 6). The closed rural community may never have considered that the solution to the Lovell's domestic turmoil may have been with the authorities. And the notion of madness was so revolting to the Tasmanian community in which the very name the 'New Norfolk asylum' connoted terror and opprobrium that no one wanted to brand Harriet Lovell as 'mad'. But where was the local doctor? Archive death records show that Dr Harold L. Cummings had carried out the autopsies on at least three of the other Lovell children, and he had treated Harriet for what he called 'epilepsy', but there is no evidence that he had ever treated Dorothy, or that he suspected she was in mortal danger.

Expert medical evidence
The focus of Dr Harold L. Cummings's expert testimony at the inquest, as reported in the *Mercury*, was not speculation that Harriet Lovell had murdered her other children, but on his findings on the death of Dorothy Lovell. He told the inquiry: 'The body was burned from head to foot, hardly any portion having escaped though the head and upper portion were more severely burned than the lower extremities.' His evidence, provided in the *Mercury*'s brief report two days earlier, had rejected Harriet Lovell's testimony that Dorothy had run towards her mother and now readers were reappraised of this evidence and also made aware that Dr Cummings had provided further evidence conflicting with what Harriet Lovell said regarding the child's boots. The mother maintained that Dorothy was wearing

boots at the time of her death. but as Dr Cummings found burn marks on the child's feet, and that the child's boots were not burnt, he concluded that the child had not been wearing foot wear. Much press space was taken up with this evidence while the coroner's summation was not reported, and the report ends with the jury returning an 'open verdict' that left the way open for further police inquiries and community speculation.

'Only a Woman'
The people of the Huon, now aware of the full coronial evidence through the *Mercury*'s press discourse, were outraged at what appeared to them to be a lack of action on behalf of the authorities. One Longley woman's rancorous letter to the *Mercury* was published the following day (18 May). She claimed the newspaper's report of the inquest had: 'caused a thrill of horror to go through the whole community. The evidence was simply shocking, and the public mind is so agitated that surely some further inquiry should be held. Jurymen and police were both there, and yet no questions asked' ('Only a Woman', Letter *Mercury* 18 May 1912, p. 10). This forensic rhetoric speaks of the community's concerns that Harriet Lovell would escape justice with a highly charged appeal: 'Surely someone will take this matter up and go carefully into the case, and have it sifted to the utmost, if only for the sake of humanity and little innocent lives, who, like Dorothy, may be exposed to brutality and danger – yours, etc (ibid.). The community pressure, along with the open verdict and an ongoing police inquiry kept the 'story' alive and on Monday 20 May the Huon correspondent filed a brief but compelling two-sentence report:

> On Sunday the body of the poor little girl, Dorothy Lovell, was exhumed for further examination. It is understood that further action in the matter is contemplated. Harriet Lovell, mother of the deceased child, is at present in the general hospital, Hobart, receiving medical treatment. ('Huon Burning Fatality', *Mercury* 22 May 1912, p. 4)

Maternal madness
Madness for the first time now entered into the news discourse as the logical explanation for Harriet Lovell's murderous actions. With Harriet Lovell's arrest for the murder of her daughter the *Mercury* ('MOUNTAIN RIVER TRAGEDY', *Mercury* 24 July 1912, p. 2) meticulously reports details of the mother's arrest before going on to repeat material previously reported on 17 May creating a morbid but compelling modern 'Medea' narrative. Readers are told that 'the mother of the victim was brought to Hobart during the week and placed in the General Hospital', from where she was arrested while 'undergoing medical observation' and taken to the Hobart Gaol, the inference being that Harriet Lovell was mentally ill. When her trial began on 22 July 1912 the 'story' about a mother allegedly brutally burning her child to death, and allegedly murdering four of her other infant children, placed this news firmly on the national news agenda and it was reported in newspapers in

every state of Australia, including the *Argus* (Melbourne) the *Adelaide Advertiser*, the *Courier Mail* (Brisbane) the *Sydney Morning Herald* and the *West Australian* (Perth), as well as in many regional newspapers throughout the country.

Harriet Lovell pleaded 'not guilty' and strenuously denied having played any part in the death of Dorothy, or of ever harming her other children. The brief 65-word *Mercury* trial report précised the evidence already heard at the inquest before Dr Harold Cummings provided the expert medical evidence that determined the trial outcome. Cummings told the jury that he had treated Harriet Lovell for 'epilepsy' and that she was not of a sound mind at the time of Dorothy's death. With this medical evidence the judge brought a swift end to the proceedings instructing the jury to return a verdict of 'not guilty by reason of insanity'. Harriet Lovell was taken down and placed in the New Norfolk Asylum.

The *Mercury* headlines of the next day (24 July 1912, p. 2) encapsulated the trial in its bold and capitalized descending headlines:

MOUNTAIN RIVER TRAGEDY.
Mrs Lovell Charged with Murder.
Question of Insanity Raised.
Found Not Accountable for Her Actions.
(*Mercury* 24 July 1912, p. 2)

The headlines provided readers with 'the crime, its punishment and its memory' (Foucault 2008b, p. 90) in four lines, assuring readers that the judicial system and medicine had 'dealt' with the maternal aberration that was Harriet Lovell.

Dorothy Lovell's death should have come as no surprise to the family, friends and neighbours in the rural district of the Huon. The family history of child deaths was well known throughout the district; the local policeman, Trooper Crosswell, knew that Benjamin Lovell had had 'trouble'; Dr Harold L. Cummings conducted the autopsy on Dorothy and on at least three of the other Lovell children and had been treating Harriet for 'epilepsy'; Rosina Banks knew that Dorothy's life had been in danger since the death of her little brother Willie; neighbouring farmers Maurice Fleming and George Manning were both well aware that little Dorothy was regularly abused by her mother, and that on at least one occasion Benjamin Lovell had been battered by his wife. Yet no one intervened. A man's home was his castle, his private domain, what happened behind closed doors, particularly in rural districts, remained behind closed doors. In apportioning blame for the tragic and horrific death of a young girl, and the deaths of her four siblings, the police, medical, judicial and welfare systems, and the community, were able to look directly to the pathology of the individual mother whose madness removed any imperative to look further into why the community had failed to act. Madness made the headlines in newspapers across the country, epitomized in the *Sydney Morning Herald*'s headlines: 'Burned to Death. Mother Demented. Tragic Family Story' (24 July 1912, p. 17).

Lilian Wakefield

Two days before Harriet Lovell went on trial in the Hobart Supreme Court for the murder of her daughter, on a bleak winter Sunday, 21 July 1912, another mother, 22-year-old Lilian Wakefield, who lived less than two miles from Harriet Lovell, allegedly killed her three young children with a razor then killed herself. The victims were Eileen Mary, seven months, Olive Ernest Adolphus, two and a half years, and Violet Eliza May, four years. The *Mercury* ran a prominent story on this shocking alleged infanticide on the day of Harriet Lovell's trial ('Dreadful Tragedy at Crabtree', *Mercury* 23 July 1912, p. 5). However, the paper made no connections between the two disturbing cases which had occurred so close to each other in the same rural district. While Harriet Lovell was depicted as a 'bad' mother and ultimately as a mad mother whose abhorrent actions had led to the death of her daughter, Lilian Wakefield's death, and the deaths of her children, were framed in press discourse before the coronial inquiry had taken place, as murder/suicide, and as a tragic example of bush madness.

'Dreadful Tragedy at Crabtree'

Lilian Wakefield was a young mother of three who resided in a remote and wretched bush cottage that could 'only be reached after descending the steep and muddy sides of a ravine, and crossing on slippery stepping stones a creek which lies at the bottom' ('Dreadful Tragedy at Crabtree', *Mercury* 23 July 1912, p. 5). Without the mother alive to answer to her (alleged) actions, the *Mercury*'s reporter took a very different approach in creating this news discourse. Without waiting for due process, for the coronial inquiry to determine the official cause of the deaths, he created a lengthy narrative using transformed indirect quotation from his observations at the scene of the crime and from interviews with the local trooper and other sources at the scene of the crime. Reported in the next day's press his subjective narrative provided the public with the explanation that this was a case of murder suicide brought on by 'madness from bush loneliness' ('Dreadful Tragedy at Crabtree', *Mercury* 23 July 1912, p. 5). There is none of the equanimity and detachment of the hard-news style he adopted in the reports of Dorothy Lovell's death by burning, in this report the journalist places himself immediately in the news discourse through the adoption of a literary approach which is strikingly different from the usual news discourses in the *Mercury* at the time.

The day after the bodies of Lilian Wakefield and her children were found, the *Mercury*'s report begins in the standard fashion of précised headlines which succinctly narrates the story that follows:

DREADFUL TRAGEDY AT
CRABTREE.
MOTHER MURDERS HER CHILDREN.
THEN COMMITS SUICIDE.
MADNESS FROM BUSH LONELINESS.
(From Our Huon Reporter)
(*Mercury* 23 July 1912, p. 5)

From here on in the discourse diverges from the standard hard-news format with
an eloquent opening paragraph:

> The little village of Crabtree, lying some eight miles distant from Huonville,
> was on Sunday the scene of a tragedy at once so shocking and so profound that
> it is no wonder that the little community among whom it happened stands at the
> moment appalled and stunned. It occurred upon a day as fair and peaceful as ever
> dawned, when all nature spoke of what was beautiful and good, and ugliness
> and crime seemed to have no place in the scheme of things. ('DREADFUL
> TRAGEDY AT CRABTREE', *Mercury* 22 July 1912, p. 5)

The writing reflects the descriptive prose style of Charles Dickens's journalism
or the New Journalism style introduced by William Stead into his reports in *Pall
Mall Gazette* in the 1880s. Dickens's habit was to heighten 'a picture by the
accumulation of minute details' (*Leisure Hour* 1883, p. 39), and here in this report
the journalist layers these minute details describing the idyllic rural environment,
heightening the sense of tragedy, and creating a sense of lost innocence in the
benign and beautiful Tasmanian bush. Reporting before the coronial inquiry had
taken place the journalist is free to use his skills of narration to formulate a very
different news story.

The *Mercury* editor, 'H. R.' Henry Nicholls, a pioneering *Argus* journalist
who had become famous for his writings from the Australian gold fields about
the poor living conditions endured by pioneering families, was sympathetic to
the challenges of bush life (and this may account for the *Mercury*'s tardiness in
fully reporting Dorothy Lovell's death). Perhaps it was under his influence that the
Huon correspondent created this moving narrative of bush murder and madness.
The mother, Lilian Wakefield, is sympathetically portrayed from the very start
of this report through the frame of 'bush madness'. The report leaves no area for
doubting that the poor, deranged mother killed her three children and then herself
while suffering from madness. There are no qualifying words such as 'allegedly'
or 'apparently' to open the way for an alternative outcome at the coronial inquiry,
leaving readers to accept this press report as the facts of what happened.

Lilian is described as a 'young' mother aged 'only' 22 years of age, who
'deliberately took the lives of her three children, and then perished by her own
hand'. She was a bush woman, a mother and a wife whose insanity, brought on by
her lonely environment, saw her fail her husband, her children, and her community.

But unlike Harriet Lovell, who was portrayed as a violent, abusive wife and mother, Lilian Wakefield, in death, is almost martyred as a tragic victim of the malevolent, omnipresent bush. The prose creates a notion of lost innocence in the benign and beautiful Tasmanian bush. The narrative uses transformed indirect quotation presenting the events not as opinion statements from witnesses, but as *the events*. Like a well-crafted fictional story, the prose paces the drama, taking the reader through the events of the day, introducing the characters: first the husband, Ernest; then Lilian and her children and finally the family boarder, Isaac Wilson. The events of the day are related chronologically through the mediated voices of Ernest and Isaac, the neighbours and Trooper Crosswell, the same trooper who just a few months earlier had dealt with the tragic death of Dorothy Lovell, and the Friday before had been in court in Hobart giving his evidence at Harriet Lovell's trial.

The day, according to the news narrative, began with Ernest Wakefield rising at seven o'clock to go shooting with a friend. As he leaves the house he shouts out '"Hooray!"' to his wife, and then through the constructed dialogue of Isaac Wilson, Lilian Wakefield and the lodger are sitting at the breakfast table, Lilian with the baby on her lap. Mid morning Isaac Wilson shaves at the fireplace then strops his razor and places it on the mantelpiece. At midday he leaves the cottage while Lilian is 'busying herself with her household duties' and 'the little ones' are 'playing innocently together'. Not long after Isaac Wilson leaves the cottage Ernest's sister, Mrs Frank Cordwell (Catherine Rebecca Cordwell), who lived nearby, briefly enters the discourse to tell how she saw Lilian outside the house, 'but neither she nor her three children were ever again seen alive'.

The narrative now shifts in time to the end of the day, and in the winter's darkness Ernest Wakefield, the husband returns to his home where on:

> Entering the house by the back door, beheld his entire family lying dead upon the floor. He ran away screaming towards the house of Mitchell, and the two men went back to the house, whose interior resembled rather a shambles than a human habitation. They could do nothing, however, but close the door upon the gruesome spectacle. ('DREADFUL TRAGEDY AT CRABTREE',, *Mercury* 23 July 1912, p. 5)

The constructed dialogue of Trooper Crosswell, at times through transformed indirect quotation, imbues the narrative with a forensic tone as the policeman enters the tragic scene:

> Proceeding into the kitchen he found the woman on the floor with her face in a pool of blood, her head being under the kitchen table. Close by her was a blood-stained razor. Upon the table was a small looking-glass bespatted with blood, and there was also blood on the table. ('DREADFUL TRAGEDY AT CRABTREE', *Mercury* 23 July 1912, p. 5)

Because of the assumption that there was no question that Lilian Wakefield was responsible for the deaths, and the finality of her own death removing *sub judice* and other legal imperatives from the news discourse, the reporter creates a remarkably unbalanced pre-inquest news narrative, which raises questions about the report's influence over the coronial inquiry that was yet to be held.

The forensic detailing gathered by the journalist from his interview with Trooper Crosswell brings a chilling particularity of detail to the narrative:

> Lying on his face next to the dead woman the officer found the body of the unhappy woman's second child, a little boy 2½ years of age, named Olive Ernest Adolphus, while on the hearth lay the corpse of the eldest child, Violet Eliza May, aged 4 years. She, too, was lying on her face, and the throats of both children had been horribly wounded. The bodies of the two children were dressed, with the exception of stockings and shoes, and the little girl had her hair plaited. ('DREADFUL TRAGEDY AT CRABTREE', *Mercury* 23 July 1912, p. 5)

The only personal descriptor in this confronting discourse is applied to Lilian Wakefield in the form of the subjective collocation the 'unhappy woman'.

The New Journalism structure paces the details, disclosing information in a manner drawn from the format of penny crime fiction:

> Amid all the horror there was still one small life to be accounted for, and Trooper Crosswell had not far to look in order to satisfy himself that it, too, had been sacrificed, for in a cradle, also in the kitchen, he found the seven months' old baby which had been called Irene Mary. Though when found it was in a sitting posture it was dead, as were all the others. Upon the mantelpiece was found the case of the razor with which the fearful deed had been committed. ('DREADFUL TRAGEDY AT CRABTREE', *Mercury* 23 July 1912, p. 5)

Unconstrained by legal imperatives, the journalist chooses the eyewitness accounts which best reflect his certainty that Lilian Wakefield killed herself and her family:

> No motive is assigned for the mother's terrible crime, and the most reasonable supposition is that it was committed under the influence of a sudden fit of homicidal mania. There is not wanting evidence that Mrs Wakefield had keenly felt her loneliness in the bush for her house is not only remotely situated, but is extremely difficult to access. It can only be reached after descending the steep and muddy sides of a ravine, and crossing on slippery stepping-stones a creek which lies at the bottom. Indeed, it is said, that Mrs Wakefield had been heard at times to bewail her loneliness, and exclaim that death was preferable to it. ('DREADFUL TRAGEDY AT CRABTREE,' *Mercury* 23 July 1912, p. 5)

In transformed indirect quotation this unattributed information, prior to the coronial inquiry, creates a certainty, shutting out any alternative discourses. But what of William Isaac Wilson, the last man to see Lilian alive, why was his story so readily accepted?

The funeral was held on 24 July a week before the full inquest (the acceptance that this had been a murder suicide is reflected in the coroner's actions in briefly convening and immediately adjourning the inquest to allow the family and the community to lay the family to rest). The funeral provided the Huon journalist with another opportunity to craft an affecting story: 'The funeral of the young married woman, Lilian May Wakefield, wife of Ernest Wakefield, labourer, of Crabtree, who on Sunday last murdered her three children and then committed suicide, took place at Ranelagh this afternoon, and with her were buried her little victims' ('The Crabtree Tragedy. Funeral of the Victims', *Mercury* 25 July 1912, p. 6). Again what is striking in this news discourse is the pre-emptive cause of deaths before the full coronial inquiry. This is a community desperate to move on from the horrific events of recent times. The 340-word report of the funeral informs readers that the entire community attended the mass outpouring of grief at the Ranelagh church where Lilian Wakefield was buried in the churchyard with 'her little victims', six miles from the miserable bush cottage. The journalist crafts another affecting narrative:

> Nearly the whole population of Crabtree followed the three coffins (the body of the 7 months old baby being contained in the same coffin as that of the mother) to the place of interment, about six miles distant, and as the procession moved along it from time to time received additions, which gradually swelled it to very large proportions. When at last it reached the churchyard gate there must have been about 50 vehicles in the train, while behind these came many followers on foot. The melancholy procession created an affecting sensation among the rural dwellers as it slowly wound its way through the dells of the Huon. ('The Crabtree Tragedy. Funeral of the Victims', *Mercury* 25 July 1912, p. 6).

The funeral of Lilian Wakefield and her children was reported as a community event that enabled the people of the Huon to not only share their collective grief and to express their collective feelings of sadness, but also to reaffirm their sense of being part of a rural community. In contrast the *Mercury* did not report Dorothy Lovell's funeral, perhaps because, with the mother and father in attendance, both of whom were culpable in the child's horrific death, it was unlikely to attract the same public outpouring of communal grief.

The inquest into the deaths of Lilian Wakefield and her three children was held on a midwinter's day at the Crabtree State School (a rather inappropriate site to inquire into the deaths of three young children, the eldest of whom was a pupil at the school) and was conducted by Sergeant Lonergan before the district coroner, W. J. Thomas, the same coroner who presided over Dorothy Lovell's inquest. According to the Huon correspondent the inquest started at 10 o'clock in the morning and lasted until late in the evening; however, the news report provides only a brief account of the evidence of the key witnesses: Ernest

Wakefield, William Isaac Wilson, George Harris (who lived between 200 and 300 yards from the house), Catherine Rebecca Cordwell, David Mitchell (Ernest's hunting companion) and Dr Cummings. In the harrowing, mediated evidence of Ernest Wakefield *Mercury* readers were told: 'His wife had not at any time been depressed, and he had had no cause to suspect that she would do anything so desperate'. However, the last man to see her alive, William Isaac Wilson, provides contradictory evidence allegedly through the voice of Lilian Wakefield herself, in his claim that two weeks' earlier:

> He was about to drive Mrs Wakefield and her children to her mother's residence, when the weather being threatening the deceased said, 'I hope it is not going to rain, because I don't like stopping here by myself. I feel so miserable.' She added. 'I suppose you would call it melancholy, but I sometimes feel that way that I could cut my throat and the children's too.' ('The Crabtree Tragedy. Inquest on the Victims', *Mercury* 31 July 1912, p. 8)

Wilson claimed he offered to stay with Lilian, but that she 'laughed it off'. He admitted he did not mention this conversation to anyone, and that he thought her 'remark was only intended for a joke'.

Dr Cummings' evidence was again influential. He is reported as saying that 'death was due to wounds in the throat. Beyond those were no marks of violence. There was nothing to indicate that the wound in Mrs Wakefield's throat was otherwise than self-inflicted'. When asked by the coroner whether he considered the deed was done suddenly or was premeditated, Dr Cummings said: 'from the surrounding circumstances the deed was undoubtedly premeditated. She would not be in her right mind when she committed it. She would premeditate the deed while in a state of melancholia. In each case death would result about a minute after the wounds were inflicted ('The Crabtree Tragedy. Inquest on the Victims', *Mercury* 31 July 1912, p. 8). The coroner returned a verdict that Lilian Wakefield had committed suicide while temporarily insane, and in the case of the children that 'they died from wounds inflicted by their mother'. The coronial findings confirmed what the journalist had reported a week earlier.

Conclusion

Lilian Wakefield, like Harriet Lovell, was a married women living with her husband and children in the densely forested foothills of Mount Wellington. Lilian shared the small bush cottage with her husband, Ernest and William Isaac Wilson. It is not known if these two bush mothers knew each other, but living in adjoining bush settlements where the community gathered at a local church for funerals, marriages and religious festivals, and the Longley hall for community events, it is more than likely that they did know each other. The circumstances of these acts of (alleged) infanticide, as described through news discourse (the only available documentary evidence of these events), were remarkably different. The temporal and geographic proximity, however, make it surprising that neither the coroner nor the press made any comment about two infanticide/child murder cases occurring within a short time of each other in the same bush community.

There were no leading articles on the broader issue of maternal and child welfare and bush life, and the two cases were reported without any reference to each other. In both cases the mothers, and not society, welfare or the community, were to blame. The guilt was contained within the family frame, in the private domestic sphere of maternal madness, requiring neither the press nor public officials to situate these events in the public sphere.

In the final chapter of this book, in the case of 21-year Edith Roberts, madness was not a focus of her defence or the news discourse. In Chapter 6 I analyse the news coverage of this young woman's infanticidal actions and expose how the press catapulted infanticide back onto the national political agenda in England in 1921–22 and in so doing brought about legislative change after 300 years.

Chapter 6
'The Hinkley Girl-Mother' and the *Leicester Mercury*

It was long past midnight on a mild spring night in 1921 when a 21-year-old unmarried factory worker in the rural town of Hinkley, in the east midlands of England, secretly gave birth in the attic bedroom she shared with her sister. Some time soon after, while her sister lay sleeping beside her, Edith Roberts strangled her newborn child with a strip of lace from her camisole and hid the body in the flock mattress. More than 50 years after the 'infanticide epidemic' of the 1860s the actions of this young Englishwoman, reported in the press, catapulted the issue of infanticide back onto the national political agenda in England. A campaign by Edith Roberts's local newspaper, the *Leicester Mercury*, to save the young woman from the ignominy of a death sentence resulted within a year in the introduction of the 1922 Infanticide Act that finally removed the death penalty from the crime of infanticide in England and the British Commonwealth. This final chapter brings the study of infanticide and the press to a close with the analysis of the *Leicester Mercury*'s coverage of the infanticide trial of Edith Roberts and the paper's subsequent campaign to bring about legislative reform to the 300-year-old infanticide law.

In 1921 Edith Roberts lived with her father and stepmother, 16-year-old sister Lily, and two half-brothers, in a modest worker's cottage in the rural village of Hinkley in the mill and market town of Leicester. Edith's father, Robert Roberts, was a foreman at the local dye works and his wife (only ever identified in the news reports under the patriarchal naming of 'Mrs Robert Roberts' or 'Mrs Roberts') was a church-going woman who was well respected in the community. As Edith Roberts went about her daily life in late 1920 and the early part of 1921 she carried with her the secret of her pregnancy, a circumstance she found so shameful she was unable to disclose the truth to her parents. Up until she gave birth on 16 April 1921 Edith disguised her swelling stomach from her family and friends by swaddling her abdomen with strips of cloth. On the night she went into labour she later told the court that she endured the 'great agony' alone and 'tormented', pacing up and down in the attic bedroom she shared with her sister, 'until she could bear the pain no longer and laid down' beside her sleeping sister and finally gave birth ('Hinkley Murder Charge', *Leicester Mercury* 7 June 1921, p. 1). What happened next would thrust this quiet, God-fearing family into the public spotlight in the most unexpected and unwelcome manner and eventually turn Edith Roberts's actions into the most publicized infanticide in the 95-year history of the *Leicester Mercury* and transform the shy factory worker into a national cause célèbre.

The *Leicester Mercury*'s coverage of Edith Roberts's infanticide is noteworthy for the newspaper's decision to establish a campaign to secure the young woman's freedom and amend the 300-year-old infanticide law, and this at a time when it was also publishing particularly lurid infanticide reports in its pages, and in two instances placed sensational infanticide reports alongside news stories about Edith Roberts.

The *Leicester Mercury* began life as the weekly *Leicester Chronicle* in 1836 and was regarded as 'staunchly non-conformist' and the forerunner of the 'free independent press' (England 1999, p. 8). It was published, printed and edited by Albert Cockshaw the son of a schoolteacher who established one of the first circulating libraries in England. Cockshaw was a 'dedicated radical and non-conformist, acutely aware of the poverty and misery that surrounded him' (England 1999, p. 8). Cockshaw used the printed word to help to change the 'order of things and along with other reformers he advocated the disestablishment of the Church, the abolition of slavery, extended suffrage and the abolition of the Church rate' (England 1999, p. 8). However, in 1897 the newspaper changed its style and format to become a 'popular' newspaper. A women's section was added, as well as serialized fiction by well-known authors, and illustrated weekly supplements became a feature of the paper. By the 1920s the *Leicester Mercury* was a popular tabloid newspaper engaging readers with gripping headlines which focused on crime and scandal, particularly murder and divorce, although it also prided itself in its comprehensive coverage of regional news. A glimpse at headlines in the newspaper in 1921 provides an insight into the paper's news priorities of the day: 'Leicester Woman's Ordeal: Murderous Attack by Unknown Assailant' (*Leicester Mercury* 16 June 1921, p. 1); 'Boy Charged with Murder: Little Girl Found Dead after Outrage: Feet and Arms Bound' (20 June 1921, p. 1); '"Other woman" Question at Ashby: Railway Policeman Sued by his Wife' (20 June 1921, p. 1); 'Policeman's Discovery: Finds Girl with Knife at Naked Breast' (11 July 1921, p. 5). Such lurid reports on murder, rape and divorce were standard fare for the tabloid newspaper.

Infanticide Coverage

During the period between Edith's arrest in April 1921 and her release in June 1922 the newspaper published several prominent – and sensational – infanticide stories. In the midst of the *Leicester Mercury*'s June 1921 coverage of Edith Roberts's ordeal in the aftermath of her trial the paper ran a sensational infanticide report on its front page on 16 June headlined: 'Baby's Body in Suitcase: Gruesome Discovery in a Leicester House: Unsolved Year-Old Mystery: Inquest Opened and Adjourned for a Week' (*Leicester Mercury* 16 June 1921, p. 1). From this report it appears that a 'young woman' who had boarded in rooms at a Leicester house for several months in 1919 and 'who had been working in Leicester, finally left the city a year ago, leaving behind her a portmanteau'. The woman had written to the landlady several times since requesting the disposal of the leather suitcase. After a year expired the landlady's curiosity got the better of her and she removed the bag from the shelf in the coalhouse, where it had been deposited, and opened it to discover, underneath clothes, the body of a child. Despite the advanced state of decomposition, the crucial evidence of the medical practitioner determined that the child had not breathed, 'the lungs apparently had not been inflated with air' ('Baby's Body in Suitcase', *Leicester Mercury* 16 June 1921, p. 1).

'Ghastly Discovery'

At the start of 1922 another gruesome infanticide story was published on the front page of the *Leicester Mercury* while the paper was continuing its campaign to free Edith Roberts. The report's sensational headlines, 'Ghastly Discovery in Leicester: Baby's Body by Parcel Post' foretold a bizarre infanticide story. Readers were entertained and informed with a news narrative that read more like a fictional murder mystery out of a penny-dreadful than a news report. A postal official at the Station-street parcel office had made a 'ghastly discovery' when he 'found a parcel which had been through the post contained the body of a newly born baby'. The coronial inquiry offered the *Leicester Mercury* the opportunity to create a compelling news narrative in constructed dialogue, telling readers how a piece of window cord had slipped off at each end of the parcel and had been placed on the postal official's desk to be re-wrapped. 'The brown paper was torn, and witness noticed blood on the inner sheet. He unwrapped the parcel, and found that it contained the body of a newly born child'. The 'stamp on the parcel showed that it had been posted at Addington-street post office, Ramsgate on January 14'. The medical doctor, Dr N. Sprigg, determined that the body was that of a premature child weighing four pounds and that it had 'incised wounds along the throat'. He told the inquest that he was of the opinion the child had had a separate existence. 'It must have breathed and it must have been fully delivered', he told the inquest. Death, he determined, 'was due to haemorrhage and shock following the wounds' ('Ghastly Discovery in Leicester', *Leicester Mercury* 21 January 1922, p. 1).

On the same day the newspaper reported a second page-one infanticide story, that of a married woman who was said to have killed her child, with the story adopting the predictable infanticidal madness trope for the reporting of a married woman's infanticidal actions: 'Demented Woman's Rash Act'. Through the reconstruction of the witness statements into a descriptive narrative the reporter told readers that a 'Mary Ann Brough (32), the wife of a collier, drowned herself and her daughter, Mabel, in the reservoir at Harrington'. A six-year-old boy had also been thrown into the water but he managed to scramble out and raise the alarm. Readers were told 'the mother had not been well recently' ('Demented Woman's Rash Act', *Leicester Mercury* 21 January 1922, p. 1). A week later the sensational 'Baby's Body by Parcel Post' story concluded when readers were told that the coroner had determined that the unknown newly born male child had been murdered. The case was adjourned 'in the hope that in the meantime the Ramsgate police, who were investigating the case, might obtain some information'. This page-one report provided further startling evidence that there had been other stories in the 'newspapers that a similar parcel, containing an infant, had been found at Southampton, that parcel also being posted at Ramsgate. It was possible there might be some connection between the two – they MIGHT BE TWIN CHILDREN, but so far as they were concerned they had nothing to do with the second body.' ('Wilful Murder Verdict: Child's Body by Post to Leicester: Inquiry into Gruesome Mystery', *Leicester Mercury* 27 January 1922, p. 1).

The *Leicester Mercury*'s Campaign

Harry Hackett, the editor of the *Leicester Mercury* at the time of Edith Roberts's trial was the right newspaperman at the right time to be leading a campaign to 'save' a young woman from what the community began to acknowledge as an injustice. Hackett was an enlightened editor who supported the franchise for women and lobbied for better conditions for the poor and disadvantaged. He was also an experienced newspaperman who had the ability to read the public sentiment of the time. He had joined the paper as a young reporter in the 1860s and by the 1870s he was chief reporter and in 1882 became the editor, a position he held for the next 30 years. During the First World War he acted as honorary secretary of a committee to grant increased allowances to the wives and children of serving men serving. With the Armistice Hackett took on the role of honorary secretary of a committee encouraging manufacturers to donate gifts of boots, hosiery and other necessities to war widows and their children, which was to become known as the War Widows' Charity. A political man, he was on the local Liberal Party committee, and such was his impact on Liberal politics in the district that when he died, Sir Winston Churchill sent a letter to his family expressing his admiration for Harry Hackett.

By 1921, when Edith Roberts became the focus of news discourse in the *Leicester Mercury*, many newspapers had begun transforming their front pages by replacing classified advertisements with news. The *Leicester Mercury* was one of the first regional newspapers in England to place news stories on its front page and by 1921 classified advertisements had been removed entirely from page one of the newspaper, to page two. Page three was primarily block advertising, while page four was half-news and half-advertising, and page five and six were predominantly news. The regional newspaper was following the lead of Lord Northcliffe who had introduced the new layout and popular format with his *Daily Mail* in 1896, a format that became known as 'the tabloid'.

The young factory hand, Edith Roberts, first entered public discourse through the *Leicester Mercury* on 18 April 1921, the day after she first appeared in court to answer to a charge of infanticide. However, the paper determined that this infanticide was of little news value and buried it in the 'police courts' column on page five ('Police Courts', 18 April 1921, p. 5) merely noting Edith Roberts's appearance before the magistrate on a charge of 'infanticide' (the only time her crime is referred to in this way). Edith was remanded and sent to trial at the June Assizes. It was not until she came to trial at the summer session of the Leicester Assizes that the *Leicester Mercury* determined that this story was newsworthy, prominently publishing the first day of the trial on its front page under the headlines:

HINKLEY MURDER CHARGE
Factory Girl's Ordeal
WOMEN JURORS CHALLENGED
(*Leicester Mercury* 7 June 1921, p. 1)

What is noteworthy in this report is that Edith, the 'factory girl', is not the focus of the report, but rather the focus is on the gender make-up of the jury in the trial of a woman charged with the gender-specific crime of infanticide. Changes to the jury system in England less than three years earlier, with the passing of the Sex Disqualification (Removal) Act in 1919, meant that when Edith Roberts came to trial charged with infanticide women were able to sit in judgment on one of their own sex. The Act, which had come into law on 23 December 1919, stated that:

> A person shall not be disqualified by sex or marriage from the exercise of any public function, or from being appointed to or holding any civil or judicial office or post, or from entering or assuming or carrying on any civil profession or vocation, or for admission to any incorporated society whether incorporated by Royal Charter or otherwise, and a person shall not be exempted by sex or marriage from the liability to serve as a juror. (Sex Disqualification (Removal) Act 1919 (9 & 10 Geo. V *c.*71) 23 December 1919)

The fact that no women were empanelled to sit in judgment on Edith Roberts was the focus of the paper's report. The opening paragraph informed readers that Edith Roberts's barrister, Mr G.W. Powers, had 'challenged all the women jurors called as they were to be sworn, and the case was tried by men alone' ('HINKLEY MURDER CHARGE', *Leicester Mercury* 7 June 1921, p. 1). The *Leicester Mercury* considered the jury selection of such news high value that it embedded it into the story's headlines and established the tone of the paper's reporting of Edith's trial. However, the paper did note that the challenge to the jurors 'was made by counsel for the accused in accordance with a long-established constitutional right'. Mr Powers, who objected to a female presence on the jury, may have done so from his belief that women, as the gatekeeper's of female morality, would have been harsher in their judgment of the young woman's actions than would a male jury, or else it was his belief in the fundamental inadequacy of women to sit in judgment in a criminal trial. Powers never disclosed his reasoning. For more than 200 years the legal profession in England had posed questions about female intellectual capacity to sit in judgment of citizens. The patriarchal profession had hung onto its belief that woman jurors raised 'a fundamental conflict between the desire to make juries truly representative and the fear that not all citizens are intellectually capable of the extended and onerous duties of jury service' (Cornish 1968, 25). The misogynistic view of Sir William Blackstone (1765–1769), an English jurist, who referred to the requirement that a jury be composed of '*liber et legalis homo*' (a free and lawful man) and argued that women were excluded from jury service '*propter defectum sexus*' (because of the defect of the sex) was still the dominant mindset for many in the legal profession.

The popular tabloid the *Leicester Mercury*, however, displayed a more enlightened view and two days after the jury selection had taken place the paper published a news story sourced from a letter written by Miss M. Mackintosh, a member of the women's section of the Leicester Labour Party. Miss Mackintosh had written to the paper in regard 'to the challenges to the women as jurors in the Hinkley child murder charge at the Assizes' ('Correspondence', *Leicester Mercury* 9 June 1921 p. 5). Significantly, the paper made the editorial decision to publish Miss Mackintosh's letter not on the 'Correspondence' page, but on a news page adjacent to the day's coverage of the Edith Roberts's trial under the headline 'Correspondence' providing Miss Mackintosh's letter with the imprimatur of the newspaper. Appropriating Miss Mackintosh's words, with attribution, the paper mediated her political rhetoric, creating its own discourse:

> She [Miss Mackintosh] thinks that if ever there was a case which should have been tried by women it is such a one as this. She expresses no opinion upon the case itself, but says 'it is quite time we women came forward with a determination to demand full representation not only on public bodies, but in all positions, especially those which refer to women'. ('Correspondence', *Leicester Mercury* 9 June 1921, p. 5)

Miss A. Mackintosh, a suffragette, whose measured discourse disavowed those who thought women were too weak-headed and emotional to sit in judgment on criminal matters, belonged to a women's sub-group of the Labour Party which also lobbied for birth control and rejected any lingering beliefs in Malthusian dogma. Although the social and political climate for women in England in 1921 allowed women to have their voices heard more often in news discourse, and saw some women even reporting news, it was still a time when the dominant discourse was vociferously paternalistic. Despite advances women were still living in a man's world.

Infanticide was no longer understood fundamentally as a crime that posed a danger to society, but rather as an example of an individual woman's deviancy, or madness. By the time of Edith Roberts's trial there had been a softening of the position towards women who killed their children, brought about for the most part because women were no longer committing infanticide in the high numbers that had been reported in the nineteenth century. After the 1871 Child Protection Act with the enforcement of the registration of births, tighter controls on pregnant women, and the development of a welfare system, the number of infanticides steadily decreased. However, in a world where illegitimacy remained a 'stain' and an unmarried mother, especially in the cities and towns of England, was still ostracized as a 'fallen' woman, desperate young women like Edith Roberts, and the mothers of the parcel post babies, did kill their babies with regularity, and their actions continued to make salacious copy for the newspapers. News discourse also reflected the changing options for young women who found themselves with an unwanted pregnancy. In August 1921 the page-one lead in the *Leicester Mercury* was a story of a police surgeon conducting 'illegal operations on women' ('Charge Against Police Surgeon', *Leicester Mercury* 3 August 1921, p. 1), while on the 5 August another page-one story reflected the increasing representation of the women's movement: 'Sex Equality: Lady Astor Asks for Simple Justice' (*Leicester Mercury* 5 August 1921, p. 1). But at the same time infanticide remained ever present with a front page report on 18 August a reminder of the ever-present political aspect of infanticide: 'Mothers Kill Their children: Unable to Watch Them Starve: Stricken Russia: Cholera Raging in Famine Areas' (*Leicester Mercury* 18 August 1921, p. 1). Infanticide in England (and Australia) was never overtly represented in news discourse as a political act; the political reading of infanticide over the 100 years of this study is my interpretation of the news discourse.

Infanticide in 1920s England

In England in the 1920s, while infanticide was no longer seen as a threat to society as a whole, and larger sections of society acknowledged the inherent injustice of men escaping censure while women's lives were irrevocable changed by an out-of-marriage pregnancy, society still named and shamed the woman and never the man. This overt discursive discrimination caused a level of discomfort that saw Edith Roberts, a young factory worker from an exemplary working-class background (who portrayed the appropriate emotional response – intense shame, and was represented in the press as fragile and contrite) regarded as a victim of an outdated and unjust system, creating the social and political climate for change.

In contrast with the *Leicester Mercury*'s immoderate, salacious reporting of other infanticides, from their first news report on Edith Roberts's case there was no overt sensationalization by the tabloid and in fact the paper's reports are uncharacteristically measured, with Edith Roberts represented as a naive ingénue, rather than as a stereotypical deviant, fallen woman. The newspaper shies away from reference to the salacious details of Edith's infanticide, and over the next year it not only does not name her crime as 'infanticide', but it rarely refers to her actions at all and when it does her infanticidal actions are referred to as 'child murder'.

The *Leicester Mercury*'s Reports

The *Leicester Mercury*'s first report of Edith Roberts's trial, once it had moved past its discourse on the make-up of the all-male jury, is in all other ways a standard prosaic infanticide report with the medical expert witness, Dr Basil Taylor, providing 'crucial' evidence that 'certain lacy material, which afterwards turned out to be a camisole, was tied round the child's mouth'. Through transformed indirect quotation the paper presents the doctor's evidence as: 'the medical opinion was that the child had breathed and had had a separate existence, and that the cause of death was suffocation' ('HINKLEY MURDER CHARGE', *Leicester Mercury* 7 June 1921, p. 1). Edith's stepmother, the matriarch of the Roberts's household who was expected to guard the family home against vice, is not presented as a woman who failed in her wifely and motherly duties to adequately patrol the moral boundaries of her home. Rather she is represented first as a powerless woman, and then sympathetically as a mother distraught by her stepdaughter's immoral actions. 'Mrs Roberts' is described as being 'much affected' when giving evidence and had to be 'accommodated with a seat'. The representation of the physical vulnerability of the key females in the case, Edith, her stepmother and her sister, is to be a common factor in the paternalistic news discourse, which consistently frames each of these women as broken and powerless. Readers are told several times that the proceedings were interrupted because the 'accused girl fainted'. At the same time as these women are constantly named and shamed in news discourse they are also represented as humbled, humiliated and broken, erasing their power and any threat they may have been to society, and allowing readers, through the sympathetic framing of the news discourse, to be empathetic to Edith Roberts and her family.

It is through the stepmother's constructed dialogue that Edith Roberts's pathetic voice comes through to the readers for the first time as Mrs Roberts tells the court that Edith told her: 'that the baby was born while she was in bed with her sister Lily, after she had walked about the bedroom in great pain during a portion of the night. The baby lay against her just as it was born. She killed it, and it was cold' ('HINKLEY MURDER CHARGE', *Leicester Mercury* 7 June 1921, p. 1). Edith's sister Lily, who was the next to give evidence, whispered from the dock that she 'was not disturbed during the night'. Then Edith's father is brought before the paper's readers as 'Robert Jos. Roberts', a 'foreman dyer' at the Hinkley dye mill. Just as his wife is not represented through a blaming discourse, the paper does not represent Robert Roberts as having failed his family and the community by inadequately supervising his wife and his daughter, although the blaming is implicit in the naming of the parents. Robert Roberts is represented throughout the paper's reports as a decent, hardworking God-fearing father, husband and member of the community.

In the report on Edith's trial on 7 June a pitiable dialogue between father and daughter is brought to readers through constructed dialogue with Robert Roberts telling the court that 'on the day after the discovery of the body he asked the girl what had made her do it, and she said, "I was frightened and ashamed"'. The brief report on Edith Roberts's trial concludes with further evidence of Dr Cecil Taylor presented in constructed dialogue and framed in the lexicon of medicine with the ancient hydrostacy test implicit in the rhetoric. Dr Taylor reportedly told the court that the post-mortem 'showed that the organs were healthy, the lungs and heart together floated', and he came to the conclusion 'that it had had a separate existence. The cause of death, in witness's opinion, was suffocation, probably through the camisole being tied tightly round the face'. This evidence had significant implications for the defendant, because if the jury accepted this evidence then Edith Roberts could not be found guilty on a lesser charge of concealing birth. However, Dr Taylor, under cross-examination, provided the jury with an alternative outcome:

> In cross-examination, the witness agreed that the camisole had not been tied over the nose, but said a newly born child breathed through the mouth. It was perfectly possible that the girl was unconscious through the pain she suffered, and that she might not realise what she was doing. ('HINKLEY MURDER CHARGE', *Leicester Mercury* 7 June 1921, p. 1)

The constructed dialogue takes the reader directly from the statement sentence that condemns the defendant, to one that mitigates her actions and provides the jury – and the *Leicester Mercury*'s readers – with the age-old alternative of parturient madness as an acceptable defence. The collocation of the words 'perfectly possible' reinforces the belief that the 'girl' (connoting youthfulness, guileless and a lack of worldliness) could have strangled her infant not aware of her actions due to the pain of birth. However, the jury was not to be swayed by such rhetoric and within 15 minutes they had returned a 'guilty' verdict. The next day's *Leicester Mercury* represented the trial outcome in bold capitalized page-five headlines: 'DEATH SENTENCE AT LEICESTER ASSIZES. Accused Girl Carried from the Dock. PAINFUL SCENE AT MURDER TRIAL' (*Leicester Mercury* 8 June 1921, p. 5). The first headline with the phrase 'death sentence' (connoting the dreaded corporeal punishment of death on the gallows, the most feared juridical phrase in the legal lexicon) allows the descriptive headlines that follow to paint an evocative picture full of pathos. The 'girl' being romantically carried from the dock by a man emphasizes Edith Roberts's vulnerability and powerlessness. Again this trial report varies from the usual infanticide news discourse in its focus and intention. It does not frame Edith Roberts, a convicted infanticidal mother, as a deviant mother, there is no report from the judge condemning her 'unnatural' and 'wicked' actions, but rather she is the 'accused' (as opposed to convicted) and again represented as a 'girl' connoting an unworldliness. The focus of the report is Edith's lawyer's final address to the jury, a break from the traditional format of court reporting whereby the defence address is usually dispensed with in a few truncated lines of news discourse, or ignored completely. Here Mr G.W. Powers is given several paragraphs to argue his case with forensic rhetoric:

> The evidence as to the child having had a separate existence was not satisfactory, and that unless that was proved there could be no crime of murder. Even if the jury accepted the evidence on this point, however, he appealed to them to say that whatever the girl did was done in the frenzy and agony of pain through which she was passing, and therefore hardly conscious of her own acts at the

time, and consequently not responsible. ('DEATH SENTENCE at LEICESTER ASSIZES', *Leicester Mercury* 8 June 1921, p. 5)

But as the reader already knew, Mr Power's efforts were in vain. At the guilty verdict Edith is framed rhetorically as 'the prisoner' and again the focus is on her physical and emotional reaction: she 'reeled backwards and was held up by two warders'. And then her voice resonates through the discourse, in direct quotes. Edith Roberts when asked 'if she had anything to say' 'murmured in a feeble voice: "I am very sorry; I didn't intend doing it"'. Her spoken contrition, brought to readers through direct speech, drains deviant agency from the young woman's crime and allows even the most hard-hearted reader to empathize with the young infanticidal woman at the moment the judge 'assuming the black cap' told the court it was his 'painful duty' to pass 'the only sentence the law allowed for the crime of which she had been convicted'. Again a scene of great emotional force is portrayed through the pathos in the news discourse: 'When the terrible words of the death sentence fell upon the girl's ears she again collapsed, and uttered loud cries and moans, which continued as she was being carried from the dock. Several ladies who were in court were much affected by the painful scene' (ibid.). This descriptive scene transforms every woman present in the courtroom into a powerless and pathetic creature, reinforcing the lingering belief that women were emotionally weak and eminently unsuited to such a solemn and important task as jury duty.

The *Leicester Mercury*'s report is particularly unusual in terms of court news discourse, which generally reflects a court's decision with equanimity. The paper inflects disapproval into its discourse through the choice of headlines and overtly through the way it chooses to report the events with the focus on the 'painful scene' with Edith being carried insensible from the dock. The tone and structure of this report provides readers with a preferred reading of the trial outcome and no doubt had a significant influence on the community outpouring of support for Edith which would show itself in the hundreds of letters the paper would receive in the following week.

In this same edition of the paper a second news discourse on Edith Roberts's trial was published embedded into the 'Yesterday's Assizes' column on page eight. In the regular court list with its spare legalistic language reflecting the sourcing of the assizes list from the law clerk's office, appeared an emotive editorial report on Edith Roberts's trial. After a report on the case of William Booth Green (50), a company secretary who was found guilty of swindling £14,000 from his employers, the Coalville Taylor Mills Mutual Self Help Money Society and the Hugglescote Money Society, and who was sentenced to 15 months hard labour, 'the other case' readers were told:

> was one of those tragic stories in which a girl momentarily goes wrong, realises
> the consequences when too late, is apparently too ashamed to throw herself
> upon the affection of those who would have befriended her despite her lapses,
> in a paroxysm of agony takes an innocent life for which she had a special

responsibility, thus bringing herself within the law in its most terrible aspects. As the law stands, and the facts being what they were and are, there was no other verdict for the jury than that they returned, and the statute had to take its course, but in this instance, as in the other, the effects, though they fall with crushing weight upon the young woman, beard down her friends almost as deeply. The man in the case cannot escape if he has a conscience, whoever he may be. The jury strongly recommended the girl to mercy, and there is small doubt that recommendation will have full weight given to it – we trust speedily, so that anguish may be somewhat assuaged. But a grave offence was committed, which we cannot for a moment minimise, though there is surely need for a reform of the law of capital punishment when the same sentence is passed in a case like this as upon Crippen. That reform ought to come soon. Meanwhile, we trust it will be long ere Hinkley, or any other place in the county, sends to the courts cases so tragically pitiful and pathetic as that of yesterday. ('Yesterday's Assizes', *Leicester Mercury* 8 June 1921, p. 7)

This report embedded in the assizes column, rather than in the newspaper's opinion statement – its leading article – uses a paternalistic rhetoric to explicitly make an editorial judgement on the trial outcome. While the paper reflects its disappointment at the judicial decision, it acknowledges that the 'girl' had gone 'momentarily wrong' and had committed 'a grave offence' which the paper 'could not minimise'. The rhetoric acknowledges that under the law as it exists no other course could have been taken by the courts, but then, extraordinarily, argues through the assizes column for a change to the law. The strength of the paper's political argument is reinforced by comparisons with the sensational case of Dr Hawley Harvey Crippen, which made news headlines around the world a decade earlier. Crippen was an American physician living in London who had been found guilty of murdering his wife, Cora, and burying her dismembered body in the cellar of their London home. He was later hanged.[1] By drawing comparisons between a young woman who murdered her newborn child to the 'evil monster' the press portrayed as Dr Crippen, was a persuasive rhetorical strategy and in the weeks and months to come the paper would return to this rhetorical trope using hyperbole ('The Respite', Editorial *Leicester Mercury* 13 June 1921, p. 5) to draw comparisons between Edith and the most notorious villain of the Victorian period prior to Jack the Ripper, Charles Peace (1832–1879). Peace was a notorious and clever burglar from Sheffield whose appearance as a well-dressed, violin-playing man allowed him to commit murders and daring burglaries in South London undetected throughout 1877–78. He was eventually caught at Blackheath and sentenced to death and just before his execution he confessed to a second murder two years earlier in Manchester.

---

[1]   DNA tests in 2008 determined that the remains found in the cellar were those of a man and experts now think the police framed Crippen.

The 'Hinkley Girl-Mother'

The overt editorializing in the Assizes column on 8 June 1921 set the tone for the *Leicester Mercury*'s sustained campaign to 'save' Edith Roberts, framed rhetorically as the 'Hinkley Girl-Mother'. The newspaper campaigned firstly to save Edith from the death penalty; then to save her from life imprisonment; and finally they campaigned to see the law amended and the removal of the automatic death penalty for all English women who killed their babies in the postpartum period. With her 'guilty' verdict Edith Roberts's news value increased rather than dissipated and the 'Hinkley girl-mother' became *the* story of the *Leicester Mercury*'s news pages for the next 12 months.

Edith Roberts was 21 when she strangled her newborn baby in the bedroom of her family's home. In 1921 in England 23.4 per cent of women were aged 20–24 when having their first child, while just 2.5 per cent were giving birth for the first time aged 15–19. The peek age was 25–29, with 31 per cent of women giving birth at this age (Goodman 1957, p. 204). Yet Edith Roberts, at 21, was consistently portrayed in the *Leicester Mercury* as a 'girl' or as the 'girl-mother'. The framing of Edith as a 'girl' and a 'mother' was perhaps on one level an allusion to her unmarried status, but it was also a deliberate rhetorical strategy used by the newspaper to represent the 21 going on 22-year-old Edith as a 'girl-like' mother, that is as a female who, even with her maternal status, was without power and therefore non-threatening. While it was acknowledged that Edith had 'done wrong' and that she had committed a 'grave offence', she was framed by patriarchy as a powerless woman, a woman to be patronized and pitied rather than feared. Additionally, in the 1920s motherhood was generally equated with wifehood, and wifehood was equated with a sexually active woman, and by framing Edith Roberts as a 'girl' or 'girl-mother', it emphasized her sexual inexperience, and therefore framed her as unthreatening. The *Leicester Mercury* consistently represented Edith Roberts throughout their campaign as a 'girl' or 'girl-mother'. In the newspaper's first story ('Hinkley Murder Charge', 7 June 1921, p. 1) she was referred to as a 'girl' five times, as opposed to the 'factory hand' once, the 'accused' four times, and the 'prisoner' once. In the following day's press report she was a 'girl' three times, a 'factory hand' once, and a 'prisoner' once. The *Leicester Mercury*'s 'Girl-Mother' moniker, which would stay with Edith Roberts for the duration of her press profile, entered the news discourse in bold headlines on 11 June 1921: 'HINKLEY MURDER; GIRL-MOTHER REPRIEVED'. From here on in headlines and news stories in the *Leicester Mercury* portrayed Edith Roberts as the 'Girl-Mother'. For example: 'Appeal Lodged for Girl-Mother' (15 June 1921, p. 5); 'Fund for Girl-Mother' (16 June 1921, p. 5); 'Hinkley Girl Mother' (5 November 1921, p. 3).

When the *Leicester Mercury* began to report on a possible reprieve for the 'Girl-Mother' two days after her conviction, the news discourse shifts from a judicial focus and onto the young woman herself. This news framing is an early example of celebrity news. Edith Roberts is now transformed into a press personality and the feminizing focus is on Edith herself and not on her crime. The newspaper reported on her personal appearance – on what she wore, how her hair was dressed, her body shape and her emotional status. Edith Roberts presented herself as the model penitent young twentieth-century infanticide, with her alluring aura of vulnerability and her natural characteristics – she was considered pretty and she was young and, importantly, demure and contrite, making her the ideal celebrity citizen to be represented in press discourse as the embodiment of the outdated and unjust Infanticide Act. At the same time as the *Leicester Mercury* was turning Edith Roberts into an infanticide celebrity, the paper was performing its Fourth Estate 'watchdog' role by scrutinizing a 'bad law' and in so doing politicized Edith Roberts's infanticide.

But as much as she was a symbol of infanticide and an archaic law, Edith Roberts was a news commodity and the *Leicester Mercury* realized the importance of keeping this commodity before the public eye and the need to build on the momentum from the highly charged report of her death sentence. To do this the paper determined to cover every aspect of Edith Roberts's life in incarceration, bringing details, however mundane, to its readers. The layering of the discourse began on 9 June when readers were told that there was 'no accommodation for female prisoners at the Leicester Gaol', and therefore the 'condemned girl' was taken to the Birmingham Prison. Edith's transportation becomes a personal narrative of the girl's traumatic experience. The discourse then reframes her from the 'condemned girl' and the 'prisoner', back to the 'Girl-Mother' who is escorted to the Birmingham Gaol by two wardresses and the Birmingham prison doctor, who 'had several times to give her stimulants during the terrible ordeal through which she passed in her trial' ('The Hinkley Murder', *Leicester Mercury* 9 June 1921, p. 5). This reminder of the role of the doctor at her trial not only reinforces the romantic aura of vulnerability the news discourse is weaving around the figure of Edith Roberts, but also alludes to the well-known trope of the hysterical, swooning female being revived with medicinal compounds and reiterates the central role of medicine in the care of women who step outside the societal boundaries of the 'normal' woman.

Readers were further apprised that Edith, 'though suffering acutely from the strain, which several times brought her to the verge of collapse', was determined to be fit enough to make the journey back to Birmingham, and that during the journey 'every possible care was taken by the sympathetic and considerate prison officials'. Edith Roberts's news values are certain to remain high on the paper's news agenda as readers are told that 'interest now centres very naturally in the next step that will be taken by those responsible for the defence of the unfortunate girl'. With the publication of personal interest stories on the 'Hinkley Girl-Mother', the best-known infanticide in the county, the *Leicester Mercury* was swamped by letters from its readers in support of Edith Roberts and demanding that something be done to save the 'girl' from the ignominy of the death sentence. One letter from a woman who signed herself 'A Mother', eloquently reflected the newspaper's position, and was therefore rewarded with the privileged status within the paper's discourse:

'A Mother' writes: the hearts of all true women are filled with horror and pity at the sentence which had to be passed upon this poor girl yesterday. Why was not the man there? In my opinion it is a stain upon English law that such cases, as these should be thus treated. Instead of being branded as a criminal, this poor girl should rather be treated with kindness and sympathy (in a home, if you like) nursed back to health, mental and bodily, helped to work, and to regain her name. In conclusion, let me say that she is not as wicked as married women who deliberately prevent motherhood. ('The Hinkley Murder', Letter, *Leicester Mercury* 9 June 1921, p. 5)

The letter-writer skilfully uses metaphor to represent Edith Roberts's position as a 'stain upon English law' rather than the girl's infanticidal actions being a 'stain' on her reputation, although there is an underlying inference in the allusion to 'a home' that she has lost her good name. The collocation 'poor girl' again emphasizes Edith's powerlessness and vulnerability. Edith Roberts, the infanticide, is not a 'criminal', but physically and mentally unwell and ultimately she is nowhere near as 'wicked' as married women who use contraception to 'deliberately prevent motherhood', illustrating that 1920s England was still very much a 'society of blood' (Foucault 1991a, p. 269).

'The respite'
It was not long before the newspaper, anxious to be the first amongst its peers, tried to pre-empt the announcement of Edith's reprieve by constructing a report based on rumour in an effort to continue to be positioned as the leader in the reporting of the Edith Roberts's case. 'We understand that an intimation has been received at Birmingham prison that the death sentence passed on the girl, Edith Mary Roberts, at Leicester Assizes this week, for the murder of her newly born child at Hinkley, has been commuted' ('Hinkley Murder', *Leicester Mercury* 10 June 1921, p. 10). In this short three-paragraph story the newspaper foreshadows the line its campaign will follow after Edith Roberts's reprieve: 'Many letters have come to hand suggesting a petition for a reprieve are now out of date, but we hear it is proposed to go on with the petition, which not only asks for a commutation of the sentence, but that there shall be as limited a sentence as possible consistent with the interests of justice' (ibid.).

When Edith's reprieve did come on 12 June the momentum for reform was such that now the newspaper transformed its campaign into a call for the abolition of the death sentence for the crime of infanticide. On Monday 13 June an editorial in the *Leicester Mercury* put it directly to its readers: 'the important question emphasized by the case will not be allowed to lapse again', and it is 'time the law was amended that stipulated for the death penalty in such circumstances, for in its inequalities the Statute does not conform to the popular sense of justice' ('The Respite', Editorial *Leicester Mercury* 13 June 1921, p. 5). The newspaper, under the editorship of Harry Hackett, established a persuasive discourse on the need for change, aware that the political and social climate saw the public wanting legislative reform. The editorial tells readers that the law, as it stands 'offends the moral sense to place upon the same plane a case like that of the Hinkley girl and to go to the other extreme, the crime or crimes of Charles Peace. Yet the law provides the same penalty for both'. The newspaper called upon the local Members of Parliament to 'take the question up', assuring readers that 'a short Bill' to amend the law 'would surely quickly pass both Houses' (ibid.).

Hinkley Board of Guardians

The next day the focus on Edith Roberts's plight is maintained in a report on a special meeting of the Hinkley Board of Guardians to register the Board's support for Edith Roberts. The great irony of this move was perhaps lost on a twentieth-century audience unaware of the role boards of guardians had held across the nation in the nineteenth century in denying relief to unmarried mothers and their illegitimate children under the old poor laws. The discourse on how the hard-hearted actions of guardians in the parishes had directly led countless starving, destitute and desperate young women to commit infanticide was perhaps lost in time. The rhetoric of one of the Hinkley guardians, Mr G. Kinton, who claimed the Infanticide Act was 'The "Un-English" English law', a catchphrase which was to be regularly woven into news discourse over the next year, has resonances with *The Times* campaign the focus of Part I of this study. In the twentieth century the elite group who represented the authoritative patriarchal power of Hinkley, whose members had once denied the mothers of 'bastard' children succour, competed to outdo each other in their pronouncements of support for the vulnerable Hinkley 'girl'. Edith's former lawyer, Mr Powers, told the meeting that 'after the suffering that the girl had passed through, she ought to have been discharged straight off. She had suffered quite enough for what she had done' and called for the support of Guardians 'up and down the country' to deal with the issue and to 'make them alter the law' ('Guardians Stand by Girl-Mother', *Leicester Mercury* 14 June 1921, p. 5).

The Guardians, in framing 21-year-old Edith Roberts as a 'poor girl', like the press, allowed for the accretion of a collective influential paternalistic discourse on infanticide to develop over the next year that not only shut out any alternative discourses, but also transformed a nation's thinking on infanticide. The moment had arrived when the infanticidal woman, symbolized in the bodily figure of Edith Roberts, was no longer represented as a universal threat to society, but rather was seen as a contained threat to herself, to her own good name, to the good name of her family and to those immediately affected by her actions. At the same time the discourse moved the focus even further away from the predominantly absent, and always anonymous, man who continued to avoid opprobrium, further removing the imperative for a broader public discourse on the topic of male sexuality and morality because in 1920s England the patriarchal rule of blood was still absolute.

Over the months to come the *Leicester Mercury* kept the community informed through its news, editorial and correspondence pages of the status of Edith Roberts's case, providing information on where readers could sign petitions and how they could donate money to the fund set up to provide the 'girl-mother' with a new start in life. The paper told readers of the effect of the campaign throughout the country: 'There is a very general desire throughout the country that every step should be taken to get a modification of the sentence in the case of the Hinkley girl tried for murder at Leicester Assizes' ('Hinkley Girl's Appeal', *Leicester Mercury* 18 June 1921, p. 7). The newspaper informed readers of the status of the petitions to the Home Secretary, which had begun as appeals to have her sentence reduced, and became appeals for Edith's release and for a change to the law. Many social, community and religious groups became involved with the campaign, and the newspaper was mindful to keep readers up to date on new developments and regularly published the names of those who played a significant part in the campaign. Numerous distinguished writers, including British novelist and playwright, Sir Hall Caine, expressed the opinion that the outcome of Edith Roberts's trial 'showed the necessity for a revision of the law governing the cases of this character' ('The News in Hinkley: Welcome Communication', *Leicester Mercury* 3 June 1922, p. 1). The *Leicester Mercury*'s list shows the breadth of support for Edith Roberts with politicians and prominent citizens adding their names to her cause, including: the 'Hon. H.D. McLaren (MP for the Bosworth Division), Mr E.A. Hawley (Conservative candidate for the division) and Rev H.H.C. Jones, Unitarian minister, Great Meeting House Hinckley, "being an especially kind friend", the Rev. Canon Elliott, Mrs Bond, J., Miss Irwin, J., and Ald Banton and significantly the support of J., Magistrate Sir Jonathan North' (ibid.). With such unconcealed support for Edith Roberts it is no wonder the 'flood of sympathy' was swelling and by 18 June, according to the newspaper, 10,000 signatures had been obtained on one petition alone ('Hinkley Girl's Appeal', *Leicester Mercury* 18 June 1921, p. 7).

In July the 'Girl-Mother' was still incarcerated, serving a life sentence, but the *Leicester Mercury* brought welcome news that the issue had finally been brought before the Parliament when Mr John Jones asked the Home Secretary in the House of Commons if now that the sentence 'passed upon the girl, Edith Mary Roberts, at the recent Leicester Assizes had been commuted to penal servitude for life', if 'in view of all the circumstances he would review the case with the object of a further reduction of sentence'. Sir John Baird replied that it was 'too soon to advise a further reduction of sentence' ('Hinkley Tragedy: A Question in the House', *Leicester Mercury* 5 July 1921, p. 1). Edith Roberts, now a national figure of infanticide, was an example to others and her profile meant that she was not going to be allowed to escape punishment for her actions as that would send the wrong message to other 'fallen' women. Jones responded plaintively to Sir John's hard-nosed pronouncements with an allusion to the ever-absent man telling the Parliament: 'She is the victim of some other person. Surely she is not to bear the whole burden?' (ibid.).

'12 soldiers in India'

On 29 July came the publication of what must be the most bizarre infanticide letter to be published in the press with 12 soldiers from the Second Battalion

Leicestershire Regiment, on duty in India, writing to the *Mercury*'s sister paper, the weekend *Illustrated Leicester Chronicle*, to record their outrage at Edith's situation. It is indeed ironic that it is a group of soldiers, who willingly represent themselves as 'not angels by a long way' (with the modifying clause 'but we are British'), who discursively bring the absent male back into the spotlight. Writing before Edith's reprieve they argue: 'It is again a case of the man being let off scot free while the girl is condemned to death.' The soldiers condemn the action of the authorities in such cases, writing that 'all Englishmen abroad feel ashamed that such treatment should be dealt out to a poor girl' and they hope their letter 'may do its full share' by being forwarded to the authorities to reprieve the girl' ('Hinkley Girl Mother: Letters of Sympathy from 12 Soldiers in India', *Leicester Mercury* 29 July 1921, p. 3).

'Standing Alone in Her Agony'

By 16 July petitions containing 30,000 signatures had been forwarded to the Government and after a public meeting on 18 July at the Leicester Market Place Edith's plight was highlighted in affecting, bold, pathetic headlines: 'STANDING ALONE IN HER AGONY' (*Leicester Mercury* 19 July 1921, p.5). This comprehensive feature allows the people of Hinkley to speak through the press about their sentiments on the Edith Roberts's case. One of the most influential voices at this meeting (the same meeting was attended by the women of the Labour movement, including Miss Lawrence) was the magistrate, Sir Jonathan North. In seconding the motion calling for a lessening of her sentence, Sir Jonathan observed that his presence might be regarded as 'AN INDISCRETION by those who might feel that it was not within the province of a magistrate to take any action which was opposed to the laws of the land' (ibid.). The use of the capitalized typeface emphasized the delicate position the magistrate had placed himself in and the newsworthiness of his disclosure. However, Sir Jonathan told the meeting that he felt so strongly about the case that it was his 'duty' to speak out. Alderman Banton also told the meeting there was a need for the law to be revised, but also (again the use of capitalized typeface providing readers with a preferred reading by pointing them to the important aspects of the report) 'a need for a REVISION OF OUR OUTLOOK in these matters'. Through the constructed dialogue of the journalist the alderman reminds the meeting that 'instead of being a disgrace to civilisation, their criminal laws should be framed in a reformative and not vindictive spirit' (ibid.).

'Darling daddy, mam, and all' – Edith Roberts speaks

The clearest voice of an infanticidal woman in the news discourse in this study is the voice of Edith Roberts. But it is not through her court appearance, or through interviews presented as constructed dialogue in press discourse, but rather through the publication of a seemingly private letter written by Edith to her father, that we hear the voice of this young infanticidal woman ('"Pray God I shall Soon Be With You" – Hinkley Girl's Pathetic Letter from Prison', *Leicester Mercury* 23 September 1921, p.7). The letter, purportedly handed by her father to the *Leicester*

Mercury, exposes her private thoughts and experiences. But are these thoughts really the innermost thoughts of the young woman? While I am not challenging the authorship of this letter, the simplicity of the sentiment and the intimate references to her family confirm that Edith Roberts was the author of this letter, but what was its intention? Was it simply a private epistolary discourse between a father and his errant, and now contrite daughter? Are the words published by the *Leicester Mercury* the innermost thoughts of a young infanticide? Her voice throughout the letter published in the *Leicester Mercury* brings to mind the notion of the internal eye, which Foucault outlines in his description of Bentham's panopticon (Foucault 1991b). This letter speaks of controlled self surveillance, it is a letter in which a disaffected young woman projects how she wishes to be viewed by her father and by society as she attempts to be reintegrated back into the family and into society. In writing to her father Edith is writing, subconsciously or not, to the society from which she has been excluded. The eyes and ears of a patriarchal Christian society have framed this discourse. This is the letter of a young woman painfully self-conscious of her wrongful deeds; she is shameful and remorseful, her contrition is poignant, she is acutely aware of her status as a female who before the eyes of God has 'fallen from grace'. Edith Roberts's inner eye casts itself over this discourse, and exposes society's control over the 'docile body' of a marginalized young woman.

Whether Edith Roberts wrote this letter under the encouragement of the *Leicester Mercury*'s special correspondent, Robert Gittoes-Davies, who had started visiting her in prison, or whether she wrote the letter independently we will never know, nor will we ever know how she felt about her pathetic private correspondence being exposed to public scrutiny through its publication in the *Leicester Mercury*. The newspaper, however, revelled in bringing this intimate discourse to its readers on 23 September 1921, and exposing a young woman's excruciating shame to the public gaze. The letter represents Edith not only as a God-fearing and dutiful daughter, but also as a brave and stoic ingénue deserving of sympathy:

> There is no need to tell you how broken-hearted I am, and I know you are all the same; but still, dears, I am going to try to make myself as contented as ever I can. I am going to live for the time when God will lift the terrible cloud, and let me come back to all those who are so dear to me.
>
> Well, daddy, I felt it very keenly leaving Birmingham, as you know what a dread I had of coming to this prison, but it is much better than what I expected. The matron is very nice, and so are the officers. I am going to work hard, dad, and do all they tell me, and you know I shall be a good girl. So I want you all to look after yourselves and pray to God that I shall soon be with you all once more.
>
> I am sure I shall never, as long as I live, do anything that will get me in prison again. There is a lot more unfortunate girls like me here, and I expect they are patiently waiting for their release, so I must do the same.

I do thank God from the bottom of my heart that you want me back home again. They do say it is always darkest before dawn, so I am going to think I have had the dark part, and I have got the bright to have. ('"Pray God I shall Soon Be With You"– Hinckley Girl's Pathetic Letter from Prison', *Leicester Mercury* 23 September 1921, p. 7)

Edith Roberts, emblematic of Foucault's 'docile body', says all the 'right' things in this discourse: she is a 'good girl' who works hard; she frames the penal institution as a rightfully fearful place, but also reflects her compliance to the institution's rules; the matron is 'very nice' and so are the officers. And then she assures her father, and society, that for the rest of her life she shall conform to society's expectations and that through God she can see the light ahead. She references other 'unfortunate girls' in her predicament, reflecting the reality that infanticide was still the lived experience for many young women impregnated outside marriage and cast out of society. The letter amplifies the importance of the family as the institution central to Edith Roberts's rehabilitation. As the 'fallen woman' she will only redeem herself through the restorative powers of her reintegration into the family. While this letter is important in this study because it is the closest we get to a discourse of length from the direct voice of an infanticidal woman, however, the hegemonic mediation of society is imbued in her every word.

In November, with Edith no closer to being reintegrated into her family, the Nuneaton and district Free Churches take up the matter, with the secretary, the Reverend W.F. Knight, writing to the Home Secretary to add their weight to the campaign for the release from prison of the 'unfortunate girl'. Reverend Knight's correspondence, forwarded to the *Leicester Mercury*, is plaintive in its tone of impatience and draws upon colourful rhetoric and collocation to persuade the rightfulness of the Nuneaton and district Free Churches' position. 'Surely', Reverend Knight contends, the 'girl' has 'suffered enough already, and it seems to us most unjust that the one who caused the crime – indirectly, at least – cannot be touched by the law, whereas the victim of young and tender age should have her life marred and almost blasted by lonely suffering and public shame. We appeal to you, sir, to bow to the just demand of public opinion in this matter, and to do so urgently' ('Hinkley Girl Mother', *Leicester Mercury* 5 November 1921, p. 3).

Almost a year from the date when Edith Roberts's strangled her newborn baby, news of her imminent release is hinted at by the *Leicester Mercury* through Robert Roberts who is informed by a *Sunday Express* (a sister paper of the *Leicester Mercury*) 'special correspondent' of the possibility of his daughter's release. '"If only I knew for a fact that she would be coming home soon, I think you would see me jump through the ceiling. It seems too good to be true. As it is, I can only say that I have been hopeful all along that she would one day be restored to us"' ('The Hinkley Girl Mother: Edith Roberts Likely to be Freed Soon: "Will Come Home", says Father', *Leicester Mercury* 27 March 1922, p. 7). In a class-based society as a working-class man, the father's position in the hierarchy of patriarchy is defined – he is reliant on the institutions of power, the Home Office and the press, to inform him of his daughter's status. A week later the *Leicester Mercury* ran a curt news story that reeks of a Home Office official breathing down the editor's neck for peremptorily reporting the possibility of Edith Roberts's imminent release from jail. The story, headlined with its usual moniker 'The Hinkley Girl-Mother', has a sub-heading: 'No Official Action Yet' and reports in a chastened tone: 'We are authorized to state that there is no official foundation for the assertion that the Hinckley girl-mother will be released at an early date.' The newspaper then diverts the blame for their hastiness to the father: 'Naturally, the girl's father is hopeful that the Home Secretary will soon see his way to order Edith Roberts's release. There is, however, reason to believe that contrary to rumours which have appeared in the Sunday press, the case had not been reviewed as yet' ('The Hinkley Girl-Mother: No Official Action Yet', *Leicester Mercury* 8 April 1922, p. 7). A less penitent tone comes into the concluding sentence with the paper returning to its watchdog role to put pressure back on the Home Secretary by suggesting that 'the probability is that the Home Secretary may feel constrained to consider the question of the girl's release on the anniversary of her conviction – June 7th – for the family is convinced that ere long the minister will advise the Crown to exercise the clemency which is a feature of British Justice in such cases as that of the Hinckley girl-mother' (ibid.).

While the press focus is on the 'celebrity' infanticide, the act of infanticide continues to have high news value in the tabloid *Leicester Mercury* and on 4 April 1922 infanticide was back on the front page with a story about the discovery of a baby's body in a culvert on the road between Aylestone and Blaby ('Baby's Body Found Near Leicester', *Leicester Mercury* 4 April 1922, p. 1). Maternity remains in the front-page news discourse when three days later a horrific maternal tragedy is reported in the paper with the death of 22-year-old Mrs Clara Octavia Brown, 'who had been confined in January' and had 'placed some methylated spirits in her mouth and set fire to it with a match' ('Young Mother's Suicide', *Leicester Mercury* 11 April 1922, p. 1).

Anniversary coverage
As had been expected, with the anniversary of Edith Roberts's sentence looming, reliable news of her imminent release was published in an 'extra special' wrap-around edition, of the *Leicester Mercury* on 3 June 1922 which was rushed to Hinkley, Earl Shilton, and Barwell early that morning. The front page declares in over-sized font: 'HINKLEY GIRL MOTHER: TO BE RELEASED IN A FEW DAYS: HOME OFFICE ACTION: GIRL'S LETTER TO HER PARENTS – Exclusive to "Leicester Mercury"'. The report begins in an authoritative tone: 'We are able to state on very high authority that Edith Roberts, the Hinkley girl mother, under sentence of penal servitude for life, for child murder, is to be released within the next few days'. It quickly reiterates its central role in the media coverage, reminding readers that 'the "Leicester Daily Mercury" was the first newspaper in the United Kingdom to announce the release of Miss Roberts'. The extensive report outlines the 'harrowing tragedy' of the previous 12 months, reminding

readers that 'the girl, who had undergone a terrible ordeal, which culminated in the awesome death sentence, was an object of public sympathy'. It reiterates in a bold sub-heading the words of the Hinkley Guardian, Mr G. Kinton, who had said that it was *Altogether Un-English*' to 'put the unfortunate girl on a par with the greatest and blackest criminal'. This report chronologically maps out the Edith Roberts's campaign drawing upon and quoting from its own reports. Sections of Edith's letter, which 'told how she was undergoing her sentence with fortitude', were, republished including the moving biblical extract 'it is always darkest before dawn'. Significantly the report made readers aware of the now imminent changes to the Infanticide Act, that as a 'result of this case' there 'was a Bill before the House, in the name of Mr A. Henderson, which will enable juries to return verdicts of manslaughter in cases of this nature' (ibid.).

It is in this report of Saturday 3 June 1922 through an oblique attribution in the *Leicester Mercury*, that readers are made aware that the news of Edith Roberts's pardon did not come from journalistic enterprise, but from Edith herself. The young woman, whose desperate infanticide actions in her attic bedroom on that spring night in 1921 thrust her into the public spotlight, swept along by a public and press campaign to be the cause célèbre for reform to the Infanticide Act, finally, momentarily, has control of her story. Through another letter Edith tells the world that the 'Governor of Liverpool prison [she had been moved from Birmingham] had informed her that she was to be released within a few days'. The letter is, however, heavily mediated through the voice of the paper's 'special correspondent', Mr R. Gittoes-Davies, who is now allowed to overtly enter the news discourse with his own by-line (a rarity at this time) as a reward for his work in cultivating Edith over the past months.

In this report Gittoes-Davies transforms Edith from the 'Girl-Mother' to 'Miss Roberts', an adult female for the first time in the news discourse. She is now represented discursively as an eligible young woman ready for the restorative powers of the institution of marriage. Mr R. Gittoes-Davies informs readers that 'Miss Roberts' has already received 'three or four offers of marriage, including one from a sailor and one from America'. Penitent, punished, reformed and now about to be released back into society, Edith Roberts is now framed as a marriageable and therefore desirable young woman. Although, according to Gittoes-Davies, her parents are not rushing her transformation: 'so far as I can learn it is the intention of the parents that the girl should return and live at Hinkley, although it is hoped that they will be able to send her away for a seaside holiday'. And finally Edith's celebrity status is taken to the next level with film offers and book deals, although Gittoes-Davies presents this information in a clipped tone, discounting rumours reported by 'some newspapers' that 'Miss Roberts, when she is released, will be engaged to play a prominent part in a film. I am authorized to state that there is not the slightest foundation for the statement' thus distancing the young woman from the disreputable world of film stardom. Coincidentally at the same time as Edith Roberts from Hinkley was undergoing her public ordeal one of the most successful stars of the silent screen in America was a woman named Edith Roberts

(1898–1935). This Edith Roberts was 23 in 1921 and had already starred in more than 150 movies. In 1921–22 when Edith Roberts the factory hand was brought into the public spotlight through her infanticidal actions, the Hollywood Edith Roberts was entertaining theatregoers in Hinkley and Leicester in such films as *Luring Lips* (1921) and *Front Page Story* (1922).

Hinkley girl-mother's homecoming
Finally, what all of Hinkley, according to the *Leicester Mercury*, had been waiting for – the return home of the 'Hinkley Girl-Mother'. On Monday 5 June 1922 the paper's 'Special Correspondent', Mr R. Gittoes-Davies, outlines the 'engineering' of Edith's homecoming in an extensive page-one report: 'Edith Roberts's Release: Leaving Liverpool Tomorrow' which shamelessly places the newspaper at the forefront of the discourse:

> The home-coming of the girl is being eagerly anticipated. Meantime, however, everybody here is wondering how the 'Mercury' managed to exclusively announce the glad news. A special edition was rushed into Hinkley early on Saturday morning and the 'Mercury' placard: 'Hinkley Girl-Mother: Happy Surprise', was soon all over Leicestershire. One paper went so far as to almost deny the statement, but, of course, we made it on unimpeachable authority. How we obtained the information must naturally remain known only to a few who engineered it in the 'Mercury' Office. ('Edith Roberts's Release: Leaving Liverpool Tomorrow', *Leicester Mercury* 6 June 1922, p. 1)

This bragging discourse with its smug allusion to journalism ethics and the practice of protecting sources, is blind to the journalist's own ethical practice in the stage-management of the homecoming. The *Leicester Mercury* was so determined to be the ultimate primary definer of Edith Roberts's story that it lost sight of the young woman at the centre of the discourse. Edith Roberts had become a press commodity. So involved were the paper's journalists and editor in the campaign to gain her release that they lost sight of the rights of the young woman and her family. In their scurry to claim the press's ultimate prize, an exclusive – 'a scoop' – the paper that had played a central role in gaining the freedom of Edith Roberts, and changing the Infanticide Act, now comes across in an analysis of their coverage as rather shabby and unethical. Their dogged mindset to beat the opposition is nowhere better reflected than in the following disclosure, published without a hint of awareness of the newspaper's unethical actions: 'Incidentally no one was more surprised than the girl's step-mother, Mrs Roberts, when, on going to do some shopping early on Saturday morning, she heard the "Mercury" special edition containing the news of the girl-mother's release being shouted in the streets.' The report, in an upbeat self-aggrandizing tone, directly quotes Mrs Roberts in what reads as manufactured dialogue:

'Everybody was talking about the "Mercury's" announcement of my daughter's release,' said Mrs Roberts. 'Why, you had actually issued a special edition within an hour of the time I received the great tidings. I hear the "Mercury's" scoop was the talk of the district on Saturday.' ('Edith Roberts's Release: Leaving Liverpool Tomorrow', *Leicester Mercury* 6 June 1922, p. 1)

The 'Special Correspondent', Mr Robert Gittoes-Davies, is overtly managing Edith Roberts's return to society. In the report on Edith's release 'from the gloomy portals of the penal settlement' he reframes Edith into 'the young Hinkley woman', in contrast to the 'girl-mother' who 'exactly twelve months ago ... was carried weeping piteously from the dock of the Leicester County Assizes after hearing the judge pronounce the death sentence' ('Release of Edith Roberts', *Leicester Mercury* 6 June 1922, p. 1). The Hinckley community, and the population of Leicester, who had so actively supported her cause, are now made aware of how tightly managed her return home was. The community who supported the young woman through the past year are now denied knowledge of the details of her return home with the paper sanctimoniously announcing that the time of Edith's arrival in Hinckley is to be kept 'a close secret, as the parents are anxious to avoid anything in the way of a demonstration'. The subtext is clear the *Leicester Mercury* is managing the biggest news prize of the year. The paper would be the eyes of the world in bringing the exclusive story of Edith Roberts's release. The stage-management was down to the last detail as readers were informed that the journalist, Mr Gittoes-Davies, the paper's photographer, Mr Robert Buchannan, and Edith's father and the Unitarian minister, Reverend H. C. H. Jones, were to be the only people to observe her release from prison. The reporter and photographer were to travel with Edith, her father and Reverend Jones (framed discursively as Edith's 'special friend') in a car from Liverpool back to Hinckley. Edith's stepmother is absent from the tableau of father and daughter, reinforcing the pre-eminence of the father in a patriarchal society of blood.

Not surprisingly the report of her release is heralded in triumphant banner headlines in the *Leicester Mercury*: 'EDITH ROBERTS' HOME-COMING' (Wednesday 7 June 1922, p. 1). Gittoes-Davies immediately inserts himself into the story through his by-line and then begins his first-person exposition of Edith's return to the 'family circle' with the press car pulling up outside the prison: 'Our car was drawn into the gaol yard, and the father waited patiently, fearful until the last that it was all nothing but a dream.' Then at the very moment the world had been waiting for, the journalist pulls down the shutters: 'It is only right and decent to draw the veil of privacy over the reunion of sorrowing father and careworn daughter, save to say it was indeed a touching scene.' Robert Gittoes-Davies did, however, provide his readers with a glimpse into the poignant scene of Edith's reunion with her stepmother later in the day (although he has the family make-up incorrect):

Just as the car drove up at the little house of sad but now happier memories, there was a partially suppressed shout of welcome. The girl herself sprang from the vehicle as though unconscious of the people around her, and dashed into the house, where there was naturally a very affecting scene. Her stepmother and her three sisters (the eldest about 17) were in tears. A few moments later Edith ran upstairs to kiss her little stepbrother. ('EDITH ROBERTS' HOME-COMING', *Leicester Mercury* 7 June 1922, p. 1)

The triumphant 'scoop', however, did not go exactly to plan, with other newspapers claiming that they also had the 'exclusive story' of Edith Roberts's release. Much aggrieved by such suggestions, the discourse of Edith Roberts's homecoming is overshadowed by the paper again imposing itself upon the narrative with a bold sub-heading immediately underneath the brief leading paragraph: 'THE MERCURY'S PART: The "Leicester Daily Mercury" was the First Newspaper'. This sub-heading was followed by another self-aggrandizing discourse in which the paper attempts to re-establish itself as the primary definer of Edith Roberts's story: 'As several misleading statements have appeared in London and provincial Press, it is necessary to state that no newspaper representative except the "Daily Mercury" correspondent has been able to converse with Miss Roberts or her family.' The paper goes on to explain that 'a number of journalists made futile attempts to meet the girl at Liverpool, while several London Press-men awaited Miss Roberts at Hinckley' but none were successful and that while 'several newspapers published reports purporting to contain remarks by the girl, and the story of the journey home' no one, other than the *Leicester Mercury*, had spoken with the girl:

> As a matter of fact the proprietors of the Leicester 'Daily Mercury' were allowed to provide a car for the journey from Liverpool. The party to greet the girl-mother on her release comprised: her father; Rev H.C.H. Jones, Unitarian Minister, Hinckley: Mr R, Gittoes-Davies, 'Mercury' special writer, and Mr Robert Buchanan, 'Mercury' and 'I. L. C.' photographer. These, of course, all returned with Miss Roberts to Hinckley. This is made clear to show that the only authentic interviews with the girl or her father have appeared exclusively in our columns. ('EDITH ROBERTS' HOME-COMING', *Leicester Mercury* 7 June 1922, p. 1)

The *Leicester Mercury* had invested so much in the campaign to 'save' Edith Roberts, had moved so far away from the press's role of objective observer and recorder of events to be a central player, that it was determined to stamp its ownership upon Edith Roberts's story.

On the first anniversary of her conviction, 8 June 1922, the final report on Edith Roberts appeared in the *Leicester Mercury*, not in a hard news format, but as an extensive human-interest story published on page four. The new journalistic format of feature stories based on interviews was just coming into vogue and in this story the difference is highlighted in the horizontal rather than vertical layout of the story beneath the banner headline: 'EDITH ROBERTS' OWN STORY (Exclusive to the "Daily Mercury")', (*Leicester Mercury* 8 June 1922, p. 7)'. The story, heavy with pathos, begins with Edith in direct quotes telling readers: '"I always cried myself to sleep ... My greatest joy came when I heard the tramcars rattling by, because it reminded me that there was a big, sympathetic world outside"'. But then Gittoes-Davies imposes himself into the discourse in the attribution to this quote: 'these words, addressed to me by Edith Roberts as we chatted in the quiet of her home, convey some idea of the agony and suspense which the Girl-Mother has known'. Momentarily Edith has been returned to her old moniker of 'Girl-Mother'. Through the voice of Gittoes-Davies, readers learn of Edith's arrival at the prison, the tasks she undertook, and then he draws allusions to Tennyson's *The Lady of Shalott* to create a romantic trope of the young woman: 'The narrow window of her cell was always kept open and – she was on the fourth floor – if she stood on the deal table she could look out upon the open fields and see mother's playing with their little ones.' The inappropriate imagery of the vision of mothers playing with their young children seems to have been lost on the journalist.

Conclusion

With Edith Roberts back in the family home, her return to the private sphere saw the focus turn to the campaign to reform the Infanticide Act. But while the *Leicester Mercury* played a prominent part in putting infanticide back on the national news agenda, in the coverage of Edith Roberts's release from prison the paper did not cover the parliamentary debate on the proposed new Infanticide Act. In a brief news story on 6 June 1922 the newspaper simply reported without fanfare the introduction of the new Infanticide Act. But it did allow the young Hinkley woman who killed her newborn baby in a desperate act in her attic bedroom on that spring night in 1921 to be rightfully credited for the changes to the 300-year-old law: 'Edith Roberts had indeed resulted in the presentation to Parliament of a Bill empowering juries to return a verdict of manslaughter where it is proved that at the time of the offence the woman had not recovered from the effects of childbirth' ('Infanticide Act', *Leicester Mercury* 6 June 1922, p. 5). While it was the regional newspaper's coverage of Edith Roberts's infanticide that transformed her into a cause célèbre and brought her case into the national spotlight, it was Edith's desperate infanticidal actions, emblematic of the desperate actions of countless young women over 300 years, that politicized infanticide in the early twentieth century and finally brought the 1922 Infanticide Act into law.

Conclusion

There she stands in the dock, the young woman charged with the crime of infanticide. She stands alone before the world, facing a sentence of death on the gallows if she is found guilty of killing her newborn child. She is considered to be representative of all that is wicked in her sex, she is an 'unnatural mother', a dangerous, deviant woman. The only women who enter the court to bear witness to her ordeal are those brought in briefly to provide evidence, which generally speaks to her guilt. Women are barred from the public galleries when indelicate matters such as the detailed sexual forensic evidence of infanticide trials come before the court (and the judge instructs the court reporter to censor his copy). And so it is that the woman charged with killing her baby soon after giving birth finds herself alone to be judged in the most patriarchal of environments, the nineteenth and early twentieth-century courtroom where she is surrounded by educated men whose discourses control her fate. The pale-faced young woman is brought to us today through news discourse that has the power to create the reality that is the infanticidal woman.

This study has argued that the production of knowledge, of 'facts', and the exercise of power are inextricably connected to discourse, particularly to press discourse which in the nineteenth and early twentieth centuries was the first mass-medium to disseminate news, knowledge, information and opinions to society. As discussed earlier, news texts are often used in historical studies as uncomplicated reflections of a historical reality, while what they offer is one (journalistic) view of a historical reality. However, this study has shown that through the close reading of news we can see that news texts are multilayered and far richer and more complex than they may at first appear. News texts are the nexus of multiple discourses, and therefore are particularly useful for exposing how knowledge and power are acquired, maintained and understood discursively at any given moment in time. It is from this perspective that this study has drawn upon news texts as a way of understanding infanticide and the young mothers who committed this desperate act.

News texts also importantly provide the rich social and political context that allows us to better understand the motivations of women who killed their babies. We have seen how laws and social moralities cast the unmarried mother out of a society ruled by the law of blood. We have seen how the introduction of the 1834 New Poor Law with its Bastardy Clause saw unmarried mothers and their illegitimate children denied parish relief. *The Times*'s reports on the appalling conditions at the Sevenoaks workhouse provided an understanding of why so many destitute young women shunned the workhouse. The grim reality of life for female convict servants in colonial Australia is better understood through the news reports of the infanticide case of Mary McLauchlan. News texts supply rich context to the lived experiences of young women charged with infanticide. We were brought into the world of Sarah Scorey, who, homeless, wandered the countryside in labour looking for a bed and finally laid down on the outside of her brother's bed before getting up during the night to secretly give birth to and kill her baby in her uncle's barn. We have seen how pregnant Newington servant Sarah Read, cast out of her London workplace, returned home to Streatham in labour travelling on the top of a stage coach on a rainy winter's day and 'suffered extreme agitation, and had undergone almost incredible fatigue' on the 14-hour journey. We were privy to the most intimate details of the married life of Sarah and Joseph Masters of Oatlands and wondered at Sarah's fortitude as she silently endured the final stages of labour while her husband lay beside her in the marital bed. Dorothy Lovell's tragic life and horrific death at the hands of her mother comes to us through news texts, and through news texts we are compelled to wonder about the deaths of Harriet Lovell's four other infant children. Young country girl, Edith Roberts, in the Roaring Twenties was constrained by social mores to stay silent about her pregnancy and in desperation killed her newborn infant by strangling it with lace from her camisole in the bed she shared with her sister. Through news texts we have seen how desperation is such a powerful motivation for women who, rejected by society, take control of their lives. Court reports, everyday histories of ordinary lives brought into the public spotlight through unlawful acts, provide us with some of the richest material about the domestic lives of poor and working-class women.

Understanding the politics of representation is crucial to an understanding of the power of any cultural text. Foucault tells us 'power produces; in fact it produces reality' (1991b, p. 194) and this study exposes the power of press discourse in the formation of the reality that is the act of infanticide and the infanticidal woman between 1822 and 1922. This study has shown how the discursive power of the press is contained within a deeply paternalistic industry that works to shut out female discourse and reinforces patriarchal ideologies. We have seen that infanticide was a particularly forceful act of resistance to the patriarchal hegemony and in a society of blood, ruled by blood, a woman's actions in killing a man's offspring threatened the very foundations of society. The analysis of infanticide press reports exposes the systemic practice of removing the infanticidal woman's voice from public discourse because to allow her a voice would be to allow her agency and no woman who killed a man's child could be allowed the power of agency.

But while this study has shown the repressive, coercive and negative role the press plays in discursively creating an understanding of the infanticidal woman and the crime of infanticide in the period 1822–1922, it has also shown that the power of the press is not only a negative, repressive force, but that, as Foucault tells us, power can also be productive, it can have a positive force in society. Through a close reading of infanticide news this study has shown that the women who killed their babies were subjugated and silenced through press discourse, but that the very act of reporting a woman's infanticidal actions gave publicity to her rebellious act and spoke to the world of a woman's potent ability to subvert a society of blood and to challenge what was regarded as the natural order of things. And when individual infanticide reports come together, when they are read collectively, infanticide becomes the most powerful, subversive political act a nineteenth-century woman could commit.

I have drawn upon Foucault to talk about a multiplicity of positions in regards to power, and throughout this study the multiplicity of positions in regards to power and news discourse is clearly demonstrated. While the infanticidal women in this study were represented in news discourse primarily as 'fallen' women, as 'weaker vessels' who succumbed to seduction, and their actions were represented as 'depraved' and 'unnatural', this study has also shown that at times, such as in the cases during *The Times*'s New Poor Law reform campaign, and in the cases of Mary McLauchlan and Edith Roberts, individual infanticidal women were also positioned in press discourse as victims of an unjust legal system and of a patriarchy that saw women carry the burden of what was seen as sexual impropriety. While the infanticidal women brought before the courts in England and Australia during the period of this study were all the product of a society where entrenched misogynistic hypocrisy and iniquitous rules and laws subjugated all women, the publication of the actions of infanticidal women, represented in press discourse, shows us that these, the most disenfranchised women in society, were not entirely without power.

Newspapers are cultural institutions, structurally integrated into a capitalist system. News has always been a commodity, it is a product sold for profit, and news discourse has a cultural, political and commercial value. The press, by publishing lurid court reports of the trials of women charged with infanticide, or reports on the inquisitions on the bodies of dead babies, played a key role in the creation of the woman society came to understand as the 'unnatural mother', 'the Infanticide'. By closely reading the news stories created by court reporters, journalists, editors and others I have exposed the duality of press discourse. Infanticide news was published because it was a highly saleable news commodity and also because it was expected to have an ideological control over the population, specifically over unmarried women, reflecting Foucault's notion of the 'docile body'. On one level infanticide press discourse provided potent morality tales warning young women of the dangers of improper sexual conduct, but the same young woman who is objectified and judged through infanticide press discourse is also made visible by that discourse. Through the application of Critical Discourse Analysis, and the use of close textual analysis, this study exposes the multiple discourses of power involved in the creation of 'the Infanticide'. Legal, medical, judicial, political, religious, economic and social discourses are embedded within news texts and provide a comprehensive insight into the young woman charged with the crime of infanticide. This study looked at the connections between these discourses, and how these interconnections created a power relationship and way of knowing the infanticidal woman that saw infanticide become one of the significant social issues in the period 1822–1922.

This study's analysis of the production of news exposes how the nineteenth-century court reporter created news from courtroom discourse, how he reconstructed dialogue from multiple discourses and mediated the 'facts' brought before the judiciary. We have seen how the medical expert witness, who made judgements upon the body of the baby, and the body of the fecund young woman in the dock, was a primary definer of infanticide news. When one medical coroner, Dr Edwin Lankester, made shocking pronouncements from the coroner's chair, claiming that 16,000 women in London were guilty of murdering their children, his forceful (but flawed) statistics saw journalists create sensational news stories in the influential *Times* newspaper that led to what I have termed a 'maternal panic'. We also saw how court reporters made decisions about which aspects of a case were the most newsworthy, and which were not, based on the ideology of news values and on personal, paternalistic opinions. Through the letters to the editor and leading articles this study has also shown how the court reporter's discourse was accepted unquestioningly as the authoritative voice on court proceedings. These historical documents, these infanticide news stories, are a portal into the patriarchal world not only of journalism in another age, but also the world of lawyers, police, and ordinary citizens caught up in judicial dramas. We have also seen the discursive power of newspaper editors in influencing public opinion and setting public and political agendas. In the nineteenth century Thomas Barnes, drawing upon reports from the court columns of *The Times*, was 'unrelenting in his condemnation of the New Poor Law' (Roberts 1972, 18). John Delane, the opinion maker of his age, exposed the appalling conditions in workhouses and the treatment of pregnant and birthing women. In 1830 Robert Lathrop Murray in colonial Van Diemen's Land used the technologies of the press to give the young Scotswoman, Mary McLauchlan, a posthumous, albeit limited and heavily mediated, voice. The Hobart Town cabal who had deceived Mary into silence on the gallows had not reckoned on one of their own giving a powerless infanticidal convict woman a platform from which to posthumously name the 'author of her destruction'. At the start of the twentieth century Harry Hackett, the editor at the *Leicester Mercury*, created a press campaign that led to legislative change to the old and unjust infanticide law. These powerful men, representatives of a hypocritical, misogynistic, patriarchal society, were also at times instrumental in empowering the infanticidal woman through prominent press coverage. But while they placed the infanticidal woman at the centre of political and social discourse they also stereotyped unmarried mothers, named and shamed them, labelled them 'wicked' and deviant, and reinforced the rules of a patriarchal society that limited, repressed and constrained women who were sexually active outside marriage, reinforcing the predominance of a society of blood. Through the platform of their newspapers these patriarchal newsmen brought infanticide to the public consciousness and created a political and social discourse that also politicized the most disenfranchised women in society.

Reading social issues *through* news texts exposes the power of news discourse in the creation of dominant ways of knowing social subjects, such as the infanticidal woman. In the case of infanticide news in nineteenth-century

England, by mapping the constancy of infanticide reports before and after the introduction of the 1834 New Poor Law, this study has created links between news and a rise in public interest. I have also shown how infanticide was used explicitly and persuasively by the London *Times* to argue the inequities of the 1834 New Poor Law in influential leading articles and in so doing allowed the cause of the most disenfranchised, marginalized women in society to be placed at the centre of political and social discourse. This discourse influenced parliamentarians, local politicians, magistrates, coroners, ministers of religion and all manner of public speakers across the nation and saw them draw upon leading articles and news reports in *The Times* to form opinions on various aspects of the law.

The study of early twentieth century newspapers in Tasmania provided insight into how the infanticidal woman and the act of infanticide was understood discursively as 'bush madness' in rural Australia. The analysis of these two disparate cases also provided insight into how the same reporter used very different practices in the creation of infanticide news. The study concluded with an analysis of the 1921–22 press discourse in the *Leicester Mercury* and showed how the young factory worker from Leicester, Edith Roberts, became the national symbol of everything that was unjust about the 300-year-old infanticide act when the regional daily newspaper ran a persuasive press campaign that finally forced the British Parliament to amend the archaic 300-year-old infanticide law.

As I have argued, news texts are often the only surviving written texts that offer a narrative of a lived experience and it is through news discourse that we know of the 'sad troubles' of the young woman from Sunny-brae, and of the desperate actions of Sarah Read, Eliza Young, Mary Smith, Sarah Elliott, Elizabeth Alert, Mary Burford and Sarah Scorey. And it is through news discourse that we know of the most intimate and distressing details of the lives of Mary McLauchlan, Sarah Masters, Lilian Wakefield, Harriet Lovell and Edith Roberts.

As Foucault reminds us the discursive and the non-discursive are inextricably linked, 'discourses are practices; they exist in a field of non-discursive practices; statements have materiality' (2002a pp. 49, 68). The analysis of discourses created from the infanticidal actions of young women in England and Australia in the nineteenth and early twentieth centuries exposes a society fearful of the power that women had over the life and death of a man's offspring. The analysis also exposes the resistance of these desperate young women who, while they were always victims, they were not merely 'docile bodies', but young women who, through the act of infanticide, took control of their lives. Through the reporting of their actions in the press infanticidal women gained a political agency which, in a society where power spoke through blood, transformed these desperate, courageous young women into political subjects.

Bibliography

Convict Records

Colonial Secretary's Office (CSO1), Tasmanian Archive and Heritage Office.
CON 18/24 Tasmanian Archive and Heritage Office.
'Executive Council Minutes Friday April 16, 1830', Tasmanian Archive and Heritage Office.

Legal Documents

An Act for the due Execution of Divers Laws and Statutes heretofore made against Rogues, Vagabonds and sturdy Beggars, and other lewd and idle Persons 1610, 7. James 1 chapter 8.
An Act to prevent the destroying and Murthering of Bastard Children 1624, 21, James 1 chapter 27.
Bastards Act 1810, 50, George III, chapter 51.
Davison v. *Duncan* 7 [E and B 229, 1957].
Infanticide Act 1810, 50, George III, chapter 51.
Infanticide Act 1922, George V, chapter 8.
Lord Ellenborough's Act 1803, 43, George III, chapter 58.
Poor Act 1575, 18, Elizabeth 1, chapter 3.
Rex v. *Wright*, 8 T.R. 293 [K.B.1799].
Sex Disqualification (Removal) Act 1919, 9 & 10, George V, chapter 71.

Hansard

Lord Brougham, House of Lords, 28 July 1834, *Hansard*, 3 ser., *xxv*, pp. 608–10.

Government Reports

'Evidence Mr Majendie, E. Surrey, Kent and Essex Poor Law Commissioners' Report 1834', in Report from H.M. Commissioners for Inquiring into the Administration and Practical Operation of the Poor Laws, London 1834, pp. 448–50.

'Poor Law Commissioners' Report into the Present State of Poor Laws. Copy of the Report made in 1834 by the Commissioners for Inquiring into the Administration and Practical Operation of the Poor Laws. Presented to both Houses of Parliament by Command of His Majesty' (London: H.M. Stationery Office 1905).

Medical Journals

'Asserted Increase in Infanticide', Editorial *Medical Times and Gazette* 2 (1867): 455.
'Coroner's Arithmetic', *British Medical Journal* 22 September (1866): 341.
'Coroner's Court', *Medical Times and Gazette* 1 (1865): 2.
'The Coroner's Court and Dr Lankester's Second Annual Report', *Medical Times Gazette* 1 (1865): 443.
Editorial, *Lancet* 12 June (1869): 824.
'The Late Dr Lankester', *Medical Times and Gazette* 1 (1875): 320.
'Third Annual Report', Medical Times and Gazette 1 (1866): 369.
'Third Annual Report of the Coroner for Central Middlesex', *British Medical Journal* 1 (1866): 448–50.

Newspapers

Adelaide Advertiser
'Burnt Her Child to Death. A Strange Case. Sensational Evidence Hobart', *Adelaide Advertiser* 24 July 1912, p. 9.
'A Child's Death. Allegations against the Mother. An Open Verdict', *Adelaide Advertiser* 16 May 1912, p. 10.
'Tasmania. Hobart', *Adelaide Advertiser* 20 May 1912, p. 9.
'Unlucky Family. A Girl Burnt to Death', *Adelaide Advertiser* 10 May 1912, p. 8.

Argus
'Women Who Work: Hard Lot of Farmer's Wives – Lino', *Argus* 13 January 1902, pp. 5–6.

Brisbane Courier Mail
'A Hobart Sensation Death of a Child. Remarkable Evidence', *Brisbane Courier Mail* 23 May 1912, p. 7.

Colonial Times
'Coroner's Inquest – Infanticide', *Colonial Times* 8 December 1837, p. 3.
'Criminal Court April 15, 1830', *Colonial Times* 16 April 1830, p. 3.
'Domestic Intelligence', *Colonial Times* 20 December 1835, p. 4.

Editorial, *Colonial Times* 7 August 1829, p. 3.
Executed, *Colonial Times* 23 April 1830, p. 3.
Editorial, *Colonial Times* 7 May 1830, p. 2.
'From the *Sydney Herald*', *Colonial Times* 10 September 1833, p. 5.
'Latest English New', *Colonial Times* 10 July 1829, p. 3.
'Law Intelligence Supreme Court', *Colonial Times* 12 May 1835, pp. 6–7.
'Law Intelligence – Supreme Court – Criminal Side; Friday 8 May', *Colonial Times* 12 May 1835, pp. 150-51..

Examiner
'Care of a Child', *Examiner* 28 May 1912, p. 6
'Little Girl's Fate', *Examiner* 16 May 1912, p. 6.

Hobart Town Courier
'Child Murder', *Hobart Town Courier* 4 September 1830, p. 2.
'Child Murder', *Hobart Town Courier* 9 October 1840, p. 4.
'Coroner's Inquest – Infanticide', *Hobart Town Courier* 8 December 1837, p. 3.
Editorial, *Hobart Town Courier* 31 January 1829, p. 3.
'Infanticide', *Hobart Town Courier* 7 April 1838, p. 3.
'Infanticide', *Hobart Town Courier* 9 October 1840, p. 4.
'Mary M'Laughland', *Hobart Town Courier* 17 April 1830, p. 2.
'On Monday', *Hobart Town Courier* 24 April 1830, p. 3.
'Supreme Court', *Hobart Town Courier* 15 May 1835, p. 3.

Leicester Mercury
'Appeal Lodged for Girl-Mother', *Leicester Mercury* 15 June 1921, p. 5.
'Baby's Body Found near Leicester', *Leicester Mercury* 4 April 1922, p. 1.
'Charge against Police Surgeon', *Leicester Mercury* 3 August 1921, p. 1.
'Correspondence', *Leicester Mercury* 9 June 1921, p. 5.
'Death Sentence at Leicester Assizes. Accused Girl Carried from the Dock. Painful Scene at Murder Trial', *Leicester Mercury* 8 June 1921, p. 5.
'Edith Roberts' Home-Coming', *Leicester Mercury* Wednesday 7 June 1922, p. 1.
'Edith Roberts' Own Story (Exclusive to the "Daily Mercury")', *Leicester Mercury* 8 June 1922, p. 7.
'Edith Roberts' Release: Leaving Liverpool Tomorrow', *Leicester Mercury* 6 June 1922, p. 1.
'Fund for Girl-Mother', *Leicester Mercury* 16 June 1921, p. 5.
'Guardians Stand by Girl-Mother', *Leicester Mercury* 14 June 1921, p. 5.
'Hinkley Girl's Appeal', *Leicester Mercury* 18 June 18 1921, p. 7.
'Hinkley Girl-Mother', *Leicester Mercury* 5 November 1921, p. 3.
'The Hinkley Girl-Mother: Edith Roberts Likely to Be Freed Soon: "Will Come Home," Says Father', *Leicester Mercury* 27 March 1922, p. 7.
'Hinkley Girl-Mother: Letters of Sympathy from 12 Soldiers in India', *Leicester Mercury* 29 July 1921, p. 3.

'The Hinkley Girl-Mother: No Official Action Yet', *Leicester Mercury* 8 April 1922, p. 7.

'Hinkley Girl-Mother: To Be Realeased in a Few Days: Home Office Action: Girl's Letter to Her Parents – Exclusive to "Leicester Mercury"', *Leicester Mercury* 3 June 1922, p. 1.

'The Hinkley Murder', *Leicester Mercury* 9 June 1921, p. 5.

'Hinkley Murder', *Leicester Mercury* 10 June 1921, p. 10.

'Hinkley Murder Charge', *Leicester Mercury* 7 June 1921, p. 1.

'Hinkley Tragedy: A Question in the House', *Leicester Mercury* 5 July 1921, p. 1

'Infanticide Act', *Leicester Mercury* 6 June 1922, p. 5.

'The "Leicester Daily Mercury" was the First Newspaper', *Leicester Mercury* 6 June 1922, p. 1.

'Mothers Kill Their children: Unable to Watch Them Starve: Stricken Russia: Cholera Raging in Famine Areas', *Leicester Mercury* 18 August 1921, p. 1.

'The News in Hinkley: Welcome Communication', *Leicester Mercury* 3 June 1922, p. 1.

'Police Courts', *Leicester Mercury* 18 April 1921, p. 5.

'"Pray God I Shall Soon Be with You" – Hinckley Girl's Pathetic Letter from Prison', *Leicester Mercury* 23 September 1921, p. 7.

'Release of Edith Roberts', *Leicester Mercury* 6 June 1922, p. 1.

'The Respite', Editorial *Leicester Mercury* 13 June 1921, p. 5.

'Sex Equality: Lady Astor Asks for Simple Justice', *Leicester Mercury* 5 August 1921, p. 1.

'Standing Alone in Her Agony', *Leicester Mercury* 19 July 1921, p. 5.

'Yesterday's Assizes', *Leicester Mercury* 8 June 1921, p. 7.

'Young Mother's Suicide', *Leicester Mercury* 11 April 1922, p. 1.

Pall Mall Gazette
'Dr Lankester', *Pall Mall Gazette* 22 August 1866, p. 6.

The Mercury
'Child's Death by Burning', *Mercury* 16 May 1912, p. 4.

'The Crabtree Tragedy. Funeral of the Victims', *Mercury* 24 July 1912, p. 6.

'The Crabtree Tragedy. Inquest on the Victims', *Mercury* 30 July 1912, p. 8.

'Dreadful Tragedy at Crabtree. Mother Murders Her Children Then Commits Suicide, Madness from Bush Loneliness', *Mercury* 22 July 1912, p. 5.

'Epitome of News', *Mercury* 10 May 1912, p. 4.

'Epitome of News', *Mercury* 24 July 1912, p. 4.

'Evidence of a Neighbour', *Mercury* 17 May 1912, p. 7.

'Farmer's Sensational Statements', *Mercury* 17 May 1912, p. 7.

'The Huon Burning Fatality', *Mercury* 22 May 1912, p. 4.

'The Huon Burning Fatality. To the Editor of "The Mercury"', *Mercury* 18 May 1912, p. 10.

'Huon Burning Fatality. Young Girl's Dreadful Death. Some Extraordinary Evidence', *Mercury* 17 May 1912, p. 7.

'Little Girl's Story', *Mercury* 17 May 1912, p. 7.

'Mountain River Tragedy: Mother of Victim Arrested. Charged with Murder', *Mercury* 23 May 1912, p. 4.

'Mountain River Tragedy. Mrs Lovell Charged with Murder', *Mercury* 24 July 1912, p.2

'Only a Woman', Letter *Mercury* 18 May 1912, p. 10.

'Shocking Accident. Child Burnt to Death at Longley', *Mercury* 10 May 1912, p. 5.

Tasmanian Austral Asiatic Review

'The First Woman Executed', *Tasmanian Austral Asiatic Review* 23 April 1830, p. 533.

'Law Intelligence Supreme Court – Criminal Side. Friday 8 May', *Tasmanian Austral Asiatic Review* 16 April 1830, p. 3.

The Times

'Adjourned Coroner's Inquest – Infanticide', *Times* 23 February 1833, p. 2 *Times* Digital Archive 1785–1985 accessed: 23 January 2009.

'The Cause of Good Sense and Humanity', Editorial *Times* 10 August 1865, p. 8 *Times* Digital Archive 1785–1985 accessed: January 16, 2008.

'Child Murder', *Times* 4 February 1823, p. 3 *Times* Digital Archive 1785–1985 accessed: 7 March 2008.

'A Coroner's Arithmetic – Dr Lankester', *Times* 23 August 1866, p. 8 *Times* Digital Archive 1785–1985 accessed: 3 January 2008.

'The Correspondence Which We Recently Published Respecting the Verdict of the Coroner's Jury at Taunton', Editorial *Times* 30 May 1837, p. 4 *Times* Digital Archive 1785–1985 accessed: 14 March 2008.

'Death from Overwork', *Times* 26 June 1863, p. 8 *Times* Digital Archive 1785–1985 accessed: 5 March 2008.

'Dr Lankester's Annual Coronial Report as an Appropriate Holyday Topic', Editorial *Times* 7 September 1869, p. 7 *Times* Digital Archive 1785–1985 accessed: 28 January 2008.

'Dr Lancaster [sic] on Child Murder', *Times* 15 August 1866, p. 7 *Times* Digital Archive 1785–1985 accessed: 13 July 2008.

'Dr Lankester on Infanticide', *Times* 24 October 1862 p. 6 *Times* Digital Archive 1785–1985 accessed: 13 March 2008.

'Dr Lankester – We Regret', *Times* 31 October 1874, p. 5, *Times* Digital Archive 1785–1985 accessed: 13 March 2008.

'Duke of Bedford and the Cabman', *Times* 11 August 1874, p. 3 *Times* Digital Archive 1785–1985 accessed: 9 June 2009.

Editorial, *Times* 25 March 1831, p. 3 *Times* Digital Archive 1785–1985 accessed: 21 November 2008.

Editorial, *Times* 25 February 1834, p. 5 *Times* Digital Archive 1785–1985 accessed: 24 June 2008.

Editorial, *Times* 16 April 1834, p. 5 *Times* Digital Archive 1785–1985 accessed: 3 July 2010.

Editorial, *Times* 23 April 1834, p. 5 *Times* Digital Archive 1785–1985 accessed: 3 July 2010.

Editorial, *Times* 9 August 1834, p. 5 *Times* Digital Archive 1785–1985 accessed: 3 July 2010.

Editorial, *Times* 5 February 1835, p. 2 *Times* Digital Archive 1785–1985 accessed: 7 July 2010.

Editorial, *Times* 9 February 1835, p. 4 *Times* Digital Archive 1785–1985 accessed: 6 July 2010.

Editorial, *Times* 14 April 1837, p. 4 *Times* Digital Archive 1785–1985 accessed: 3 July 2010.

Editorial, *Times* 2 December 1837, p. 5 *Times* Digital Archive 1785–1985 accessed: 3 July 2010.

Editorial, *Times* 22 December 1837, p. 5 *Times* Digital Archive 1785–1985 accessed: 3 July 2010.

Editorial, *Times* 8 February 1838, p. 2 *Times* Digital Archive 1785–1985 accessed: 6 July 2010.

Editorial, *Times* 4 December 1838, p. 5 *Times* Digital Archive 1785–1985 accessed: 9 July 2010.

Editorial, *Times* 13 April 1841, p. 4 *Times* Digital Archive 1785–1985 accessed: 18 July 2010.

Editorial, *Times* 29 November 1841, p. 4 *Times* Digital Archive 1785–1985 accessed: 12 July 2010.

Editorial, *Times* 1 August 1865, p. 8 *Times* Digital Archive 1785–1985 accessed: 2 May 2009.

'Exchequer Chamber 7 May *Winsor v. The Queen*', *Times* 8 May 1866, p. 8 *Times* Digital Archive 1785–1985 accessed: 6 June 2009.

'Extraordinary Case of Infanticide', *Times*, 18 November 1823, p. 3 *Times* Digital Archive 1785–1985 accessed: 22 November 2008.

Grayston, J. 'The Poor Law Amendment Act', Letter *Times* 24 December 1838, p. 2 *Times* Digital Archive 1785–1985 accessed: September 2010.

'House of Commons', Editorial *Times* 19 April 1834, p. 4 *Times* Digital Archive 1785–1985 accessed: 14 July 2009.

Humphries, J., Letter *Times* 18 October 1862, p. 12 *Times* Digital Archive 1785–1985 accessed: 4 May 2009.

'Infanticide', *Times*, 15 December 1823, p. 3 *Times* Digital Archive 1785–1985 accessed: 22 November 2008.

'Infanticide', *Times* 15 February 1827, p. 4 *Times* Digital Archive 1785–1985 accessed: 22 May 2008.

'Infanticide', *Times* 27 November 1827, p. 3 *Times* Digital Archive 1785–1985 accessed: 4 June 2009.

'Infanticide', *Times* 30 November 1863, p. 11 *Times* Digital Archive 1785–1985 accessed: 13 September 2011.

'Infanticide – The King v. Mary Smith', *Times* 31 July 1833, p. 6 *Times* Digital Archive 1785–1985 accessed: 7 June 2008.

'Infanticide', Letter *Times* 4 August 1865, p. 12 *Times* Digital Archive 1785–1985 accessed: 6 August 2008.

'Infanticide in the Metropolis', *Times* 9 September 1862, p. 6 *Times* Digital Archive 1785–1985 accessed: 7 January 2009.

'Infanticide and Mutilation of a Child', *Times* 9 January 1841, p. 6 *Times* Digital Archive 1785–1985 accessed: 16 July 2011.

'Infanticide and Suicide', *Times* 19 January 1833, p. 4 *Times* Digital Archive 1785–1985 accessed: 2 September 2009.

'Inhuman Atrocity', *Times* 29 October 1822, p. 3 *Times* Digital Archive 1785–1985 accessed: 1 May 2010.

'Inquest', *Times* 11 August 1874, p. 4 *Times* Digital Archive 1785–1985 accessed: 16 June 2008.

'A London Coroner's Work – Dr Lankester', *Times* **16 April 1867, p. 11** *Times* Digital Archive 1785–1985 accessed: 1 June 2008.

'London Monday', *Times* 23 June 1834, p. 4 *Times* Digital Archive 1785–1985 accessed: 1 October 2009.

'A Member of the Royal College of Surgeons', Letter *Times* 3 August 1825, p. 3 *Times* Digital Archive 1785–1985 accessed: 3 November 2008.

'Mr Roworth', Editorial *Times* 4 January 1841, p. 5 *Times* Digital Archive 1785–1985 accessed: 23 October 2008.

'Mortality of Infants', *Times* 6 January 1863, p. 10 *Times* Digital Archive 1785–1985 accessed: 18 January 18, 2009.

'New Poor Law Murders', *Times* Letter 15 August 1838, p. 6 *Times* Digital Archive 1785–1985 accessed: 7 November 2009.

'Numerous Meeting at Rochdale to Petition for a Repeal of the New Poor Law Act', *Times* 6 February 1838, p. 6 *Times* Digital Archive 1785–1985 accessed: 23 April 2009.

'One of the Most Atrocious Cases of Child-Murder', *Times* 24 February 1841, p. 6 *Times* Digital Archive 1785–1985 accessed: 12 July 2010.

'The Papers Upon Hindoo Infanticide', *Times* 25 October 1824, p. 3; 30 December 1824, p. 3, 31 December 1824, p. 3; 6 January 1825, p. 3 *Times* Digital Archive 1785–1985 accessed: 2 January 2011.

'Poor Laws Administration Bill', *Times* 25 June 1847, p. 4 *Times* Digital Archive 1785–1985 accessed: 15 May 2008.

'The Public Mind Has of Late', Editorial *Times* 1 August 1865, p. 8 *Times* Digital Archive 1785–1985 accessed: 13 May 2008.

'A Report from Dr Lankester on the Sanitary State of the West-end Workrooms', Editorial *Times* 26 June 1863, p. 11 *Times* Digital Archive 1785–1985 accessed: 13 January 2009.

'Respite of the Two Females Ordered for Execution at Chester on Saturday (This Day), 1 September 1838', *Times* 1 September 1838, p. 5 *Times* Digital Archive 1785–1985 accessed: 17 July 2008.

'S.G.O.' 'Infanticide', Letter *Times* 5 August 1865, p. 7 *Times* Digital Archive 1785–1985 accessed: 18 January 2008.

'Shocking Case of Infanticide', *Times* 19 December 1831, p. 4 *Times* Digital Archive 1785–1985 accessed: May 24, 2008.

'Shocking Infanticide!', *Times* 30 June 1830, p. 3 *Times* Digital Archive 1785–1985 accessed: May 24, 2008.

'Social Science Congress – Dr Lankester's Report', *Times* 6 October 1866, p. 12 accessed: 2 December 2009 *Times* Digital Archive 1785–1985.

'Social Science Congress – The Following', *Times* 19 August 1869, p. 8 *Times* Digital Archive 1785–1985 accessed: 12 December 2008.

'Spring Assizes, Oxford Circuit', Letter *Times* 14 March 1838, p. 7 *Times* Digital Archive 1785–1985 accessed: 7 November 2009.

'Surrey Winter Assizes: Charge of Infanticide', *Times* 3 January 1824, p. 3 *Times* Digital Archive 1785–1985 accessed: 4 April 2009..

'Suspected Infanticide', *Times* 12 February 1824, p. 4 *Times* Digital Archive 1785–1985 accessed: 7 June 2010.

'Sussex Parson'. 'Infanticide', Letter *Times* 10 August 1865, p. 7 *Times* Digital Archive 1785–1985 accessed: 3 July 2009.

'The Torquay Infanticide', Editorial *Times* 1 August 1865 p. 6 *Times* Digital Archive 1785–1985 accessed: 28 January 2010.

'The Traveller', Letter *Times* 8 August 1865, p. 7 *Times* Digital Archive 1785–1985 accessed: 9 December 2008.

'R.R.', Letter *Times* 10 August 1865, p. 7 *Times* Digital Archive 1785–1985 accessed: 9 December 2008.

'Winchester Assizes – Infanticide', 12 March 1827, p. 4 *Times* Digital Archive 1785–1985 accessed: 1 May 2010.

'Worcester – Infanticide', *Times* 9 March 1832, p. 3 *Times* Digital Archive 1785–1985 accessed: 7 October 2008.

'Year's Work of a Coroner – Dr Lankester', *Times* 12 June 1864 p. 9 *Times* Digital Archive 1785–1985 accessed: 12 February 2008.

Secondary Sources

Ackermann, J., *Australia from a Woman's Point of View* (London: Cassell and Company, 1913).

Ajroud, H. (ed.), *Dualities*, English Studies Series (Tunis: University of Tunis Press, 2001).

Altick, R.D., *Victorian Studies in Scarlet: Murders and Manners in the Age of Victoria* (New York: Norton, 1970).

Andrejevic, M., 'Power, Knowledge, and Governance: Foucault's Relevance to Journalism Studies', *Journalism Studies* 9 (2008): 605–14.

Andrews, A., *The Newspaper Press: The Press Organ*, vol. 3 (London: E.W. Allen, 1869).

Bartky, S., 'Foucault, Femininity, and the Modernization of Patriarchal Power', in I. Diamond and L. Quinby (eds), *Feminism and Foucault: Reflections in Resistance* (Boston: Northeastern University Press, 1988): 65–86.

'Bedford, William (1781–1852)', *Australian Dictionary of Biography* (Canberra: National Centre of Biography, Australian National University, 1966). http://adb.anu.edu.au/biography/bedford-william-1760/text1963 accessed: 18 October 2011.

Behlmer, G.K., 'Deadly Motherhood: Infanticide and Medical Opinion in Mid-Victorian England', *Journal of the History of Medicine and Allied Sciences* 34 (1979): 403–27.

——, 'Toward a New Political Narrative', *Journal of Communication* 35 (1985): 156–71.

Blackstone, W., *Commentaries on the Laws of England: In Four Books with an Analysis of the Work*, 2nd Edition, 18th London Edition (New York: Collins and Hannay, 1832).

Bourne, H.R., *English Newspapers: Chapters in the History of Journalism* (London: Chatto & Windus, 1898).

Boyce, G., J. Curran and P. Wingate (eds), *Newspaper History: From the 17th Century to the Present Day* (London: Constable, 1978).

Braddon, M.E., *Lady Audley's Secret* (London: Tinsley Bros., 1862).

Broude, N. and M.D. Garrard, (ed.), *Feminism and Art History: Questioning the Litany* (New York: Harper & Row, 1982).

Carlyle, T., *On Heroes, Hero-Worship, and the Heroic in History*, 5th Edition (London: Chapman & Hall, 1907).

A Century of Journalism: The Sydney Morning Herald and Its Record of Australian Life 1831–1931 (Sydney: Fairfax, 1931).

Chibnall, S., *Law and Order News* (London: Tavistock Publications, 1977).

——, 'Chronicles of the Gallows: The Social History of Crime Reporting', in H. Christian (ed.), *The Sociology of Journalism and the Press* (New Jersey: University of Keele Press, 1980).

Clark, S., 'Deeds against Nature': Women and Crime in the Street Literature of Early Modern England', *Sederi XII* (*Valladolid: Sociedad Espanola de Estudios Renacentistas Ingleses*, 2001): 9–30.

Cohen, S., *Folk Devils and Moral Panics*, 3rd Edition (London: Routledge, 2002).

Cohen, S. and J. Young (eds), *The Manufacture of News: Social Problems, Deviance and the Mass Media* (London: Constable, 1981).

Collins, W., *The Woman in White* (New York: Harper & Brothers, 1860).

Conley, C., *The Unwritten Law: Criminal Justice in Victorian Kent* (New York: Oxford University Press, 1991).

Cornish, W.R., *The Jury* (London: Penguin, 1968).

Curran, J., 'Capitalism and Control of the Press 1800–1975', in J. Curran, P. Wingate and G. Boyce, *Newspaper History from the Seventeenth Century to the Present Day* (London: Constable, 1978).

Curran, J., P. Wingate and G. Boyce, *Newspaper History from the Seventeenth Century to the Present Day* (London: Constable, 1978).

Dasent, A.I., *John Thadeus Delane, Editor of 'The Times': His Life and Correspondence*, vol. 1 (London: John Murray, 1908).

Davies, S.D., 'Child-Killing in English Law: Part II , *The Modern Law Review* 1 (1938): 269–87.

Davis, R.P., *The Tasmanian Gallows* (Hobart: Cat & Fiddle Press, 1974).

Diamond, E., *Good News, Bad News* (Cambridge: MIT Press, 1980).

Diamond, I. and L. Quinby (eds), *Feminism & Foucault: Reflections on Resistance* (Boston: Northeastern University Press, 1988).

Dickens, C.,'"Some Recollections of Mortality", by "The Uncommercial Traveller"', *All The Year Round* 16 May 1863 (London: Chapman & Hall, 1863).

Emmerichs, M.B., 'Trials of Women for Homicide in Nineteenth-Century England', *Women and Criminal Justice* 5 (1993): 99–109.

England, S., *The Magnificent Mercury: History of a Regional Newspaper: The First 125 Years of the Leicester Mercury* (Leicester: Kairos Press, 1999).

English, M.P., *Victorian Values: The Life and Times of Dr. Edwin Lankester* (Bristol: Biopress, 1990).

Faubion, J.D. (ed.), *Michel Foucault: Power: Essential Works of Foucault 1965–84*, vol. 3 (London: Penguin, 2000).

Felson, M.K., *Crime and Everyday Life* (California: Pine Forge Press, Thousand Oaks, 1994).

Flinn, E. 'Melville, Henry (1799–1873)', *Australian Dictionary of Biography*, vol. 2 (Melbourne: Melbourne University Press, 1967).

Foucault, M., 'The Birth of the Asylum', in P. Rabinow (ed.), *The Foucault Reader* (London: Penguin 1991a): 141–67.

——, 'The Body of the Condemned', in P. Rabinow (ed.), *The Foucault Reader* (London: Penguin 1991a): 170–78.

——, 'Docile Bodies', in P. Rabinow (ed.), *The Foucault Reader* (London: Penguin 1991a): 179–87.

——, 'The Great Confinement', in P. Rabinow (ed.), *The Foucault Reader* (London: Penguin, 1991a): 124–40.

——, 'The Politics of Health in the Eighteenth Century', in P. Rabinow (ed.), *The Foucault Reader* (London: Penguin 1991a): 273–89.

——, 'Right of Death and Power over Life', in P. Rabinow (ed.), *The Foucault Reader* (London: Penguin, 1991a): 258–72.

——, 'We "Other Victorians"', in P. Rabinow (ed.), *The Foucault Reader*, in (London: Penguin 1991a): 292–300.

——, *Discipline and Punish: The Birth of the Prison* (London: Penguin, 1991b).

——, 'About the Beginning of the Hermeneutics of the Self: Two Lectures at Dartmouth', *Political Theory* 21 (1993): 198–227.

——, 'What is Enlightenment?', in P. Rabinow (ed.), *Michel Foucault, Essential Works: Volume 1 (Ethics)* (England: Harmondsworth, 1994).

——, *Archaeology of Knowledge* (London: Routledge, 2002a).

——, *Foucault: The Order of Things* (London: Routledge 2002b).

——, *The History of Sexuality*, vol. 1 (London: Penguin, 2008a).

——, *The Spectacle of the Scaffold* (London: Penguin, 2008b).

Gaskell, E., *Ruth* (London: Chapman & Hall, 1853).

Goc. N., ——, 'Mothers and Madness: The Media Representation of Postpartum Psychosis', in P. Twohig and V. Kalitzkus (eds), *Interdisciplinary Perspectives on Health, Illness and Disease* (New York: Rodopi, 2004).

—— 'Monstrous Mothers and the Media', in N. Scott (ed), *Monsters and the Monstrous* (Oxford: Inter-Disciplinary Press, 2007).

——, 'Framing the News: "Bad" Mothers and the "Medea" News Frame', *Australian Journalism Review* 31 (July 2009a): 33–47.

——, 'Medea in the Courtroom and on the Stage in Nineteenth-Century London', *Australasian Journal of Victorian Studies* 14 (1) (2009b). www.nla.gov.au/openpublish/index.php/AJVS accessed: 21 January 2011.

—— 'Motherhood, Murder and the Media: Joanne Hayes and the Kerry Babies case' in E. Podnieks (ed.), *Mediating Moms: Mothers in Popular Culture* (Quebec: McGill-Queens University Press, 2012): 125–143.

Graham, L., 'Discourse analysis and the critical use of Foucault', Paper presented at Australian Association for Research in Education Annual Conference, 27 November – 1 December 2005, Sydney, Queensland University of Technology.

Grant, J., *The Newspaper Press: Its Origin – Progress – and Present Position*, vol.2 (London: Tinsley Brothers, 1871).

Greg, W.R., 'The Newspaper Press', *Edinburgh Review* 102 (October 1855): 470–98.

Gregory, M.V., 'The Violent Rhetoric of Paternal Child-Murder in *The Times* (London), 1826–49', in J. Thorn (ed.), *Writing British Infanticide: Child-Murder, Gender, and Print, 1722–1859* (Newark: Delaware University Press, 2003).

Hall, S., C. Critcher, T. Jefferson, J. Clarke, and B. Roberts, *Policing the Crisis: Mugging, the State and Law and Order* (London: Macmillan, 1978).

Hall, S., 'Encoding/Decoding', in David Graddol and Oliver Boyd-Barrett (eds), *Media Texts: Authors and Readers* (Clevedon: Open University Press, 1994), pp. 42–77.

Haller, D., 'Bastardy and Baby Farming in Victorian England', *History Journal* (1989). www.loyno.edu/–history/journal/1989–0/haller.htm accessed: 5 December 2008.

Harris, M. and A. Lee (eds), *The Press in English Society from the Seventeenth to the Nineteenth Centuries* (Rutherford: Fairleigh Dickinson 1986).

Hastings, G.W. (ed.), *Transactions of the National Association for the Promotion of Social Science Belfast Meeting* (London: Longmans, Green, Reader and Dyer, 1868).

Hekman, S. (ed.), *Feminist Interpretations of Michel Foucault* (Pennsylvania: Pennsylvania State University, 1996).

Henriques, U.R.Q., 'Bastardy and the New Poor Law', *Past & Present* 37 (1967): 103–29.

Hilson, J., *The Newspaper Press in Nine Papers* (Kelso: Murray, 1858).

History of 'The Times', Volume 1: 'The Thunderer' in the Making 1785–1841 (London: *The Times*, 1935).

History of 'The Times', Volume 2: The Tradition Established 1841–84 (London: *The Times*, 1939).

'How the Newspaper is Made,' *Leisure Hour* (London: Religious Tract Society, 1883): 38–42.

Humble, H., 'Infanticide, Its Cause and Cure', in O. Shipley (ed.), *The Church and the World: Essays on Questions of the Day* (London: Longmans Green, Reader and Dyer, 1866).

Jackson, M. (ed.), *Infanticide: Historical Perspectives on Child Murder and Concealment 1550–2000* (Aldershot: Ashgate, 2002).

Jones, A., *Powers of the Press and Newspapers in Nineteenth Century England* (Aldershot: Scholar, 1996).

Jones, M., 'Fractured Narratives of Infanticide in the Crime and Execution Broadside in Britain, 1780–1850', in J. Thorn (ed.), *Writing British Infanticide: Child-Murder, Gender, and Print, 1722–1859* (Newark: Delaware University Press, 2003).

King, H., 'Four and Twenty Hours in a Newspaper Office', *Once A Week*, 26 September 1863 (London), pp. 369–73.

Knelman, J., *Twisting in the Wind: The Murderess and the English Press* (Toronto: University of Toronto Press, 1998).

Lankester, E., 'On Prison and Workhouse Dietaries', in G.W. Hastings (ed.), *Transactions of the National Association for the Promotion of Social Science Belfast Meeting* (London: Longmans, Green, Reader and Dyer, 1868a).

——, 'The Repression of Infanticide', in G.W. Hastings (ed.), *Transactions of the National Association for the Promotion of Social Science Belfast Meeting* (London: Longmans, Green, Reader and Dyer, 1868b).

——, 'The Registration Systems', in E. Pears (ed.), *Transactions of the National Association for the Promotion of Social Science Bristol Meeting 1869* (London: Longmans, Green, Reader and Dyer, 1870): 205-17.

MacDonald, H., *Human Remains: Episodes in Human Dissection* (Melbourne: Melbourne University Press, 2005).

McEvoy, K., 'Newspapers and Crime: Narrative and the Construction of Identity', in John Morison (ed), *Tall Stories? Reading Law and Literature,* (Dartmouth: Ashgate, 1996): 179–198.

McNay, L., *Foucault and Feminism: Power, Gender and the Self* (Cambridge: Polity Press, 1992).

Malthus, T., *An Essay on the Principle of Population, as It Affects the Future Improvement of Society with Remarks on the Speculations of Mr. Godwin, M. Condorcet, and Other Writers* (London, J. Johnston, 1798).

Marousi, J., *Depraved and Disorderly: Female Convicts, Sexuality and Gender in Colonial Australia* (Melbourne: Cambridge University Press, 1997).

Martin, R. M. *Statistics of the Colonies of the British Empire* (London: William H. Allen and Co 1839): 443.

Martineau, H., *History of the Peace: Pictorial History of England during the Thirty Years' Peace 1816–46* (London: W. and R. Chambers, 1858).

Mayhew, H., *London Labour and the London Poor* (London: Charles Griffin and Company, 1862).

Meredith, L.A., *My Home in Tasmania During a Residence of Nine Years in Two Volumes* vol. 1 (London: John Murray, 1852): 153.

Millman, M., 'The Influence of the Social Science Association on Hospital Planning in Victorian England', *Medical History* 18 (1974): 122–37.

Mills, J., *Womanwords: A Vocabulary of Culture and Patriarchal Society* (Harlow, Essex: Longman, 1989).

Mills, S., *Feminist Stylistics* (London: Routledge, 1995).

Milner, L.S., *Hardness of Heart / Hardness of Life: The Stain of Human Infanticide* (Lanham: University Press of America, 2000).

Murray, C.R., 'Murray, Robert William Felton Lathrop (1777–1850)', *Australian Dictionary of Biography*, vol. 2 (Melbourne: Melbourne University Press 1967).

Murray, L.A., *New Oxford Book of Australian Verse* (Melbourne: Oxford University Press, 1991).

Nochlin, L., 'Lost and Found: Once More the Fallen Woman', in N. Broude and M.D. Garrard (eds), *Feminism and Art History: Questioning the Litany* (New York: Harper & Row, 1982).

Oastler, R., *Fleet Papers: Being Letters to the Right Hon. Sir J. Graham, Bart. M.P. Her Majesty's Principal Secretary of State for the Home Department; from Richard Oastler, His Victim in the Queen's Prison* (London: W.J. Cleaver, 1843).

Oberman, M., 'Mothers Who Kill: Cross-Cultural Patterns in and Perspectives on Contemporary Maternal Filicide', *International Journal of Law and Psychiatry* 26 (2003): 493–514.

Olssen, M., *Michel Foucault: Materialism and Education* (Westport: Bergin & Garvey 1999).

Parker, H.W., *Van Diemen's Land: Its Rise, Progress and Present State with Advice to Emigrants* (London: Simkin and Marshall, 1834).

Patmore, C., *The Angel in the House* (London and Cambridge: Macmillan and Co., 1863).

Pears, E. (ed.), *Transactions of the National Association for the Promotion of Social Science Bristol Meeting* 1869 (London: Longmans, Green, Reader and Dyer, 1870).

The Penny Cyclopædia of the Society for the Diffusion of Useful Knowledge, 'Saltcoats', vol. 20, (London: C. Knight, 1842): 369.

Piers, M., *Infanticide* (New York: Norton, 1978).

Quinlan, M.J., *Victorian Prelude* (New York: Columbia University Press, 1955).

Rabinow, P. (ed.), *The Foucault Reader* (London: Penguin Books, 1991).

Rae-Ellis, V., *Louise Anne Meredith: Tigress in Exile*, 2nd Edition (Hobart: Blubber Head Press, 1990).

Reekie, G., *Measuring Immorality: Social Inquiry and the Problem of Illegitimacy* (Cambridge: Cambridge University Press, 1998).

Reisigl, M. and R. Wodak, *Discourse and Discrimination* (London: Routledge, 2001).

Richardson, J.E., *Analysing Newspapers: An Approach from Critical Discourse Analysis* (London: Palgrave, 2007).

Ritchie, J., 'Newspaper People', *About London* (London: William Tinsley, 1860).

Roberts, D., 'More Early Victorian Newspaper Editors', *Victorian Periodicals Newsletter* 16 (5) (1972): 15–28.

Roberts, D.F., *The Social Conscience of the Early Victorians* (California: Stanford University Press, 2002).

Rose, L., *Massacre of the Innocents: Infanticide in Great Britain 1800–1939* (London: Routledge, 1986).

Ryan, W.B., *Infanticide – Its Law, Prevalence, Prevention and History* (London: Churchill, 1862a)

——, 'September 1861', *Lancet* (1862b): 232–46.

Simons. J., 'Foucault's Mother', in Hekman, S. (ed.), *Feminist Interpretations of Michel Foucault* (Pennsylvania: Pennsylvania State University, 1996).

Smith, A., 'The Long Road to Objectivity and Back Again: The Kinds of Truth We Get in Journalism', *Newspaper History from the Seventeenth Century to the Present Day*. J. Curran. P. Wingate and G. Boyce (eds.) (London: Constable, 1978): 153-71.

Smith, S., 'The Periodical Press', *The Edinburgh Review*, 38 (Edinburgh and London: Constable and Company and Longman, Hurst, Rees, Orme and Brown 1823): 364–365.

Stevenson, K., '"Crimes of Moral Outrage": Victorian Encryptions of Sexual Violence', in J. Rowbotham and K. Stevenson (eds), *Criminal Conversations: Victorian Crimes, Social Panic, & Moral Outrage* (Ohio: Ihio State University Press, 2005): 232–246.

Stubbs, M., *Text and Corpus Analysis: Computer-Assisted Studies of Language and Culture* (Oxford: Blackwell, 1996).

Surette, R., *Media, Crime and Criminal Justice: Images and Realities* (Pacific Grove, CA: Brooks, 1992).

Symonds, D.A., *Weep Not for Me: Women, Ballads, and Infanticide in Early Modern Scotland* (Pennsylvania: Pennsylvania State University Press, 1997).

Thorn, J. (ed.), *Writing British Infanticide: Child-Murder, Gender, and Print, 1722–1859* (Newark: Delaware University Press, 2003).

'*The Times* Newspaper', *Leisure Hour* 1863 (London): 541–43.

Trollope, F., *Jessie Phillips: A Tale of the New Poor Law* (London: Henry Colburn, 1843).

Twohig, P. and V. Kalitzkus (eds), *Interdisciplinary Perspectives on Health, Illness and Disease* (New York: Rodopi, 2008).

Van Dijk, T.A, *News as Discourse* (Hillsdale: Lawrence Erlbaum, 1988).

——, *Racism and the Press* (London: Routledge, 1991).

——, 'Discourse, Opinions and Ideologies,' in C. Schaffner and H. Kelly-Holmes (eds), *Discourse and Ideologies* (Clevedon: Multilingual Matters Ltd, 1996): 7–37.

——, 'Discourse Analysis: Its Development and Application to the Structures of News', *Journal of Communication* 33 (2) (1997): 20–43.

Vicinus, M. (ed.), *Suffer and Be Still: Women in the Victorian Age* (London: Indiana University Press, 1973).

Wakley, T., Editorial *Lancet* vol. 1 issue 2389 (London, 12 June 1869): 824

Ward, T., 'Psychiatry and Criminal Responsibility in England 1843–1936', Dissertation, De Montfort University, Leicester, 1996.

——, 'The Sad Subject of Infanticide: Law, Medicine and Child Murder, 1860–1938', *Social and Legal Studies* 8 (1999): 163–80.

West, J., *The History of Tasmania*, vol. 2 (Launceston: Henry Dowling, 1852).

Wilkerson, M., *News and Newspapers* (London: Batsford, 1970).

Williams, F., *Dangerous Estate: The Anatomy of Newspapers* (London: Longmans, 1957).

Wiltenberg, J., *Disorderly Women and Female Power in the Street: Literature of Early Modern England and Germany* (Charlottesville and London: University of Virginia Press, 1992).

Woods, O. and J. Bishop, *The Story of 'The Times'* (London: Michael Joseph, 1983).

Woodyatt, G. (ed.), *Transactions of the National Association for the Promotion of Social Science Manchester Meeting* (London: Hastings, 1867).

Index

References to notes consist of the page number followed by the letter 'n' followed by the number of the note, e.g. 89n1 refers to footnote no.1 on page 89.

Victorian values, and the infanticidal
    woman 4–6

Wakefield, Lilian (infanticide case) 2, 18,
    95, 96, 126, 127, 138–43
Wakley, Dr Thomas 72–3, 90
Walter, John, II 49
Webb, R. K. 12
West Australian 137
West, John 104
Whalley, Sir S. 52
Wilmot, Sir Eardley 93
Wiltenberg, J. 5, 21
Winsor, Charlotte (Torquay infanticide
    case) 80–82, 84
womanhood
    and Australian bush mythology 125–6
    British vs aboriginal woman 95
    and chastity 4, 6, 8, 21, 50–52, 84–5
    domestic ideal of 2, 4–5
    and maternity 57

and sexual knowledge 26
and Victorian conception of the family
    4–5
see also convict women; domestic
    servants; 'fallen woman';
    infanticidal woman ('The
    Infanticide'); patriarchy;
    prostitution; sexual politics;
    'society of blood'; unmarried
    mothers
women jurors 149–50, 154
women's movement 151
    see also Mackintosh, A.
workhouses
    improved standards (1840s) 93
    Jane Grayston's story 62–3
    Sevenoaks workhouse inquiry 4, 65–8,
        171

Young, Eliza (infanticide case) 36–7
Young, Fanny (infanticide case) 84

For Product Safety Concerns and Information please contact our
EU representative GPSR@taylorandfrancis.com Taylor & Francis
Verlag GmbH, Kaufingerstraße 24, 80331 München, Germany